ROUTLEDGE LIBRARY EDITIONS: DEMOGRAPHY

Volume 1

POPULATION GROWTH AND LEVELS OF CONSUMPTION

POPULATION GROWTH AND LEVELS OF CONSUMPTION

With Special Reference to Countries in Asia

HORACE BELSHAW

Routledge
Taylor & Francis Group

LONDON AND NEW YORK

First published in 1956 by George Allen & Unwin Ltd.

This edition first published in 2024
by Routledge
4 Park Square, Milton Park, Abingdon, Oxon OX14 4RN

and by Routledge
605 Third Avenue, New York, NY 10158

Routledge is an imprint of the Taylor & Francis Group, an informa business

British Library Cataloguing in Publication Data
A catalogue record for this book is available from the British Library

ISBN: 978-1-032-53819-8 (Set)
ISBN: 978-1-032-54833-3 (Volume 1) (hbk)
ISBN: 978-1-032-54836-4 (Volume 1) (pbk)
ISBN: 978-1-003-42769-8 (Volume 1) (ebk)

DOI: 10.4324/9781003427698

Publisher's Note
The publisher has gone to great lengths to ensure the quality of this reprint but points out that some imperfections in the original copies may be apparent.

Disclaimer
The publisher has made every effort to trace copyright holders and would welcome correspondence from those they have been unable to trace.

POPULATION GROWTH AND LEVELS OF CONSUMPTION

*With Special Reference to
Countries in Asia*

BY

HORACE BELSHAW

*Macarthy Professor of Economics
Victoria University College, Wellington
New Zealand*

ISSUED UNDER THE AUSPICES
OF THE
INTERNATIONAL SECRETARIAT
INSTITUTE OF PACIFIC RELATIONS

LONDON
GEORGE ALLEN & UNWIN LTD
RUSKIN HOUSE MUSEUM STREET

THE INSTITUTE OF PACIFIC RELATIONS

The Institute of Pacific Relations is an unofficial and non-partisan organization, founded in 1925 to facilitate the scientific study of the peoples of the Pacific area. It is composed of autonomous National Councils in the principal countries having important interests in the Pacific area, together with an International Secretariat. It is privately financed by contributions from National Councils, corporations, and foundations. It is governed by a Pacific Council composed of members appointed by each of the National Councils.

The Institute as such and the National Councils of which it is composed do not advocate policies or express opinions on national or international affairs. Responsibility for statements of fact or opinion in Institute publications rests solely with the authors.

PRINTED IN GREAT BRITAIN
in 12 point Fournier type
BY THE WHITEFRIARS PRESS LTD
LONDON AND TONBRIDGE

TO MARION

FOREWORD

This essay is part of a wider study on the economic development of under-developed countries, which I have hopes of completing some day, and is not intended to be a comprehensive
analysis of development problems. Its central theme is the relationship between population growth and levels of consumption.
This relationship is, of course, of paramount importance, and it
necessitates consideration of capital requirements and problems of
capital formation, the rôle of innovations and the problems of
promoting them, and many other questions. Indeed, to begin with
population aspects is one way of introducing a discussion of the
whole process of economic development. But I have endeavoured,
no doubt unsuccessfully, to exercise restraint by confining attention to the more important relationships affecting levels of consumption when a population is increasing, and have not pursued
assiduously each line of enquiry opened up. For example,
although it is necessary to say something about investment
criteria, I do not pretend that the treatment is exhaustive. On the
other hand, I have pursued some lines of enquiry, such as into
'non-economic' conditions affecting innovations, which economists usually avoid.*

Especially if we do not take the rate of population growth as
given, but consider the conditions which affect it, the central
theme of this essay brings out the dilemma facing the economist
when considering problems of economic development. Economic
development is a social process, and not simply an economic
process if, indeed, there is such a thing as the latter. Many if not
most of the applied problems to which attention must be given if

* *Explorations in Entrepreneurial History*, Research Center in Entrepreneurial History, Harvard University, Cambridge, Mass., are an important
attempt to extend knowledge of such conditions.

economic development is to be promoted, raise questions outside the field with which the economist is normally concerned.

The economist may confine himself austerely to the discreet questions which by convention are his special province. He then places into the residuals many of the things which matter, and which must be the specific concern of the practical man. There is the danger that this will lead to an artificial dichotomy, a pseudo-precision in the interpretation of real problems, and the attempt to apply models designed for one society to another where they don't work at all well. The answers are sometimes given as though the non-economic factors took care of themselves, or were entirely somebody else's business. Thus dynamic models sometimes assume away population changes.

On the other hand, the economist may venture into the preserves of other social scientists, drawing on their knowledge when he can, and making the best of things when he can't, and in consequence has to explore the dark places of the residuals, sometimes with very little guidance. He then runs the risk of being convicted of scientific naivety. I have preferred to run the latter risk, with, I hope a proper humility and, being neither historian nor sociologist, demographer nor econometrician, have strayed into their pastures—in the last two instances with some guidance—in the hopes that even if the attempted synthesis is unsuccessful the solecisms will not be too blatant, and that lines of enquiry may be suggested to those more competent in such fields, which will fill in the residuals. As Rostow has it, questioning in other fields may 'provide a focus for the efforts of non-economic analysts interested in economic phenomena, which would permit them to bring their techniques and data to bear in such a manner that their conclusions might be absorbed directly into the general analysis of the growth and fluctuations of economies.'* The economist can hardly blame other social scientists because they don't provide answers to the

---

* W. W. Rostow, *The Process of Economic Growth*, Oxford University Press, 1953, p. 11. See also Talcott Parsons, *The Structure of Social Action*, Free Press Glencoe, Illinois, 1949, p. 19; and John E. Sawyer, 'Social Structure and Economic Progress', *American Economic Review*, Vol. XLI, No. 2, May, 1951, pp. 321–23.

questions of importance to him, if he doesn't pose the questions. One way of getting answers is to provoke other people by honest, even if not altogether successful, attempts at finding the answers oneself.

My approach has been coloured by several years' service as a member of the staff of the United Nations Food and Agricultural Organization, and later as chairman of a United Nations Mission which surveyed community organization and development in a number of countries in South and South-East Asia. In the former capacity it was my duty to organize and direct various types of programmes concerned with the 'social' approach to economic development in rural areas—essentially with the problem of organizing rural people the better to help themselves. In both capacities my work took me to the villages in under-developed countries in various parts of the world. These experiences— possibly reinforced by the pessimism associated with occasional intestinal afflictions which have the same general characteristics whether picked up in Guatemala, Egypt, India or China—have convinced me more than do statistics, that 'the Malthusian Situation' is something more than a bogey, and that the need to exorcise the Malthusian devil is rather urgent. Emphasis on the 'social' approach will, I think, be apparent in the following pages.

The essay is, in part, a development of ideas expressed in an earlier study on *Agricultural Reconstruction in the Far East*, written in 1947, under the auspices of the International Secretariat of the Institute of Pacific Relations. I am glad of the opportunity to acknowledge my indebtedness not only to the studies published by the Institute which are referred to in the following pages, but also to a much larger number of objective scholarly treatises on a wide variety of Asian problems which have been published under its auspices. These have provided background even where they are not directly quoted. In particular, I wish to express my thanks and appreciation to Mr. W. L. Holland, Secretary-General of the Institute, for arranging the publication of this essay, and for many useful suggestions.

I have benefited a great deal from the critical suggestions or Mr. J. V. T. Baker, Census Department, Wellington; my departmental colleagues, Associate Professor J. O. Shearer, and Mr. F. W. Holmes of Victoria College, Professor C. B. F. Simkin of Auckland University College, and Dr. Irene Taeuber of the Office of Population Research of Princeton University, to all of whom I express my sincere thanks and appreciation. I gratefully express also my great indebtedness to Professor E. de S. Brunner of Teachers' College, Columbia University, not only for critical help, but also for advice and assistance on publication, and to Dr. R. M. Campbell, C.M.G., Official Secretary to the High Commissioner of New Zealand in London, for similar advice and assistance. Mrs. Pauline Petersen and Miss Rona Arbuckle have earned my appreciation and sympathy for their patient and successful efforts to decipher and make order out of a typically professorial manuscript. My indebtedness to Professor Simkin and Dr. Taeuber is especially great. Professor Simkin was especially helpful in Part II, where an attempt is made to introduce a discussion of the fundamental relations in economic development by means of the Cobb-Douglas production function. He first drew my attention to the possibilities in this approach, and has taken great pains to clarify its meaning and interpretation in subsequent discussion and correspondence. Any merit which the exposition possesses is therefore due largely to his suggestions and guidance, especially in view of my ineptitude in handling econometric models. But my indebtedness goes much further. He has criticized the argument in detail, and made constructive suggestions on so large a number of points that it is hardly possible to acknowledge each one of them, or adequately convey how much the exposition owes to him, not simply in the chapters referred to, but throughout the essay as a whole. Dr. Taeuber gave similar help in safeguarding my demographic references, and in drawing on her wide knowledge of population conditions in Asian countries, especially Japan, for my benefit. I have not included reference in the text to all matters on which I have made changes in response to her suggestions, but give this general, inadequate acknowledgement. Needless to say, I alone am responsible for errors, or inadequacies in exposition, especially as I have not always followed the advice of my mentors. I wish to thank Professor James S. Duesenberry and *Explorations in Entrepreneureal History* for permission to use the long quotation which appears in Appendix I.

Finally I make grateful acknowledgement to the Institute of Pacific Relations for financial assistance towards publication, and to the Social Science Research Committee of the University of New Zealand for making a grant for secretarial and other assistance from funds made available by the Carnegie Corporation of New York. The author alone is responsible for any statements of fact and opinion expressed in the study.

HORACE BELSHAW

Victoria University College
Wellington
New Zealand
March, 1954

CONTENTS

INTRODUCTION

I

The scope of this essay is restricted to a consideration of the relationship between population growth and levels of consumption in so-called 'under-developed' countries in Asia. I shall regard economic development as a social process which results in a cumulative increase in levels of consumption. The selection of Asian countries for consideration is determined partly by the fact that I have had more opportunities for personal observations in Asia than in other under-developed areas, and am more familiar with the literature dealing with this region than with others, so that more information about Asian countries is at present available to me; partly because many of them illustrate rather clearly the nature of population problems. Of course, conditions differ from country to country, but to consider each country separately would require an encyclopædia volume and more *detailed* information than is available from most of them. But conceptually or analytically the problems are similar in all, and with the usual reservations as to the necessity for taking account of national differences in approaching the applied problems, it seems possible to formulate generalizations which provide a framework within which these problems can be considered in all of them.

It is useful by way of introduction to draw attention to some well known data. Between 1940 and 1950, estimated world population increased from 2,213 million to 2,410 million, or by nearly 200 million.* The estimated population of Asia (excluding U.S.S.R.) increased from 1,176 million to 1,281 million, or by over 100 million. Over a short period of ten years the number of additional people throughout the world exceeded the total popu-

---

* *United Nations Demographic Year Book*, New York, 1953.

lation of North America, and half of them lived in Asia. At present rates of growth, the population of Asia will have increased by a further 130 million in ten years, and 360 million, or nearly the present population of India, in twenty-five years.

Throughout the vast areas of Asia, levels of consumption among the great masses of the people are very low. This fact is well documented and generally known, so that a detailed discussion is not necessary here.* The prevailing poverty in Asian countries is linked in the public mind with rates of population growth and population density. But it is misleading to think simply in these terms. The annual compound rate of growth in Asia as a whole, according to United Nations' estimates, is slightly under 1 per cent, about the same as for world population. The averages conceal marked differences from country to country; but in many developed countries the rate of increase is much higher than in many which are under-developed. The former have high consumption levels and in most cases are able to improve them, even though their populations are growing fast. The latter are poor and even to sustain existing levels of consumption may present some difficulty. Thus, over the past ten years, the cumulative increase in population in New Zealand has exceeded 2 per cent, but available goods per head have shown a substantial cumulative increase so that they are some 25 per cent higher than before the war.† In India, with a population increase of 1¼ per cent, the prospects of improvement are precarious and relatively much less, even with the special efforts embodied in the Five Year Plan.‡

For the world as a whole, and even for developed countries, even a low rate of increase of 1 per cent would eventually bring trouble. In an exercise of astronomical arithmetic, which dramatically brings out the effects of compound rates of growth, Putnam writes, '. . . if the race had sprung from a couple living in 10,000 B.C. and if its numbers had expanded at the rate of 1 per cent per year since then, there would to-day be a sphere of living flesh many thousand light years in diameter, whose surface would be

* Certain indicators of poverty are discussed in Chapter I below.
† *New Zealand Official Year Book*, 1953, pp. 580 *et seq.*
‡ Cf. below, Chapter VI, p. 106, and Chapter VII, p. 114.

expanding into space many times faster than light.'* Long before
10,000 years hence, a sustained rate of growth of 1 per cent would
be checked by food shortages. Over a shorter period of a few
decades however there is no need to be alarmist over the possibility of increasing *world* food production at a sufficient rate, or
over the economic prospects of developed countries, even at much
faster rates of population growth than 1 per cent per year. But
equally there are no grounds for optimism over the prospect of
increasing consumption at current rates of growth in under-
developed countries.

We must be cautious also in drawing inferences from population densities. On the average for Asia (excluding U.S.S.R.)
estimated density is 48 per square kilometre as against 81 for
Europe.† It is 196 per square kilometre in Germany, and 320 in
the Netherlands as against 112 in India; but levels of consumption are markedly higher in the former countries. Certainly population density has a bearing on levels of consumption; but it
should be defined in terms of the relationship between size of
population and the resources which can be utilized with existing
capital at existing levels of technology, as affected by (and
influencing) economic and social structure and organization. In
the same way, the problem of improving levels of consumption
is not merely one of population growth, but of the rate of growth
in relation to the rate of increase in capital formation and the
rapidity and effectiveness of technological improvements in the
utilization of natural resources, as affected by (and influencing)
changes in economic and social structure. These, however, are the
problems with which this essay is concerned.

II

Although, for Asia, the current over-all rates of population
growth are not rapid, the increase in absolute numbers is one of

* P. C. Putnam, *The Future of Land Based Nuclear Fuels* (U.S. Atomic
Energy Commission, Technical Information Division, Oak Ridge, Tenn.,
1950. Preliminary Draft), p. 18. Quoted M. K. Bennett, *Population, Food and
Economic Progress*, Rice Institute Pamphlet, Vol. XXXIX, July, 1952, No. 2,
p. 1.
† *United Nations Demographic Year Book*, 1953.

the major demographic phenomena in world history. The growth is geographically located in an area subject to strong political disturbances. There seems little ground for correlating poverty with revolution. What is significant is that population growth hampers improvement among people who are becoming increasingly conscious of poverty and of economic differences. Their aspirations towards economic betterment have been raised and their tolerance of prevailing poverty has been greatly reduced by a greater perception of differences in levels of economic well-being between Asia and the West, and among different strata in their own countries. With it, there is a growing consciousness of the exploitation made possible by existing social relations and institutional arrangements, and increasing reluctance to submit to them. Here is a situation fraught with explosive political consequences for the world, as is shown by events in China, Indo-China and Malaya.

Since this is an economic and not a political essay, I do not propose to consider all the implications for world peace in the situation referred to, but only to express one or two opinions in summary and rather dogmatic fashion.* They are relevant to the problems with which we deal, both because political and social unrest are impediments to economic development, and because a major motive of international capital aid and technical assistance is to promote world peace by contributing to social harmony and political stability in the separate countries in Asia. It is becoming increasingly recognized that the spread of international communism will not be checked by military preparedness alone, but requires progress in satisfying the aspirations of Asian people.

Perhaps the most overt expressions of motives are to be found

* I have dealt somewhat more fully with the issues raised in *Some Social Aspects of Economic Development in Under-Developed Countries in Asia*, N.Z. Institute of International Affairs, Paper No. 2, August, 1954, Second Annual Conference of N.Z. Institute of International Affairs; and Twelfth Conference of Institute of Pacific Relations, Kyoto, Japan, September, 1954. This is reprinted in *Civilizations*, Vol. IV, No. 4, 1954 (Brussels). A fuller and more systematic discussion of political implications of economic development received after this manuscript was completed is: Eugene Staley, *The Future of Under-Developed Countries*, Harper and Brothers, New York, 1954.

in statements on United States foreign policy,* though these motives are very little different from those which inspire other nations to participate in bi-lateral programmes, or in the Technical Assistance programmes of the United Nations, or in the Colombo Plan. The over-riding motive is to establish a 'just and lasting peace'. To this end economic policy of the United States is directed to promoting military strength, the development of stable democracies which approach closer to the ideal of its own 'free' society, reducing social as well as economic pressure, and raising levels of consumption.

It is my conviction that the satisfaction of aspirations towards an improvement in levels of consumption is a necessary, but not sufficient, condition for the removal of social and political stresses. The trend of argument in this essay indicates that such an improvement will be extremely difficult to bring about, and that international capital aid and technical assistance are urgently important to promote a break through.

But international aid will fail unless it sets in motion an indigenous cumulative process of innovations and capital formation, which increases productive power more rapidly than population growth. While capital aid for specific projects and technical assistance programmes directed to specific technological improvements have their place, the conception of a cumulative process implies changes in attitudes, institutions, organizations and social relationships; an Oriental renaissance to which specific technological improvements may contribute, but with which they must be consistent at any particular time and place, if their effects are not to be ephemeral.

While the case for technical aid rests substantially on the acceptance of western techniques, and some western value judgments and forms of organization, dangers arise if the ethnocentric preconceptions of the West are unduly pressed. Dangers either that aid may be rejected because such preconceptions are repug-

---

* As expressed, for example, in *Report to the President on Foreign Economic Policies*, Washington, 1950; and *The Mutual Security Programmes for a Strong and Free World*, First Report to Congress, Washington, December, 1951.

nant to those whom foreign help is designed to benefit, or that if accepted the aid cannot be absorbed in the culture, so that failure results which leads to disillusionment.

'In many areas of the world and among large groups of people,' states a recent United States Report,* 'the Soviet Union is making a desperate effort to capitalize, even though cynically and with false promise, on the swelling social and economic pressures now dominant throughout the world. We must hold the initiative in this field; a persistent application of the principles of our free and democratic society can provide the only answer.' Such expressions of the efficacy or desirability of extending the American way of life (or the British or Dutch way of life for that matter) provoke such retorts as the following: 'The United States is, however, evidently interested at the same time in upholding a social philosophy which, whatever its merits in a rich country with special tradition, is highly inimical to the whole planning effect. Therefore, even if the unexpected happens and large investments are intelligently made, for the development of countries like India these appear likely, in existing circumstances, to lead immediately not to desirable social objectives, but to the strengthening on the one hand of the forces of monopoly, and to an increase on the other of social discontent and conflict.'†

Such observations have a bearing even in respect of investment criteria which may appear to be politically neutral. Thus capital intensive investments in heavy industry which, in the long run, may increase income and capital formation more than less intensive forms, may defer the time when levels of consumption are raised, and by concentration of wealth and economic power, strengthen 'the forces of monopoly'. The social and political consequences may then outweigh the advantages referred to, even in terms of long run consumption levels, and strengthen the forces making for non-democratic solutions.

Restraint is necessary both in attempting to apply western

* *Report to the President on Foreign Economic Policies*, p. 20.

† D. R. Gadgil, Foreword to *Planning of Post-War Development in India.* by N. V. Sovani, Gokhale Institute of Politics and Economics, and Institute of Pacific Relations, 1951, p. xi.

stereotypes of democracy, or economic organization and relationships, to very different societies, and in tying economic aid too overtly and closely to politico-strategic aims. 'The current witticism that the U.S. does not interest herself in any country unless there are enough communists around,' writes N.V. Sovani,* 'reflects reality to a greater extent than would appear at first sight.... Giving aid on the basis of immediate political or military considerations as is being done at present, amounts to patching up the rent for the time being only. It does not advance the American cause. It also does not further the policy of halting the communist tide.' Opinions of this sort may be unfair; for humanitarian motives and enlightened economic self-interest are influential, as well as political and strategic objectives. But such views are by no means uncommon, even amongst opponents of communism in Asian countries. Minimum requirements as to stability in Government, and efficiency and integrity in the disbursal of funds, may very properly be required before assistance is given; but political and strategic conditions may be refused, especially among societies still resentful of colonialism and experiencing a sensitive emergent nationalism, thereby defeating the best of intentions. Difficulties are reinforced also by fluctuations in financial aid and technical assistance programmes. Budgetary uncertainty and changes from which the technical assistance agencies suffer, both national and international, may not only increase the difficulties of the administering authorities, but also prejudicially affect the attitudes of recipient countries.

It seems apparent also that the mere increase in productive power is not sufficient to remove internal discontents and stresses. The socio-economic changes and dislocations which were taking place before the war, and have been increased by it, will be further accelerated by economic development. The further disruption of existing value systems which is bound to occur, may well create a vacuum which the increase in levels of consumption alone is not enough to fill. If occasions are not to be provided for communist leadership, the nature of the process by which such

* *Op. cit.*, p. 89.

an improvement occurs is just as important as the material end product. Even in the interests of economic development therefore, plans and programmes must be so devised as to promote the emergence of new and satisfying value systems for those which are being undermined. The character of the indigenous cumulative process of innovations and capital formation referred to earlier must satisfy other aspirations as well as those for material improvement, if Asian peoples are to be relieved of the pressures to attempt revolutionary solutions.

In essence the process requires approaches which stimulate and provide opportunities for active participation by the people, in both planning and implementing programmes for their own betterment. This is not entirely inconsistent with the 'persistent application of the principles of (the American) free and democratic society' provided that we think in terms of the ideal rather than the specific forms in which these principles are expressed in the United States. It implies, for example, free participation in electing political leaders who are tolerably honest; but in the agrarian sector especially, it goes much further in placing less emphasis on the 'atomistic' individual pursuit of self-interest, and more emphasis on developing the potentialities for self-help and mutual help which already exist, through the more effective organization of group activities, the removal of institutional impediments such as systems of land tenure which provide opportunities for exploitation, and emphasis on social reform, both as a direct contribution to satisfying aspirations towards economic betterment and as a means to improve individual capacities. Since this theme is developed more fully later, we do not enlarge upon it here.

III

We may express the viewpoint in another way by saying that although the theory of economic development might be the same for economically advanced as for under-developed countries, the problems of application are of a different order. This arises not only because of differences in the economic data such as the ratio of population to resources, or the rate of capital formation, but also because the whole culture* of under-developed societies is different.

To consider the precise characteristics of an 'under-developed' country would provide a tempting field for definitional polemics; but this would be unfruitful. For the time being I shall regard an under-developed country as a relatively poor country in terms of real income per head, but in which there are potentialities for improvement. I should consider virtually all the countries in Asia with the exception of Japan and possibly Israel as coming within this category. Many of the characteristics of these countries as they affect the population-consumption relationship, and the main requirements if potentialities for improvement are to be realized, are considered in the following pages. We can get along (and avoid recapitulation) without discussing them in detail here. It is sufficient to mention one or two.

Usually one difference in under-developed countries is in the attitudes of people towards family limitation. Another allied difference is that, while the current rates of growth of population in 'developed' countries may affect the rates of improvement in consumption levels, there are few if any such countries in which it is so rapid as to prevent such an improvement altogether. On the other hand there is a strong presumption that in many under-developed countries in Asia, and elsewhere, current or prospective rates of growth may be such as to prevent improvement in levels of consumption, or even cause regression, apart from substantial changes in non-demographic factors in the development equation, for example, in the rate of growth of capital. Especially important differences, which we shall stress, are in the propensity to innovate, and in the degree of receptivity to innovation.

We must give attention to the requirements for changes in these if development is to occur, to some problems in meeting these requirements, and to the utilization of resources at present idle,

---

* Culture may be described as, 'That complex whole which includes knowledge, belief, art, morals, law, customs and any other capabilities and habits acquired by man as a member of society.' Edward B. Tylor, *Primitive Culture*, Murray, London, 1891, p. 1.

particularly labour; but as mentioned in the foreword, many aspects of the problem such as changes in the barter terms of trade or the stabilization of export receipts, will not be considered or will be given only passing reference.

There are conceptual and statistical difficulties in measuring changes in the volume of production and consumption, the amount of capital, labour, national resources and so on, but these do not affect the general tenor of the argument, and we shall not do more than touch on them as the occasion arises.*

We shall regard a rising trend of levels of consumption and of output per head as meaning much the same; but they are not identical, if only because the proportion of national real income devoted to capital formation or to defence may change from time to time. Moreover, the distribution of the national dividend may be such that though a sort of average of productive power and consumption per head increases, large masses benefit very little, if at all. The distribution of the product is a matter of great importance and may have indirect effects on the problem before us, but except for these effects it is not a matter of primary concern in this essay. In terms of the particular problem with which we are concerned, no great harm will be done for the time being by regarding a rising trend of consumption per head and of output per head as coming to the same thing.

The notion of levels of consumption requires a little elucidation. In current discussions the phrase 'standard of living' is commonly used to connote what we have in mind. This is unfortunate because four different concepts may be covered by the phrase. These are: (1) The Level of Consumption; (2) The Standard of Consumption; (3) The Level or Plane of Living; (4) The Standard of Living. It is useful to follow Joseph S. Davis

---

* For an important if somewhat iconoclastic discussion of conceptual difficulties, cf. S. Herbert Frankel, *The Economic Impact on Under-Developed Societies:* especially Chapters III-V. Basil Blackwell, Oxford, 1953. For one of the most suggestive of recent attempts to set up a conceptual *framework* for the analysis of problems of economic development, cf. W. W. Rostow, *op. cit.*, Chapters I-VI. Marshall's *Principles*, Book IV, is also worth re-reading.

in distinguishing between them.* By the *level of consumption* is meant a 'sort of aggregate' of goods and services used up by an individual or a group. It would include services consumed, such as medical attention, or schooling, as well as consumption goods as ordinarily understood. The *standard of consumption* is the level of consumption accepted or aspired to by an individual or a group. It is a measure by which the adequacy of the existing level is judged. The *level or plane or content of living* includes more than the level of consumption. It covers all elements in well-being, 'immaterial' elements, such as political security, or the pleasures of family life, as well as goods and services.† The *standard of living* 'is the plane—of living which an individual or group earnestly seeks and strives to attain, to maintain if attained, to preserve if threatened, to regain if lost.' It embodies the whole complex value system of the individual or group. The selection of terms is not entirely happy, though it is the best to hand, and the distinctions are not always clear cut. But sufficient has been said to bring out that levels of consumption and standards of consumption are only a part of the corresponding levels and standards of living. Levels, or planes, or content, relate to what is. Standards are norms to which people aspire. But standards are also formulated by leaders, or observers, to indicate what they think people ought to want, or a society should aim at.

The distinctions also serve to bring out that the population question is a moral one. People may resist attempts to raise levels of consumption by propaganda in favour of family limitation, because this is inconsistent with the value systems embodied in their standard of living. A major difficulty in promoting economic development may be that the existing standard of living is such

---

* Joseph S. Davis, 'Standards and Content of Living', *American Economic Review*, Vol. XXXV, No. 1, March, 1945. See also M. K. Bennett, 'Disparities in Consumption Levels,' *op. cit.* For a further consideration of the problems of definition and measurement, cf. *Definition and Measurement of Standards of Living*. Report of a Conference of U.S. Experts, Public Administration Clearing House, Chicago, 1953.

† For an attempt to classify these, cf. *Essentials of Rural Welfare*, United Nations Food and Agriculture Organizations, Washington, D.C., 1949.

that economic betterment requires sacrifices which people are not prepared to make. Changes in attitudes may be required, not only in respect of family limitation, but also in respect of the propensity to work, innovate, consume, save and invest. Having regard to the current tendency to emphasize the importance of capital and technology without reference to people, it is important also to lay specific stress on the significance of human motivation as expressed in these propensities. Thus in many Asian countries' changes in attitudes towards family limitation are among those to be aimed at if *levels* of consumption are to rise sufficiently to satisfy existing *standards* of consumption, and even more, the higher standards of consumption which may be expected in the near future, as the result, *inter alia*, of the intensifying demonstration effect of western levels and standards.* But the resistance to such changes in attitudes is strong.

The observer also has his standard or moral philosophy, and with the best of intentions may find it difficult to avoid being influenced by it in the selection of questions and data, or even in his conclusions. It therefore seems proper to state briefly the viewpoint of this essay. My normative approach is to accept the very general opinion that an increase in levels of consumption is a desirable objective; but I recognize that this does not necessarily lead to an increase in over-all welfare, i.e., in levels of living. I concern myself with the relationship between population growth and levels of consumption, without passing judgment on the effects on levels of living as a whole of measures to increase consumption of material goods and services. I have no moral objection to birth control.† I am not therefore *predisposed* to sup-

---

* For a useful discussion of the importance of this demonstration effect, which, however, seems to require some qualification, cf. Ragnar Nurske, *Problems of Capital Formation in Under-Developed Countries*, Chapter III. Basil Blackwell, Oxford, 1953.

† I am a little bothered to find a suitable term. Positively, I should favour 'planned parenthood', which may imply a large family in some instances. But it is in respect of negative measures by the use of contraceptives that most emotion is generated. I use birth control more particularly to connote chemical or mechanical means to prevent birth, but to exclude abortion and

port or oppose birth control and slant the economic argument accordingly; but the economic data and this argument lead me to the conclusion that, as a general rule in the countries under consideration, birth control which retarded the rate of growth of population would make it very much easier to raise levels of consumption and to that extent is good. The viewpoint is that of a mildly optimistic neo-Malthusian, who recognizes and respects moral objections to birth control on the part of the people concerned, and notes these as obstacles to economic betterment which may have to be modified if the rate of increase in levels of consumption is to rise, or often even if consumption per head is to increase at all. As Dr. Taeuber very aptly phrases it, in a personal communication, we cannot project demographic movements in Asian countries 'straight to catastrophe'. There may be significant demographic innovations facilitating family limitation, just round the corner. Nevertheless, the difficulties in changing demographic attitudes point to the necessity for increased emphasis on non-demographic approaches.

The scope of the essay is also restricted in time. Our major interest is in the problems and prospects over the next few decades —say, three or four—and especially in the problems involved over the next five or ten years in promoting a 'break through' from conditions of virtual stagnation to a process of growth in real income per head. The data will have changed so much a 100 years hence that it is fruitless to speculate. Moreover, unless current schemes of international collaboration show some result within a reasonable period, people in the wealthier countries may grow weary of well-doing—there already are hints of this in the United States—and the recipients of foreign aid may become cynically sceptical of its value. The enhanced possibilities of political unrest consequent on failure are also of some importance, not only directly, but also because they may create additional impediments to economic improvement.

infanticide. I should not be prepared to take up a *general* moral position on sterilization or abortion, especially the latter, having regard to the danger to life and health of the individual mother.

There are some aspects of the population problem with which we shall not deal. One of these is the optimum rate of growth of population. In some developed countries such as Australia or New Zealand, where the sizable volume of immigration is a controllable element in population growth, an analysis of the factors which might be expected to determine the optimum rate of growth of population in terms of consumption levels might be highly suggestive.* In addition further discussion of the nature and meaning of optima might promote a better understanding of the terms over- and under-population.†

Nor shall we engage in arithmetical exercises as to what population the world or any country could 'support', or base comparisons on population densities. In the present state of knowledge such estimates are too conjectural to be of much use, and they may divert attention from the main determinants of economic development as they can be influenced by changes in human behaviour.‡

---

* The writer has made a preliminary attempt at such an analysis for New Zealand in *Immigration Problems and Policies in New Zealand* (Pamphlet); *New Zealand Financial Times*, Wellington, June, 1952; and in a series of articles in the *Financial Times* (commencing November, 1953) on 'Economic Development, Population Growth and the Future of Agriculture.'

† Among discussions of the concept, cf. Hugh Dalton, 'The Theory of Population,' *Economica*, March, 1928. E. F. Penrose, *Population Theories and Their Application*, Food Research Institute, Standford University, 1934. Chapters II and III; and Joseph J. Spengler, 'Population Theory' in *A Survey of Contemporary Economics*, Vol. II (Bernard F. Haley, Editor), Stanford University, 1952, and his bibliographical note, p. 113. See also, *The Determinants and Consequences of Population Trends*, United Nations, New York, 1953, pp. 233 *et seq.*

‡ Colin Clark, in 'Population Growth and Living Standards,' *International Labour Review*, Vol. LXVIII, No. 2, August, 1953, attempts such an exercise. After a discussion the gist of which is that diminishing returns in agriculture may be offset by more capital and improved technology, he estimates that at Danish productivity and dietary levels, a square kilometre of cultivable land would provide for about 200 people, or a square mile about 500 people. 'On this standard,' he asks, 'how much of the world is over-populated, or how much additional population can it support?' He then comes up with the following answers: The only countries of any size in the world which are overcrowded on this basis are Japan, the Netherlands, Belgium and probably Switzerland. The world's total cultivable area is

The urgent contemporary problem in most under-developed countries is not how many people they could feed at levels of nutrition comparable with those in Denmark if their people were as efficient as the Danes, nor even to promote an optimum line of growth in terms of consumption levels, but of somehow managing to bring about any cumulative increase at all. In this endeavour an improvement in levels of nutrition is of primary importance, but a 'bread and butter' or a 'rice bowl' consumption standard is hardly likely to be acceptable; for of recent years particularly, standards of consumption have risen and expanded to include not only more and better material things of familiar kinds, but also new material things, and better health, educational and other services. The gap between levels and standards of consumption has increased.

24 million square miles, and the world could support 12,000 million people at Danish levels of production and consumption instead of the 2,300 million it now supports. Elsewhere, however, Colin Clark, draws attention to the precarious nature of attempts at standardization of acres of land which would be necessary for estimates and comparisons of the above types (*Review of Economic Progress*, Vol. 4, Nos. 4, 5 and 6, April-June, 1952, p. 7).

PART I

ASPECTS OF THE POPULATION
SITUATION IN ASIAN COUNTRIES

CHAPTER I

THE POPULATION SITUATION

A. The Malthusian Dilemma

Writing in 1945, Warren S. Thompson* makes recurrent use of the phrase 'the Malthusian dilemma' in reference to Asian countries. Since the validity or otherwise, of the description is germane to the problem of promoting improvement, and since some writers tend to treat the Malthusian Law of Population with ridicule, or regard it as a form of reactionary economic witchcraft perpetrated in a pre-scientific age,† some brief reference to the degree of appropriateness of the Law as a description of conditions in countries in Asia is needed.

While Malthus had his forerunners, modern speculation on population problems begins with his *First Essay on Population*

---

* *Population and Peace in the Pacific*, University of Chicago Press, 1945.

† Colin Clark, 'Population Growth and Living Standards,' *op. cit.*, p. 100, regards many Malthusians as being 'propagandists' and suffering from 'anti-religious preconceptions'. 'Their point of view, they say, is purely scientific. If that is so there cannot be any group of scientists so ill-informed on the facts with which they are supposed to deal. Many Malthusians have no knowledge of the simplest facts about population; and those who do know some demography seem to be almost universally uninformed on economics.' This seems going a bit far, even about Malthusians. See also Kenneth Smith, *The Malthusian Controversy*, Routledge and Kegan-Paul, 1951, for an account which, though useful, is marred at times by a derisive tone and generally by the appearance of being more concerned with scoring off Malthus and proving him wrong than with a balanced appraisal. For more objective, if rapid and incomplete surveys of population theory, cf. Paul Douglas, *The Theory of Wages*, Chapters XIII–XVI, Macmillan, 1934; and Edmund Whittaker, *A History of Economic Ideas*, Longman Green, 1950, Chapter VII. For a most comprehensive survey of modern population theory and approaches, cf. Joseph S. Spengler, 'Population Theory,' *op. cit.*; and *The Determinants and Consequences of Population Trends*, op. cit., especially Chapter III.

(1798). We need only summarize the main elements in his Law of Population: like other living things, human beings if left unchecked tend to increase in geometric progression. Experience in the American colonies showed that population might double itself in twenty-five years, an annual geometric rate of increase of 3 per cent. But nature shows a niggardly response to man's efforts, so that the production of commodities, especially food, does not increase as rapidly. Food increases in arithmetical ratio. The dramatic numerical contrasts should be taken as illustrative rather than literal. Malthus was concerned to show that the means of life cannot increase as fast as population growth, if this is unchecked. Other values, for example, a geometric rate of increase of food supply smaller than of population would serve as well. Unless population growth is restrained by preventive checks it will be prevented by the means of subsistence, or other positive checks, i.e., it cannot in fact grow faster than food supply can be increased. The main preventive checks are delayed marriage and voluntary restraint within marriage. The main positive checks are 'vice' (in which he would include artificial control of conception,* and infanticide), disease, war and famine.

The essential elements in his theory of population are, then: (1) Diminishing returns to population growth, i.e., the tendency for a growing population to produce less food per head, which would follow if the numerical relationships held: (2) The tendency for population to grow at such a rate that the operation of the law results in positive checks round about the level of subsistence.

The falsification of Malthus's anticipations of the future in respect of western societies resulted, first, from innovations† which

---

* Whether the use of contraceptives is a preventive or a positive check then depends on one's moral viewpoint. I prefer to regard it as a preventive check.

† The term innovation is broadly understood (cf. below, Chapter XI). Joseph A. Schumpeter, *The Theory of Economic Development*, George Allen & Unwin, 1951, gives *discontinuous* innovations the key rôle in economic development. He lists five types of innovations (p. 66): (1) The introduction of a new good, or a new quality of a good; (2) the introduction

he did not foresee, second, from the increased capital formation which became possible out of the increased income resulting from innovations. These changes enabled productive power to grow more rapidly than population. The third factor operating at a later stage, for reasons to be discussed, was a decline in the birth rate, the mechanism being an increase in the age of marriage, but even more the extension of 'vice', i.e., in the form of a more wide-spread use of methods to prevent conception. So population in Western Europe displayed the logistic S-shaped curve of growth, made familiar by Pearl and others,* a slow rate of increase at low consumption levels, being followed by a decline in mortality (of which improved health measures as well as improved economic conditions were an important cause), unaccompanied by a corre-sponding decline in fertility, but with such an increase in produc-tive power as exceeded the rapid increase in population; and eventually by such a decline in birth rates as caused the rate of increase in population to flatten out. Since we shall refer later to the logistic curve, we may add that it does not describe a 'Law of Population' but merely what has happened in various societies.

It is of some importance that the changes in attitudes which caused the birth rate to decline do not seem to have been origi-nating causes of an improved ratio of production to the increase in population growth. Rather they were delayed effects of other changes including those which had a prior influence on produc-tion per head. When primitive societies have become dispirited and lost their *elan vital* because disrupted by contact with more powerful societies, fertility may decline. It would be helpful to

of a new method of production; (3) the opening of a new market; (4) the conquest of a new source of supply of raw materials or semi-finished goods; (5) the carrying out of a new organization of industry. We would include in the concept any change affecting the efficiency of labour, capital or organiza-tion other than one resulting from a change in the ratio of population to capital and natural resources, or economies of scale, and would not require the innovations to be discontinuous.

* Raymond Pearl, *The Biology of Population Growth*, Knopf, 1930, and *The Natural History of Population*, Oxford University Press, 1939, Chapter VI.

have a socio-economic analysis of such cases,* but they are exceptional and the biological generalization of Malthus would appear to be the norm in the absence of a social process which included quite important economic innovations. We should expect this biological trend of population towards subsistence level to be typical, except for marked and rapid improvements in technology, and for changes in attitudes which resulted from, or were concomitants of, the process of which an increase in production per head was a part. The innovations must be of such a magnitude as to offset any tendency to diminishing returns to population growth, or else there must be a rate of capital accumulation in excess of the biologically feasible rate of population increase.

The failure of Malthus to assess the significance of the technological changes, which were to occur and increase productive power, caused him to see little hope save in population limitation, and to justify economic inequality because of its bearing on the accumulation of capital. While, as will be suggested, his main generalizations are not so very far from describing the current situation in many Asian countries, the greater appreciation which historical experience has made possible of the rôle of innovations and of capital, warrants a somewhat less pessimistic view, and (incidentally) provides a stronger argument for international capital aid and technical assistance. But attempts to retard the prospective rate of growth must be given some importance, if consumption levels are to rise. In most developed countries the acceleration of the rate of population growth of recent years need not be the occasion for jeremiads. It may create difficulties and retard the rate of increase in income per head, but innovations and capital formation seem likely to permit a trend of increase in levels of consumption for some time. On the other hand current and prospective rates of increase in many under-developed countries are such that a small diminution in the rate of increase of population may make a big difference to the chances of raising levels of

* This appears to be exemplified among Andean Indians and for a time among the New Zealand Maoris. But we should require to distinguish between such effects and the effects of new diseases before immunity was gained.

consumption. With these observations in mind we consider the demographic situation in a number of countries in Asia.

B. Demographic Conditions

The 'Malthusian dilemma', to which Thompson refers, consists in the marked tendency of population increase to absorb any increase in national real income. It is in this sense that the phrase is used rather than of a rigid relationship between size of population and the means of subsistence.

JAPAN. The only non-western society in which a break through has occurred leading towards an S-shaped population growth is Japan. Here innovations enabled consumption levels to rise, and this with the accompanying changes in social and economic structure affected fertility. In other countries in Asia evidence of any continued decline in fertility appears to be rare—populations were doing their best to follow the biological law of Malthus. The main control was through mortality.

As Taeuber and Notestein point out, Japan is the one nation outside western culture which has achieved a substantial degree of industrialization and an appreciable decline in fertility.* But 'from the first settlement by Neolithic man to the beginning of the eighteenth century . . . the slow and irregular growth of the Japanese population . . . was similar to that of all other agrarian peoples for whom even approximate documentation is possible. . . . Population always tended to expand beyond the limits of permanent subsistence within the existing economic and technological system.'† The significant word here is agrarian. Other Asian countries have not yet broken through the framework of agrarian society in which generally there seems no strong tendency for birth rates to change, and fluctuations in population growth result mainly from changes in death rates.

CHINA. In the opinion of Warren Thompson, 'The intimate relationship that obtains between population and means of subsistence, for any given people is, perhaps, nowhere more clearly

---

* Irene B. Taeuber and Frank W. Notestein, 'The Changing Fertility of the Japanese,' *Population Studies*, Vol. I, No. 1, June, 1947. Reprint, p. 1.
† *Ibid.*, pp. 4–5.

illustrated than in China.'* Of recent centuries, supported by the extension of agriculture on steeper slopes and into unused regions, the population seems to have expanded. Within the past century, however, it has increased very little, and some students believe that it has not grown at all.† Apart from marked changes in techniques little more land appears to be tillable. Such statistical evidence as is available indicates marked fluctuations in natural increase, with death rates exercising the dominant rôle. In addition to wars, famine and the ravages of disease have imposed positive checks, with extreme poverty, little if any relieved by economic growth, always exerting its pressure. The following table gives crude birth and death rates and natural increase per 1,000 in Hsaio Chi, Kiangyia, Kiangsu:

Years	Birth rates	Death rates	Natural increase
1931–35 . .	45·1	38·7	6·4
1934–35 . .	48·0	23·8	24·2
1933–34 . .	40·0	52·0	—12·0
1932–33 . .	44·1	37·2	8·0
1931–32 . .	48·3	41·4	5·5

In years when harvests are good and there are no epidemics, we should expect birth rates to be higher and death rates lower; but, as Thompson properly comments, the violent fluctuation in death rates, much greater than that in birth rates, is probably characteristic of all populations which, like that of China, have practically no health service and live close to the subsistence level even in good years.‡ The figures in the table are quoted from a small area and so may not be representative for China as a whole. Nevertheless the correlation between good harvests and both

* *Op. cit.*, p. 176.
† Cf. *Public Health and Demography in the Far East*, by M. C. Balfour, R. F. Evans, T. W. Notestein and Irene B. Taeuber. Rockefeller Foundation, New York, 1950, p. 73. I have no information on demographic conditions in China under the present régime.
‡ *Op. cit.*, p. 181.

birth rates and death rates might be expected to be close in poor agrarian societies. Confirmation for an earlier phase in Europe in respect of birth rates is given in the following passage: 'For northern European agrarian communities of the eighteenth century it has been shown that years of abundant harvests were followed by years with high birth rates, and years with crop failure were followed by years with low birth rates. While marriage rates as well as birth rates fluctuated with food conditions, the fluctuations in birth rates were not due merely to fluctuations in marriage rates. Among other things, variations in physical stamina which might influence the ability to carry pregnancies to successful completion seem to have operated to produce the rather close correlation between food conditions and both legitimate and illegitimate fertility. During the nineteenth century this correlation decreased in importance.'* Similarly, there used to be a close connection in Europe between famines or food shortages and mortality.†

INDIA. Conditions in India show a similar pattern. As in the figures quoted for China, changes have shown considerable fluctuations.‡

Decade	Births	Deaths	Natural increase
1881–91 . .	48·9	41·3	7·6
1891–1901 . .	45·8	44·4	1·4
1901–11 . .	49·2	42·6	6·6
1911–21 . .	48·1	47·2	0·9
1921–31 . .	46·4	36·3	10·1
1931–41 . .	45·2	31·2	14·0

* The Determinants and Consequences of Population Trends, op. cit., p. 84.
† Ibid., p. 51.
‡ After Kingsley Davis, The Population of India and Pakistan, Princetown University Press, 1951, p. 85. See also D. Ghosh, Pressure of Population and Economic Efficiency in India, Indian Council of World Affairs and Oxford University Press, 1946, pp. 62–63. See also Kingsley Davis, 'Demographic Fact and Policy in India,' in Demographic Studies of Selected Areas of Rapid Growth, Milbank Memorial Fund, 1944, pp. 40–42.

The 1951 census gives the following changes between census years in Lakhs of people* :

1891					
1901	.	.	. −4	1931 .	. . +274
1911	.	.	. +135	1941 .	. . +373
1921	.	.	. −9	1951 .	. . +441

The fluctuating death rate to which this population behaviour is 'mainly attributable is an index of the fitful and inadequate control over environment.'† A substantial increase in national output has led to a commensurate growth in population, so that though in some respects conditions of life have improved, 'large numbers still live on the borderline of existence between life and death.'‡ The important single factor responsible for the high death rate is malnutrition, a natural product of poverty. This directly occasions nutritional diseases and increases susceptibility to other diseases. Together with dirt it reduces resistance to the fluctuating hazards of crop failure and epidemics.§

Commenting on the accelerated growth of recent years the Census report‖ attributes the improvement to a reduction in 'abnormal' deaths. Normal death rates have slightly diminished as a result of improved hygiene and medicine, but severe famines, plague and localized epidemics of malaria, kala-azar and other 'fevers' have been brought under greater control thereby reducing

---

* *Census of India*, 1951, Vol. I, Part 1–A, Report, p. 122. These results are not exactly consistent with those of Kingsley Davis quoted above, e.g., over the period 1911–21. One Lakh = 100,000.

† Ghosh, *op. cit.*, p. 63.

‡ *Op. cit.*, p. 63.

§ *Op. cit.*, *loc. cit.* This vulnerability was tragically brought home to the writer during a recent mission to villages in many parts of India, for example in Madras where the failure of monsoons and poor harvests set large numbers on the move for work, many to succumb from cholera. One who has seen poverty and its concomitants in rural areas in India, China or Egypt does not doubt the reality of Malthusian checks, even though he may cavil at Malthusian arithmetic.

‖ *Op. cit.*, pp. 124–34.

abnormal deaths. The report also draws attention to the relationship between abundance of harvests and mortality. Kingsley Davis also lists control of famine and epidemic disease and the reduction of war and banditry as the major causes of a decline in mortality. He draws attention to the 'surprising fact' that the percentage decline in infantile mortality has not been as great as the general mortality.*

As will be discussed later, industrialization has not been sufficient over the past fifty years to reduce the proportion of population dependent on agriculture. There has been some tendency for net area sown per caput to decline,† and evidence conflicts as to whether yields of food crops have remained virtually stable or declined. According to Dr. S. R. Sen,‡ yields 'do not show any definite trend either way—while the fertility of the soil or standard of husbandry has not perhaps gone down, it has not gone up either.' On the other hand, Dr. Baljit Singh gives area and production per head of population in British India as follows over the period 1921–22 to 1941–42:

Years	Area per head	Production per head
	(Acres)	(Lb.)
1921–2 . .	0·678	524
1931–2 . .	0·611	436
1941–2 . .	0·529	347

(*Population and Food Planning in India*, Kind Kitabs, Bombay, 1947, p. 62.)

Yields for individual years will be affected by climatic conditions, but Dr. Singh reports that the gap between population and food supply was constantly widening over the period. The Census

* *The Population of India and Pakistan*, pp. 39 et seq., and p. 35.
† Dr. S. R. Sen, 'Population and Food Supply in India,' *Agricultural Situation in India*, Vol. VII, No. 8, New Delhi, November, 1952, p. 448.
‡ *Op. cit.*, p. 449.

report* gives changes in the area of cultivated land in 'cents' per caput as follows.

1891	.	.	. 109	1931	.	.	. 104
1901	.	.	. 103	1941	.	.	. 94
1911	.	.	. 109	1951	.	.	. 84
1921	.	.	. 111				

There is no evidence of under-utilization of land, but on the contrary, evidence of excessive use. Since 1921, the rate of population growth in towns has been somewhat greater than in villages, but the rate of growth of rural population has substantially outstripped the rate of progress of cultivation. It seems very unlikely that there has been a growth of rural industries and services to offset this difference. The relative dependence on agriculture for employment has not declined in the country as a whole and there has been an increase in cultivators, and cultivating labourers working on a given area of land, and in non-earning dependants. In or about 1880 India was usually a surplus producer of grain, but more recently has been a net importer. This is not the result of a shift in agricultural production away from food grains.† Kingsley Davis concludes that with the growth of population, more and more people have sought to find a living in farming, there has been and can be no great increase in the total supply of cultivated land, and there has been no real rise in the farmland's productivity. There has been a trend towards less and less land per cultivator. He states 'there is one economic fact of sufficient duration to have some connection with population—it is generally admitted that even in recent decades the standard of living, if it has risen at all, has risen very little.'‡

Sen § gives the following table comparing estimated availability of food for consumption in pre-war and post-war years with the composition of a balanced diet:

* *Op. cit.*, p. 141.
† Census Report, pp. 152–75, also p. 33.
‡ *Ibid.*, pp. 205 *et seq.*
§ Sen, *op. cit.*, p. 451.

Food	Ounces per adult per day			
	Compos-ition of a balanced diet (per consump-tion unit)	Estimated availability for consumption in India		
		Pre-war[1] average (1934–38)	Post-war[1]	
			(1949–50)	(1950–51)
Cereals	14	16·3	13·7	13·0
Pulses	3	1·9[2]	1·9[2]	1·9[2]
Leafy Vegetables	4 }	3·7	2·0	1·6
Other Vegetables. . . .	6 }			
Ghee and Vegetable Oil . .	2	0·25	0·35	0·36
Milk and Milk Products . .	10	7·3	4·9	4·8
Meat, Fish and Eggs . . .	4	0·6	0·4	0·4
Fruit and Nuts	3	3·3	1·9	1·9
Sugar and Jaggery . . .	2	1·6[3]	1·4[3]	1·5[3]

[1] Undivided India.   [2] Includes grain.   [3] In terms of gur.

(Source S. M. Roy, 'Food Consumption in India', *Agricultural Situation in India*, 1952, p. 87.)

India requires to import food, but nutritional levels are inadequate, so that the gap between production and requirements has not been met by imports.

The Indian Census* report makes estimates and observations as to future population growth in relation to food supply. If current shortages are to be made good and *current* levels of consumption maintained, the minimal estimates of population growth in rounded figures, compared with food requirements, are as follows:

Years	Population (Millions)	Tons of food grains (Lakhs)
1951. . .	361	
1961. . .	408	850
1971. . .	453	960
1981. . .	516	1,080

* Pp. 181 *et seq.*

The report states that unless the rate of growth of population is checked by the use of contraceptives or a breakdown of food supply, it will proceed at a faster rate during 1951–80 than during 1921–50. After assessing the prospects of increased yield due to increased acreage, an increase in the area under irrigation, and methods other than irrigation, the conclusion is expressed in the following terms: 'Of course there will never be a point of time at which it can be said that the last improvement has been effected. But if we draw the moral correctly from the *many unmistakable signs which go to show that the law of diminishing returns is in effective operation*, we should make up our minds to the fact that *our effort to keep pace with unchecked growth of population is bound to fail at some point*. If the analysis of the subject . . . is even approximately valid, we should be able to go one step further and *fix* this point by saying that it is the time at which our total number reaches and passes 45 crores'*—i.e., 450,000,000.

In considering the matter further, use is made of an index of 'improvident maternity', i.e., births occurring to mothers who have already given birth to three or more children, expressed as a percentage of all births. The following compares the index of improvident maternity in various countries:

India	42·8
Japan	33·9
U.S.A.	19·2
France . ' . .	19·7
U.K.	14·3
Germany . . .	12·3

Since, in the absence of family limitation, checks might be anticipated in the form of declining food consumption per head, the report considers the problem of family limitation and adds: 'Let us then define our general aim to be—*so to limit the number of births that they do not materially exceed a substantially stationary population before our number exceeds 45 crores* (i.e., 450 million). That would be a first step towards a crystallization of ideas on targets and priorities.'† This would be achieved substantially by

* *Op. cit.*, p. 207
† *Op. cit.*, p. 216.

putting an end to improvident maternity. The Indian evidence leaves little doubt of the existence of a Malthusian dilemma.

JAVA AND MADURA. In Java and Madura improved agriculture, health and hygiene, public order and the availability of land enabled the population to increase from an estimated 5 millions in 1816 to 41 millions in 1930, a growth comparable with that in Europe since the Napoleonic wars.* But before the second world war the pressure of population, for whom 'the sheer mass and the poverty . . . made individual migration impossible',† had already caused the Dutch Government to plan colonization schemes to the outer islands. Improvements in health and economic conditions enabled the population to grow as long as land remained available, but the end result is that Indonesia is now faced with a population crisis presenting grave difficulties,‡ for a young and inexperienced independent administration. As Thompson points out, the lowering of the death rate is in itself indicative of a certain amount of improvement in the level of living. But there is no evidence of a decline in the birth rate. The technological improvements which occurred, including plantations, the oil industry and some few other industries, were not sufficiently marked either to lead to any substantial improvements in levels of consumption (in a sense which would exclude health and some schooling) or so to modify the agrarian structure as to affect the birth rate to any degree.

I have confined specific reference to the above countries, partly because there is more information about them, but also to avoid overloading the text. The same sort of story may be told of Korea and Taiwan.§ In Malaya and Ceylon the position is modified by the development of export crops. In Burma, Thailand, the Philippines and Ceylon, the Malthusian dilemma may be deferred because there is still land available, provided that the economic

* *Public Health and Demography in the Far East*, p. 90.
† *Ibid.*, p. 95.
‡ *Ibid.*, p. 97, and Thompson, *op. cit.*, p. 257.
§ Cf. *Public Health and Demography in the Far East*; Thompson, *op. cit.*; *Demographic Studies of Selected Areas of Rapid Growth*; and A. M. Carr Saunders, *World Population*, Oxford University Press, 1936.

costs of new settlement can be met as rapidly as the need to settle more people. But at this point we are met with the prospect of acceleration in the rate of population increase, a question which we discuss shortly.

INTERNATIONAL COMPARISONS. Comparisons of birth rates and death rates in individual countries according to the degree of economic development, will be modified by factors such as the age compositions of the population, which are not always particularly germane to our present enquiry. Thus in some developed countries, crude death rates are high because of the high percentage of aged persons. So the inverse correlation of economic development with birth rates is usually higher than with death rates. But as a general rule both crude birth rates and death rates are higher in under-developed countries. This is shown by the following regional comparisons:

Estimated Crude Birth Rates and Death Rates per 1,000 and Annual Increase in Numbers

Regions	Round about 1947		Annual increase in numbers
	Birth rates	Death rates	
World. . . .	35–37	22–25	26–32 million
Africa	40–45	25–30	2·5–3 ,,
America:			
Northern America .	25	10	2·3 ,,
Latin-America . .	40	17	3·5 ,,
Asia	40–45	28–32	12–18 ,,
Europe . . .	24	13	5·3 ,,
Oceania . . .	28	12	0·2 ,,

(After *United Nations Preliminary Report on World Social Situation*, E/CN.5/267, New York, 1952, pp. 10, 21 and 27.)

In North America and Oceania, the average annual increase was round about 15 per 1,000 between 1947 and 1949, as against 9 per 1,000 in Europe, and 23 per thousand in Latin-America. In Africa and Asia coverage is less complete, but the estimates are 10–15 per 1,000 in the former region and somewhat lower in Asia, but it will be noted from the table that the *absolute* increase in numbers in Asia is very great, say 50 per cent of the world increase. Link this to poverty, and aspirations for betterment, and international expression of responsibility to help towards betterment, and it becomes one of the significant movements in human history.

The *United Nations Demographic Year Book* gives figures for crude birth rates, crude death rates, and for the annual rates of increase in a number of Asian countries. These must be based on official figures. In Ceylon, Japan, and Taiwan estimates are probably reliable; but in other countries, registered vital statistics are subject to such wide margins of error as to be of little value. Accordingly we quote from United Nations' sources only the following for the countries mentioned:

Country	Crude birth rates per 1,000	Crude death rates per 1,000	Annual percentage rate of increase over various years
Ceylon .	37·3 (1951)	11·6 (1951)	2·62 (1946–53)
Japan . .	25·4 (1951)	10·0 (1951)	2·13 (1947–50)
Taiwan .	46·6 (1952)	9·9 (1952)	2·41 (1935–40)

(After *United Nations Demographic Year Book*, 1953. Various Tables.)

It would be interesting, if adequate data were available, to examine the correlation between current levels of real income or current growth in real income and rates of population increase. Of equal, and probably even greater importance, are differing degrees of extension of preventive health measures.

NUTRITION. Nutritional levels should be considered in the setting sketched out in the preceding paragraphs. The *World Food Survey* published by F.A.O. in 1946* drew attention to widespread pre-war deficiencies in food consumption below the levels needed for health and efficiency, and the association of this condition with deficiency diseases, increased susceptibility to other

* *World Food Survey*, Food and Agriculture Organization of the United Nations, Washington, D.C., 1946 *passim.*

diseases and high mortality. The areas of greatest deficiency were Central America and most of Asia, and probably parts of South America and Africa not covered by the survey. National averages concealed uneven distribution among different economic strata of the population. While other causes also existed, poverty was the main cause of deficiency. The most recent *Review of the World Food Situation** indicates that for the first time since 1939, though as yet insecurely, global food production has caught up with the population increase. But the increase has been in the 'agricul- turally more advanced countries.' In the less developed areas as a whole food production has not kept pace with population increase so that there has been some deterioration of the pre-war situation. Thus for the Far East, excluding China, the index numbers of food production per caput are given as follows (base 1934-38 = 100):

1948/9–1950/1 . . 83	
1951/2. . . . 82	
1952/3. . . . 82	

For an increase in global supplies to become permanently avail- able to the poverty stricken areas (an eleemosynary solution can- not but be precarious), would require not only in many cases that food habits would have to be changed, but also ability to purchase food out of exports—in short, a successful process of economic development. With the tendency for population growth to accelerate in many Asian countries the position becomes more serious, and the regional disparities more marked.

The *Second World Food Survey* published in 1952† makes esti- mates which take account of environmental temperature, body weight and age and sex compositions of a population. Estimated calorie supplies measured against requirements for health and efficiency are then given as follows for certain Asian countries for most recent years:

* 'The State of Food and Agriculture, 1953,' Part I, *Review and Outlook*, Rome, August, 1953.
† Food and Agriculture Organization, Rome, November, 1952.

Calories

Country	Recent level	Estimated requirements	Per cent difference
Ceylon	1,970	2,270	—13·2
India	1,700	2,250	—24·4
Japan	2,100	2,330	— 9·9
Pakistan	2,020	2,300	—12·2
Philippines.	1,960	2,230	—12·1

In addition to calorie shortages there are deficiencies in proteins and protective foods.*

OTHER INDICATORS. The following comparisons of fibre consumption provide another indication of relative poverty, even though it might be demonstrated that fibre consumption is higher in Asia than bare requirements for subsistence:

Fibre Consumption
(Kilograms per Caput)

Region	Cotton	Wool	Rayon	Total
Europe	3·7	1·4	1·4	6·5
North America	11·8	1·9	3·2	16·9
Central and South America	2·8	0·4	0·5	3·7
Asia	1·4	0·08	0·1	1·6
Africa.	1·1	0·2	0·2	1·5
Oceania	3·9	2·7	1·5	7·7

(*Per Caput Fibre Consumption Levels.* Commodity Series Bulletin No. 21, December, 1951. Food and Agriculture Organization of the United Nations, Rome, January, 1952.)

* In *Population, Food and Economic Progress, op. cit.,* pp. 25–26, and in other writings, M. K. Bennett issues a caution against drawing inferences from statistical tabulations as to the prevalence of hunger or starvation and mentions differences in bodyweight and other factors as affecting requirements. It will be noted that the estimates given above make an attempt at correcting for such differences.

The needs for food and fibre will be affected by climate and other conditions, and so are subject to qualifications as indices of relative poverty. But there are other indicators which confirm the general picture, such as those summarized in the following comparative table for India and New Zealand:

Indicators	India	New Zealand
Literacy	9·1[1]	over 95 %
Per cent School Enrolments to total population		
Primary	4·6	14·9
Post-primary	1·4	3·5
Inhabitants per radio set	500[2]	5[3]
Inhabitants, per copy of daily newspaper .	100–500	5[3]
Annual consumption of newsprint per person.	0·6 Kgs.	11–20 Kgs.

[1] Able to read and write.   [2] At least.   [3] Not more than.

(After *United Nations Preliminary Report on World Social Situation*, 1952. Various tables.)

As a further indicator we note that there are fewer than 2,000 persons per physician in the United States, United Kingdom and New Zealand, but 5,000–10,000 in Ceylon and Malaya, 10,000–50,000 in Pakistan, and over 50,000 in Indonesia and Indo-China.* In an important study which attempts to provide a more reliable basis for international comparisons of levels of consumption, M. K. Bennett† rates a large number of countries in pre-war years according to 19 indicators. The following table gives the relative score for some selected countries‡:

* *United Nations Preliminary Report on World Social Situation*, p. 56.

† 'Disparities in Consumption Levels,' *American Economic Review*, Vol. XLI, No. 4, September, 1951, pp. 632–649.

‡ Among the data included are total calories at retail level consumed per 100 lb. of humanity per day; proportion derived from grain and potatoes; reciprocals of infantile mortality rates; physicians per 1,000 of population; non-industrial utilization of non-human energy; consumption of textile fibres; percentage of school-age population attending school. For a full list and discussion, cf. work quoted, pp. 638 *et seq.*

Country	Unweighted	Weighted
United States . . .	100	100
Canada	80·6	83·7
United Kingdom . .	75·6	76·6
Philippines . . .	25·7	21·6
India	20·8	16·8
China	18·0	13·8

These selected comparisons are not intended as precise measures of differences in levels of consumption, still less of welfare, but merely to remind the reader of the rough order of size of the differences in developed and under-developed countries. There is no doubt that these are considerable. While any single indicator may be open to criticism, the general picture is one of levels of consumption which are so low that it would not seem to unduly strain the use of words, or be an undue concession to Malthus to describe the population in many Asian countries as living pretty close to the subsistence level, especially if account be taken of the prevalence in many countries of deplorable conditions of housing and sanitation.*

RATES OF POPULATION GROWTH. Reference was made earlier to the tendency for the future rate of population growth to increase. We base this on the expectation that (for reasons which must be discussed at some length) birth rates are not usually likely to decline significantly for some time, and that the extension of preventive health measures will reduce mortality. Mass vaccination, the use of DDT, and other means for large scale malaria control have already shown important results in some countries since the war.

The following table gives crude birth rates and death rates at five-yearly periods since 1937, and in the latest year for which figures are available for countries in South and South-East Asia for which the coverage is complete, and for Japan:

* On housing, cf. *Low Cost Housing in South and South-East Asia*, United Nations, ST/SOA/3, New York, March, 1951.

Crude Birth Rates and Death Rates per 1,000 in certain Countries in Asia

Country	Year	Birth rates	Death rates
Ceylon . . .	1933	38·6	21·2
	1938	35·9	21·0
	1943	40·6	21·4
	1948	40·6	13·2
	1951	37·3	11·6
Japan	1933	31·5	17·7
	1938	27·1	17·7
	1943	30·3	16·3
	1948	33·7	12·0
	1951	25·4	10·0
Federated Malay States .	1933	37·6	21·1
	1938	41·2	20·4
	1943	—	—
	1948	40·4	16·3
	1952	44·4	13·6
Singapore . . .	1933	41·9	22·5
	1938	44·9	21·4
	1943	—	—
	1948	46·2	12·4
	1952	47·5	11·2

(After *United Nations Demographic Year Book*, 1953. Tables 5 and 9.)

As the following table shows, there has been a general tendency for the gap between crude birth rates and crude death rates to increase since pre-war years.

Excess of Crude Birth Rates over Crude Death Rates
(Rates per 1,000)

Country	1933	1938	1943	1948	Latest year
Ceylon	17·4	14·9	19·2	27·4	25·7 (1951)
Japan	13·8	9·4	14·0	21·7	15·4 (1951)
Federated Malay States .	16·5	20·8	—	24·1	30·8 (1952)
Singapore . . .	19·4	23·5	—	33·8	36·3 (1952)

Preventive health measures seem already to have shown their effects, and with the drive for malaria control and other mass approaches (supported by the World Health Organization), we may expect improvements in mortality to continue for the region as a whole. In wealthier societies there is such a saturation of health facilities, both preventive and curative, that further declines in mortality are likely to be slow. Changes in fertility are more flexible and important. But in under-developed countries the extension of mass programmes, with little immediate response in fertility, may cause a marked increase in the rate of population growth before productive power takes care of the larger numbers. Recent changes in Ceylon serve to indicate the potential significance of population increases resulting from comparatively simple and inexpensive methods. Crude death rates fell from 20·3 per 1,000 in 1946 to 14·3 per 1,000 in 1947, as a result of the anti-malaria campaign with DDT, costing 15 cents per caput. The death rate declined still further in subsequent years, but the birth rate remained high at about 40 per 1,000. So in one year the annual rate of growth per 1,000 rose from 14·5 to 25·1. In 1951 population was increasing at the 'alarming' rate of 3 per cent as against 1·5 per cent during 1931–46. At the 1951 rate, the population would reach 14 million by 1970.*

* *Economic and Social Development of Ceylon*, 1926–50. Ministry of Finance, Colombo, 1951, p. 4. See also Samuel W. Anderson (Assistant Secretary for International Affairs, U.S. Dept. of Commerce), ' The Effects of Population Trends on Economic Development.' *Foreign Commerce Weekly* October 12, 1953.

CHAPTER II

DEMOGRAPHIC ATTITUDES

A. Changes in Western Countries

Declining birth rates have been characteristic of countries of western civilization during the past 100 years.* In some countries, for example the United States and France, the decline began earlier, in others later. Since the 'thirties birth rates have tended to become higher in these countries, but it is not yet clear how enduring the change will be. We are concerned, however, with the causes of declining birth rates in so far as they may throw light on the prospective changes in under-developed countries. It is possible that humanity experiences large cycles of basic biological change affecting fertility, but I am aware of no convincing evidence that the causes of the decline referred to are biological in this particular sense.

To some extent the decline was due to the higher percentage of population in the older age groups as the average life lengthened; but this would account for only a small proportion of the change, and the causes lie deeper. The increased knowledge, and availability of means to control birth is undoubtedly a factor, but methods of family limitation are not new, and the knowledge was not applied on a sufficient scale over the preceding centuries

---

* Among the studies of population changes in western civilization to which reference may be made, the following works already referred to may be noted: A. M. Carr-Saunders, *World Population;* Raymond Pearl, *The Natural History of Population* and *The Biology of Population Growth;* United Nations, *Preliminary Report on the World Social Situation;* and Rockefeller Foundation, *Public Health and Demography in the Far East.* See also Frank C. Lorimer and Frederick Osborn, *Dynamics of Population,* Macmillan, New York, 1934, and *Determinants and Consequences of Population Growth,* Chapter V, which gives a comprehensive summary of views on factors affecting fertility.

to reduce birth rates. So the real causes must be sought in changes in the socio-economic environment affecting the spread of knowledge, the availability of means, and even more, the motives to apply them. In this connection some weight must be attached to the increased availability of mechanical or chemical contraceptives, the economic capacity to purchase them, and the diminution in embarrassment over their purchase as moral sanctions against their use have weakened.

Birth control propaganda usually anticipated the decline in birth rates among the mass of the people by many decades, though not necessarily among selected groups. It may have gradually prepared a public opinion, but the sequence suggests that such propaganda is not likely to be effective until the ground has been prepared by other socio-economic changes. The emergence of such propaganda is of some significance, however, as indicating the awareness among an 'élite' of the existence of a population problem. They may have a function in spreading such an awareness, and the knowledge to cope with the problem in its personal or family aspects. So, to some extent they may accelerate the changes in public attitudes determined primarily by other causes.

Declining juvenile mortality would increase the size of family. So if a generally accepted view of the optimum size of family remained unchanged, and if it were strongly held, a higher survival rate would be conducive to a lower birth rate. This may possibly prove of some importance in the 'familial' societies of under-developed countries, a matter to which we return. But in western societies the change went further, towards a pattern of *smaller* families. Indeed, as is well known, it went so far that in the 'thirties, on the eve of a reversal of the trend, there was widespread anticipation of stable or declining populations in some countries.

The generally accepted view is that the decline in birth rates was the result of industrialization and urbanization. Undoubtedly there is a relationship, but its precise nature is by no means clear. We may indicate probable causes with some degree of confidence, but they appear to be many and we are by no means sure of their relative importance. Raymond Pearl appears to link the change with population density,* but density is an ambiguous term and there are too many exceptions for us to feel satisfied with this explanation. New Zealand began to experience a similar trend of birth rates eighty years ago when neither greatly industrialized nor urbanized, nor densely populated. The trend appears to have begun earlier in the United States than in the industrially more advanced and urbanized British Isles. So it is safer to regard changes in attitudes as arising out of the process of which industrialization and urbanization were a part, as well as out of the actual effects of these latter. In relevant respects the *mores* of the people of New Zealand were similar to those of the industrialized British Isles, and were kept roughly consistent by immigration. Also, the socio-economic changes occurring in the United States were similar in kind to those in the British Isles but more rapid. Both these societies were part of a civilization of which urbanized industry was one distinguishing characteristic, and were carried along on its current of socio-economic change.

An innovation affecting a society is seldom exhausted in its direct effects, and this must be borne in mind in connection with the intensified impact of western technology and culture on under-developed countries in this present era. This is a matter to which we return.† We think of innovations as ideas. They sometimes become embodied in material form as technical innovations influencing productive power and income. Such technological changes influence human beliefs and relationships. Often, however, the ideas impinge more directly or immediately on beliefs and relationships, though these are seldom without economic effects. These observations are relevant to the population problem, for they raise a caveat against too exclusive a concentration on the *derived* effects of technological innovations on demographic

* Cf. for example, *The Biology of Population Growth*. In *The Natural History of Population*, p. 277, he writes: 'The higher the degree of industrialization, urbanization and *consequent* population density that characterizes a whole population, the lower is that population's fertility and growth rate, and *vice versa;* this, on the whole and with few apparent exceptions.' For a critique, cf. Paul Douglas, *op. cit.*, Chapter XIII.

† Cf. below, Chapters IX and X.

attitudes. The French Revolution was not primarily a technological revolution, but a politico-economic revolution which destroyed feudalism and substituted for it peasant proprietorship, and led to a decline in religious beliefs. This last weakened moral sanctions against the application of methods of contraception already known, so that the desire for security in the peasant society and to avoid excessive fragmentation under the 'code civil' led to a reduction in birth rates before this happened in the more rapidly industrialized neighbour across the channel. The phenomenon took place in the rural areas. This is atypical but it illustrates the influence of ideas as distinct from the by-products of technological changes leading to an urban-industrial society.*

There is a natural tendency to stress the technical innovations in the Industrial Revolution, but this was also a revolution in ideas, not always or necessarily resulting from the technological changes. We are still not at all sure of the causal relationship, for example, between religious changes, the Renaissance and the rise of capitalism. No doubt it was a complex relationship, but the point is worth making that changes in religious attitudes and the emergence of new sects, the growth and extension of a more scientific attitude, and the rise of individualism are all expressive of the greater receptivity to change in general during the era we designate as the Industrial Revolution, equally with technological innovations and the emergence of new economic institutions and

---

* Cf. Carr-Saunders, *op. cit.*, Chapter IX; and the brief reference by Alva Myrdal, 'Population Trends in Densely Populated Areas,' *Proceedings of American Philosophical Society*, Vol. 95, No. 1, February 13, 1951. See also R. R. Kuzynski, *Population Movements*, Oxford University Press, 1936, pp. 39–41, where he points out that there is no evidence of any other European country than France where the fertility was lower in 1870 than before. I am informed that recent studies by French demographers, to which I do not have access, indicate that the decline in family size in France began before the revolution. This would indicate that the above passage over-stresses the rôle of the French Revolution in affecting birth rates and attitudes towards size of family, though it probably gave strength to changes in attitudes. Nevertheless, the findings referred to do not do damage to the main point, that changes in attitude were not a consequence of the derived effects of technological change.

forms of economic organization. The rôle of the first group of changes—supported by and supporting the more specifically economic elements in the composite social process—must not be neglected in its influence in increasing the receptivity towards the demographic innovation of changed attitudes towards birth control. A similar change in under-developed countries, if it occurs, will be part of a similar composite social process affecting value systems in many ways, and of a similar increased receptivity to change in general, and not *merely* a by-product of industrialization and urbanization.* But industrialization and urbanization will have their effects as well as the more general social change of which they are a part.

The corollaries of greater industrialization are a change in the ratio of urban to rural populations, changes in the relationships of people towards their work, and in their organization for work, and usually an increase in income per head on the average for the society. The decline in birth rates usually began in urban areas, and spread later to rural areas with increasing mechanization, education and closer contacts with urban areas. It began among higher income groups and those with more education, and spread to other groups. In rural areas the family continued for longer as the unit of economic activity centred on the farm and the home. Children and women participated as producers in the family enterprise. Children were an economic asset among landless labourers as well as occupying owners, and the large family had advantages from the point of view of both economic effort and economic security. The larger family had status and prestige value, and conservative tradition was normally strong among agrarian groups. Although technological improvements in agriculture were equally important with others in the Industrial Revo-

* On the theme that technical change means a change in the whole pattern of life, cf. H. S. Frankel, 'Some Conceptual Aspects of Technical Change,' *International Social Science Bulletin*, UNESCO, Vol. IV, No. 2, 1952. On the disruptive effects of the impact of the West on ways of life in Asia, cf. Guy Wint, *The British in Asia*, Faber and Faber, 1947; and J. S. Furnivall, *Colonial Policy and Practice*, Cambridge University Press, 1948. See also Chapters IX and X below.

lution, they had less effect for some time in undermining traditional conservatism and the economic and social value of the large
family. Technological improvements did destroy the family
handicrafts, and reduced the proportion of population needed to
provide food and agricultural materials, a change intensified in
Europe by importation of agricultural produce. But the labour
power released by these events in large degree drifted to the cities
where receptivity to change was greater.

The dislocation of people and their transfer to a new environment in which relationships were more anonymous and less
subject to the social pressures of kinsfolk or the village, the
lengthening of family ties and the lessening of family responsibility by distance and non-participation in family affairs, would be
conducive to a weakening of traditional attitudes. So also would
the more stimulating atmosphere of ideas, arising from closer
juxtaposition of large numbers of people, the attraction to the
cities of the more venturesome as well as the less fortunate, the
necessarily faster tempo of activity, and the smaller hold of religion in such an environment with its less intimate institutional
groupings.

To these must be added the more specifically economic effects.
Employment became no longer a family affair, but individual, in
economic enterprises in which relations were more competitive
and impersonal. Economic and social hazards were then less
cushioned by kinship groups, and until the more recent extension
of public social security schemes must be met by the majority out
of personal earnings. Such changes further made for an individualistic outlook. Women found employment outside the family
enterprise to a greater degree, and this was conducive to greater
economic independence and the progressive emergence of greater
social freedom. Children were less of an economic asset and at
times even more of an economic liability, especially when laws
were exacted against child labour and requiring compulsory
schooling, as the social conscience became more sensitive, or
organized, and the need for better education and training was felt
by employers. These changes would also promote receptivity to
new ideas. To such influences all operating in the same direction

must be added the effects of higher income (with perhaps a greater consciousness of its precariousness as the fluctuating character of economic growth became more apparent), the desire to maintain it, improve the prospects of economic welfare for children, and reduce the effects on the health of women of too much child-bearing. In some urban areas also, conditions of housing have been an undoubted deterrent to large families.

With the higher income, new wants competed with the desire for children. The demonstration effect of higher consumption levels does not stop at its effects on the propensity to consume, as brought out by Duesenberry,* but also is conducive to the smaller family which makes it easier to improve economic and social status. One factor in the changes has been an increase in the age of marriage, but with a few exceptions, this has been much less important than that married women of a given age bear fewer children.† Indeed, in some under-developed countries, for example, India, in the earlier stages, as will be suggested later, an increase in the age of marriage may increase the rate of increase of population.‡

The foregoing analysis is neither original nor complete. It might be refined by further consideration of rural-urban differentials, and birth rates according to occupations, income groups, educational status and so on; in the main such differentials have tended to narrow. Further consideration would throw some light on the sequence of change but we should expect in the main that it would confirm the general picture.

B. Changes in Japan

Japan is of special interest because it is the only country outside of western civilization which has proceeded far in the growth of

---

* James S. Duesenberry, *Income, Saving and the Theory of Consumer Behaviour*, Harvard University Press, 1949.

† Carr-Saunders, *op. cit.*, p. 95. The authors of the *Determinants and Consequences of Population Trends* (p. 73), state: 'It is evident also that the decline in the crude birth rate does not reflect to any considerable extent, a change in the tendency to marry, or the age at which marriage takes place.'

‡ *Infra*, p. 32 (this Chapter).

an urban-industrial civilization. We need not consider the demo-graphic concomitants of this growth in detail but mention only the salient points. In 1872 about 85 per cent of *families* were reported as dependent on agriculture. In 1920 only 50 per cent of *persons gainfully employed* were in agriculture. The number of *males* gainfully occupied in agriculture declined from 46 per cent in 1920 to 41 per cent in 1930, and 34 per cent in 1940.* Criticizing incomplete official statistics prior to 1920, which show a fluctuat-ing increase in birth rates from 26·3 per 1,000 in 1875 to 32·4 over 1915–19, Taeuber and Notestein† consider, on the basis of pro-bable death rates, that a birth rate exceeding 38 or 40 is consistent with the rate of growth of population in the earlier years, so that an actual decline in birth rates very probably occurred by 1920. There is less ground for differences of opinion over more recent changes. Crude birth rates declined from 36 per 1,000 in 1920 to 32·4 in 1930, and 26·6 in 1939.‡ While, as in the West, the decline in mortality preceded the decline in fertility, there is a reasonable and strong presumption, but no certainty, of some decline in birth rates between 1875 and 1920. Thereafter the comparability with the demographic sequence in the West is closer.

The transition to an urban-industrial society was more rapid in Japan than in Europe and so also was the demographic transition. So, despite Government action to offset the prospects of a declin-ing population, students of Japan's population problems were able to write: 'The projection of Japanese birth and death rates into the future indicates that, even in the absence of war, Japan's period of accelerated growth would have lasted only a century and a quarter and would have produced only a three- to fourfold increase in total population. Europe's transition had occupied three centuries and resulted in a sixfold increase.'§ Nevertheless it is a matter of some interest that birth rates were still higher in

---

* *Public Health and Demography in the Far East, op. cit.,* pp. 16–17.

† *The Changing Fertility of the Japanese, op. cit.,* p. 10.

‡ *Public Health and Demography in the Far East* (quoting S.C.A.P.), p. 23, and *United Nations Demographic Year Book,* 1951, p. 160.

§ Taeuber and Notestein, *op. cit.,* p. 2.

pre-war years than in western countries, though the gap was narrowing:

Crude Birth Rates per 1,000

Country	1932–4[1]	1939[2]
Japan	31·5	26·6
France	16·8	14·8
Italy	23·7	23·6
Netherlands . . .	21·3	20·6
Sweden	14·0	15·4
England and Wales .	14·8	14·8
U.S.A.	17·1	17·3
New Zealand[3] . .	16·7	18·7

[1] After *Preliminary Report on World Social Situation*, pp. 39 and 42.
[2] *United Nations Demographic Year Book*, 1951, Table 7.
[3] Excluding Maoris.

As in most western countries, the decline in birth rates began in the cities and spread to the rural areas later. The causes of the differential were similar,* but the differential appears to have been reduced because of the maintenance of peasant conditions in the cities.† By contrast with Carr-Saunders' interpretation of the situation in the West, an increase in the age of marriage appears to have played a more important, perhaps even a dominant rôle, at least until 1952, but the decline in marital fertility was also important, especially after that date. Another difference of some importance is the continuance of a peasant society engaged in small agriculture in which mechanization plays a small, and family labour a large part. This seems likely to continue for some time and retard the changes in urban areas, because peasants who go to the cities carry with them their familial attitudes. But there is still a differential between urban and rural areas. The gross reproduction rates in city and non-city areas in pre-war years are given as follows:

* Cf. *Public Health and Demography in the Far East*, *op. cit.*, p. 23.
† Cf. Taeuber and Notestein, *op. cit.*, p. 21.

Year	City	Non-city
1920	2·07	2·86
1925	2·02	2·76
1930	1·82	2·56
1935	1·75	2·49

(Taeuber and Notestein, *op. cit.*, p. 21.)

Moreover, recent public opinion surveys reveal the persistence of differences in attitudes.*

Percentage Distribution
(Men)

	Six major cities	Other urban	Rural
Expectation to depend on children in old age .	24·5	35·5	56·6
Natural and worthwhile to bear the burden of bringing up children	30·9	31·4	35·0
Families having two children who do not want more	40·9	46·5	29·8
In favour of contraception	75·4	69·1	64·0
Sufficient knowledge of contraception to practice	47·8	41·6	28·3

A comparison with a survey made only two years earlier indicates that the rate of diffusion of contraceptive experience was increasing, but this was higher in urban areas, so that the gap between urban and rural areas is not narrowing as yet. The survey showed a large majority in favour of state measures to decrease births.†

* The following illustrative data are from *Public Opinion Survey on Birth Control in Japan*, Population Problems Series, No. 7, The Population Problems Research Council, The Mainichi Newspapers, Tokyo, 1952.

† *Ibid.*, p. 44. Percentages in favour among men were: six major cities 75·2, other urban areas 73·7, rural areas 66·0. Dr. Taeuber draws my attention to the fact that abortion, contraception, and sterilization were legalized in the Eugenic Protection Law of 1948, and that abortion was a major element in the decline in fertility.

C. *Prospective Changes in Under-developed Countries*

We have regarded it as tolerably certain that the extension of preventive health measures, particularly those amenable to mass methods such as malaria control or vaccination, will have an important effect on mortality. We are then concerned with the factors influencing the decline in birth rates, and given a significant decline in death rates, with the consequent effects on population growth. Here it is useful to reiterate the references to Ceylon. The crude death rate fell from 20·3 per 1,000 in 1946 to 12·6 in 1950, the corresponding crude birth rates being 38·4 and 40·3 respectively. As a rough indication, we may put it that crude birth rates would have to fall to about 31 per 1,000 to maintain the same rate of increase per 1,000 of population in 1950 as in 1946. This indicates the possible order of size of the problem in some under-developed countries if population is not to increase at a very rapid rate. It would appear that it took about forty-five years (1875–1920) for crude death rates in Japan to fall from 38–40 per 1,000* to about 20 per 1,000. Thereafter the decline was slow from 19·4 in 1921–25†, to 18·2 in 1930, and 17·8 in 1939.‡ With the growth of medical knowledge, especially of preventive methods which can be applied cheaply, and with national programmes to apply it, there is a reasonable expectation that hereafter the improvement in mortality rates will be more rapid in many under-developed countries than it was in Japan, until recently. After 1947 there was a precipitate drop in the Japanese death rate as a result of the use of DDT, penicillin, and other measures.

A trend towards an urban-industrial society in under-developed countries might be expected to have similar effects on birth rates to those in Europe and Japan. It is not necessary to recapitulate the possible or likely causal influences. The pattern may well be similar though not identical, and there will be differences from

* Taeuber and Notestein, *op. cit.*
† Taeuber and Beal, 'The Dynamics of Population in Japan,' *Demographic Studies of Selected Areas of Rapid Growth*, p. 15.
‡ *United Nations Demographic Year Book*, 1951, Table 14.

country to country. Thus there is evidence of a rural-urban differential in birth rates in India, but according to Kingsley Davis, the same differential existed in 1931 as in 1891, and there was no tendency for the effect to spread and bring about a decline in birth rates over the country.* In his later study† Davis reaffirms the same conclusion, bringing the data to 1941. He draws attention to the persistence of the urban-rural differential, and to the fact that it is greater the larger the size of the city. But there has apparently been no diffusion effect, so that while urbanization may be expected to have some influence in decreasing total fertility, this is not likely to be large. Among possible reasons suggested for the differential are greater infantile mortality in the cities, the return of pregnant women to their villages to bear children, and the greater use of contraceptives. Chandrasekar, however, attributes the differential not so much to family planning as to an adverse sex ratio, i.e., an excess of males‡ resulting from immigration from the countryside.

The complexity of the process out of which the small family emerged in the West should be a warning against undue simplification, or sanguine expectations that the same result will follow in a short space of time. Industrialization had been taking place over a long period before this result followed in the West. The patterns in separate western countries and in Japan show that there is no uniformity in the speed of transition, but experience in Japan indicates that, under certain circumstances, it can be more rapid than occurred in Europe.

We touch on factors likely to affect the rate of change, considering first those having a retarding influence. First among these is the fact that a predominant proportion of the population are agrarian, and that, as stated earlier, cultural obstacles, sometimes religious,§ but more often 'familial' are deeply embedded among

* 'Demographic Fact and Policy in India,' *Demographic Studies of Selected Areas of Rapid Growth*, pp. 48–50.

† *The Population of India and Pakistan*, pp. 70–73.

‡ S. Chandrasekar, *Demographic Disarmament for India*, Family Planning Association, Bombay, 1952, p. 7.

§ As far as my limited knowledge goes the Catholic Church is among the them. These are not necessarily stronger than in Medieval Europe, but there is no reason to suppose that they are weaker, or less resistant to pressure of the same kinds and intensity. In many countries the poverty-stricken populations, their health affected by under-nourishment and endemic disease, and faced with natural and economic hazards, are listless and fatalistic. It is not an observer from the West, but a senior Indian Official who writes: 'Why will the villager not respond? (i.e., to family planning propaganda). For the same reason that he does not respond to scores of other piecemeal blandishments for the cure of his condition, from the composting of manures to domestic hygiene. He suffers from a profound listlessness of spirit, sunk into a state of utter hopelessness, in a perpetual twilight of the senses, which does not evoke normal reactions to ordinary stimuli. The biological urge is robbed of its rich human significance in such a context. Reproduction becomes an animal function, a proliferation which leads as much to death as to life.'*

Similarly a Philippino report states (in a more general connection), 'The progress in the sciences, in literature, and in arts which foreign influences have brought into the Philippines and which has seeped into the life of the people in the urban areas has not yet affected, to noticeable degree, the somnolence of life in the rural communities. For lack of inspiration, leadership, guidance, and direction, the individual has tenaciously held on to his old ways and modes of living, using the same implements in agriculture, in fishing and in the native industries as those which his parents have used. His mode of leisure, his enjoyments, his likes and

few great religions which oppose the use of contraceptives on moral grounds. There is no such opposition among most other large Christian sects. Chandrasekar, *Demographic Disarmament for India*, pp. 49–50, states that it is not opposed to Hindu beliefs, and the General Convention of American Jewish Rabbis endorsed birth control in 1930. (Chandrasekar, *op. cit.*, p. 42.) The Moslem hierachy is not opposed, as is evidenced by the *Fatawa* issued some years ago by the Grand Mufti of Egypt and other leaders. (W. Wendell Cleland, 'A Population Plan for Egypt,' *Demographic Studies of Selected Areas of Rapid Growth*, p. 135.)

* S. K. Dey (Development Commissioner for West Bengal), *Population Control in India: Ends and Means*. Reprint from *The Statesman* (undated).

dislikes, and even his vices are the same as those of past generations. On top of all this, he views his lot with contempt and
ignores the future with the philosophy of: 'Let the future take
care of itself.'*

I have quoted at length these descriptions by nationals regarding
some characteristics of their rural populations, to re-emphasize
that *general attitudes* and *inertia* may perhaps be just as important
as specific resistance to family limitation. It is significant also that
both writers urge the necessity for an integrated or 'multi-
purpose' approach to rural betterment. The Indian authority in
particular expresses the conviction that villagers can only be
persuaded to adopt family planning as part of a programme which
'promises a complete transformation of the villager's living environment in terms he can readily grasp, which are within his reach.'
In short, family planning must be part of a programme of promoting innovations affecting all important aspects of living.

To these characteristics must be added the inferior status of
women, and general ignorance and illiteracy. While literacy is not
an open sesame to betterment, and in early stages may be less
effective in encouraging change than education of the 'extension'
type, it does promote receptivity to new ideas by extending the
range of enquiry, and some new vistas are opened up even during
the educative process of becoming literate. But ignorance is more
specifically related to our problem in the lack of knowledge of the
means of family limitation coupled with the non-availability of
contraceptives which can be used under village conditions, and
are cheap enough and acceptable within the culture. It may also
be an impediment in the form of a lack of perception of the
relationship between size of family and poverty. But of greater
significance is the probability that desire for security in later life
is more influential than for higher levels of consumption now;
and that on the typical small holding, as long as existing techniques are applied, the labour of the whole family may be required
at times of planting and harvesting. Simple improvements in

---

* *The Community School of the Philippines*, Memorandum No. 77S, Bureau
of Public Schools, Department of Education, Manila, 1952.

techniques might reduce the size of family economically necessary to provide the labour force at these times.

This last consideration leads to the further point, that over a few decades, no conceivable degree of industrialization, at least in Asian countries, is likely to destroy the small-scale peasant structure of the rural sector, or reduce the absolute numbers on the land to any significant extent. Even where land for settlement is available, as in Ceylon, the Philippines Republic and Thailand, it is likely to be settled by small peasant proprietors, and in Ceylon there is a movement to convert plantations into peasant holdings. It will be remembered that the small farming economy still persists in Japan. As in Japan, improvements in equipment and in cultural practices may increase the yield, but the predominance of small farms will set the limit to mechanized, in substitution for labour-intensive, methods. As a corollary, farms will remain as family enterprises, dependent on family labour. To a greater degree than in the West subsistence is still likely to be drawn directly from the farm, so that commercial relations, and their effects on general attitudes towards life are likely on the whole to be less important. So we may expect the 'familial' structure to remain strong and persistent, but with the prospect that farm technology will reduce the size of family needed for a typical holding. This is more likely to occur (as the experience of Japan suggests) than any significant increase in the size of holdings over the period of three or four decades in which we are mainly interested. It may possibly affect attitudes towards size of family by reducing the number needed to cultivate a holding, but much less than would an agrarian revolution expressed in larger commercial farm enterprises.

Such an end result as is suggested above would indeed be a significant achievement, in that it would mean more farm produce with somewhat smaller numbers, and a smaller ratio of farming to non-farming populations. The emphasis in this interpretation is different from that commonly advanced by those who advocate industrialization as a means of enabling the size of holdings to be increased by drawing people off the land in large numbers. A greater relative emphasis is placed on the effects of technological changes within the existing farm structure in reducing labour demands, than on the pull of industrialization. I suspect that the hopes of those who place main reliance on the pull of industrialization in reducing the number and increasing the size of holdings, are doomed to disappointment and that, as experience of India shows after fifty years of industrialization, even the form of agrarian demographic relief we suggest as more likely, will be very difficult to bring about. Indeed, I should consider as gratifyingly successful, a development programme over a few decades which took care of growing numbers with no absolute increase in agricultural population.

There is also the question of the urban-rural differential. We can anticipate that this will occur, but as is shown in Japan, the peasants who migrate to the cities may carry with them their cultural attitudes,* and to that extent retard the rate of change in urban areas. The continuance of the small family holdings which we have assumed will, we anticipate, contribute to some persistences of these attitudes in urban areas until changes occur in the rural areas themselves. Nevertheless, we cannot rule out the possibility that when industrialization and urbanization, as well as receptivity to change in rural areas proceed beyond a certain point, there may be a much more rapid acculturation of peasants to urban values and activities. As an increasing proportion of urban dwellers are urban born, there may be an increased tempo of change in attitudes towards family limitation.† Except in Japan, however, the time for such changes does not appear close. Moreover the observations on the differential in India suggest that for quite some time its effects may be slight, depending on the increased proportion in cities rather than on the influence of diffusion into rural areas.

Another question touched on earlier is the effect of a higher age of marriage should this be brought about by industrialization or other factors. Ghosh‡ points out that the usually held view, that a delay in the age of marriage reduces fecundity, depends on the

* *Supra*, Chapter II, p. 31, in respect of Japan.
† I am indebted to Dr. Taeuber for this suggestion.
‡ D. Ghosh, *op. cit.*, pp. 70–71.

assumption that specific fertility at higher ages remains un-changed, and that the child-bearing period remains unchanged. He then argues convincingly that an increase in the age of mar-riage in India from 13 or 14 to 20 might be expected to increase fertility, first because those who commence child-bearing prema-turely end it prematurely; second because the improvement in health from later marriages will exercise a favourable influence on fecundity.* So the probable effects must be judged in terms of the circumstances in each country, and the possibility allowed for that for a time an increase in the age of marriage may increase fertility.

In terms of the effects of industrialization and urbanization *per se*, as distinct from those of the whole composite process of which these are a part, we must examine the prospects that substantial industrialization and urbanization will in fact occur. We shall argue that an increase in their *relative* importance requires that the over-all process of economic development shall increase real income per head. The mere increase in industrialization and urbanization *pari passu* with population may have some effect, since the increase in *absolute numbers in cities* and *size of cities* may have a qualitative as distinct from a relative quantitative influence; for the trend towards lower birth rates seems usually to be higher in larger than in smaller urban areas.† But the major significant change in the present connection must come from an increase in the *relative* importance of non-farming occupations and of urban populations. This increase, be it noted, is normally one require-ment for the increase in levels of consumption aimed at; but the persistence of high rates of population increase is itself an obstacle.

Finally, in respect of impediments to change, is the question of the effectiveness of education and propaganda. First, as Kingsley Davis points out,‡ no all-out government campaign 'backed by

---

* In the case of India we should also take account of the effects of a weak-ening of the taboo on the marriage of widows. On the importance which this might have, cf. Chandrasekar, *Demographic Disarmament for India* pp. 19–20.

† Cf. *supra*, Chapter II, p. 33, in respect of attitudes in Japan.

‡ 'Population and the Further Spread of Industrial Society' in *Problems of Development of Densely Settled Areas*, Proceedings of the American Philo-sophical Society, Vol. 95, No. 1, February, 1951.

every economic inducement, educational device, and technical assistance to diffuse contraception has ever been tried.' In some few countries, such as India, support to family limitation is given in development plans, and there are important groups promoting education, propaganda and research into attitudes and techniques; but India is among the exceptions. Often there are similar groups whose philosophy is resistant to family limitation, or to the use of contraceptives, and who exert a counteracting influence. Thus the followers of Gandhi would support family limitation, but by moral restraint. They oppose the use of contraceptives. Being active in rural betterment programmes, they carry influence in the areas where family limitation is most needed and difficult to induce. Since a democratic approach to development is being attempted such groups cannot be suppressed. In areas under communist control, where such suppression is possible, emphasis seems to be on the positive aspects of development with little concern for the population aspects. Second, the resistances and economic and technical difficulties to be overcome are so strong that a direct approach to family limitation by education and pro- paganda is no more likely to achieve quick results than it did in the West. On the other hand, even though effects may not be immediately felt, a family limitation programme covering research into attitudes and practicable means which are not repugnant to the culture, as well as education and propaganda, should hasten the time when receptivity to family planning affects birth rates, and indeed seems a necessary preparation for it in Asian countries.*

There are other factors which may shorten the period of tran-

---

* For a similar view, which is critical of the Government of India for not having a sufficiently positive population policy, cf. C. N. Vakil and P. R. Brahmananda, *Planning for a Shortage Economy*, Vora & Co., Bombay, 1952, pp. 304–6. The authors' suggestions include :

(*a*) An awakening of the national consciousness.
(*b*) Economic discrimination *against* those with large families.
(*c*) An increase in the age of marriage.
(*d*) Education of women, especially in relation to family planning.
(*e*) Intensification of urbanization.

sition. Although the impact of the West has not, as yet, markedly changed family attitudes, its dislocative effect is somewhat analogous to the dislocations which preceded the demographic transition in the West. By the weakening of old value systems the western impact *in the past* may make it easier *now* to accept the idea of family limitation.* In short, it is not as if a beginning must be made from scratch in changing value systems. Moreover, the demonstration effect of western consumption and value systems is becoming more powerful in the post-war years. In addition, to use a happy phrase of Alva Myrdal, the 'velocity of communication' is now much higher,† not simply in stimulating the desire for new or better forms of consumer goods which compete with having children, but even more in the impact of western ideas and technology which may induce a more general receptivity to change.

Some surveys, indeed, show a greater receptivity to birth control at the present time than might have been expected. Thus a recent survey made in Baroda city (population 211,000) showed that from 63 per cent to 77 per cent of women classified according to language groups favoured birth control, and between 44 per cent and 62 per cent favoured either contraception or an operation. Those favouring control of size of family by one method or another (including moral restraint and those favouring, but ignorant of methods) varied from 70 per cent to 82 per cent. Those favouring control of size of family by moral restraint as well as contraception, grouped according to income instead of languages, were between 69 per cent and 100 per cent of the total in each income group.‡ Many more surveys of this character are needed before there is a basis for generalization in various countries, and in any case, an attitude is one thing and the practice of family limitation another. The reference is made simply to suggest

* We hasten to add that in expressing the above view, we are not arguing that the over-all effects of the western impact have been beneficial.

† 'Population Trends in Densely Populated Areas,' *Problems of Development of Densely Settled Areas*, op. cit., p. 5.

‡ S. Chandrasekar, 'Attitudes of Baroda Mothers towards Family Planning,' *Third International Conference on Planned Parenthood*, Bombay, 1952, pp. 68–72.

the possibility that attitudes may be less resistant than is commonly supposed, in which case increasing the availability of the means might greatly expedite transitions in practice.* The problem of finding means acceptable to the culture and cheap enough is yet to be solved, however.

The 'velocity of communication' depends a great deal on the existence and adequacy of development plans. Despite variations from country to country these, in essence, are national efforts to promote economic and social changes similar in very important respects to those which occurred in the West, particularly in the increase in capital formation and application of improved technology, the development of economic institutions better suited to these ends, and the changes in economic attitudes deemed necessary for them. Plans usually cover also direct measures to promote social welfare, including health measures, and the spread of general education and education of the extension type.† The overall social changes hastened by the development process increase the possibility of a speeding up of changes in demographic attitudes. Health measures may have a more direct effect, for with the increase in the survival rate among infants and juveniles, families of the present size may be ensured and familial responsibilities and aspirations preserved with a smaller birth rate. It seems unlikely that attitudes toward birth rates will be completely unaffected. If plans succeed in raising incomes, in reducing the size of family

* Since writing the above I have been able to read an article by S. Chandrasekar on 'The Prospect for Planned Parenthood in India,' *Pacific Affairs*, Vol. XXVI, No. 4, December, 1953, which is even more optimistic as far as India is concerned. His view is that 'The nationwide response and support from the public and press' to the All-India Conference on Family Planning 'were so spontaneous and abundant as to surpass the fondest hopes of the organizers. The conference offered conclusive proof that the country was disposed to endorse planned parenthood.' But the writer also mentions the practical difficulties of introducing methods of family limitation into the villages. On the other hand, I am advised that the WHO Government of India experiment in the rhythm method of family limitation did not succeed. I have not, however, had access to the report on this experiment.

† It has now become fashionable to describe extension education as 'fundamental' or 'mass' education.

needed to cultivate a typical holding, and in promoting industrialization and urbanization, the demographic effects will be all the stronger. All this, again, however, relates to general attitudes, and assumes a rational weighing of consequences. Such may exist as a sort of background, but not be strong enough to lead to sufficient control of sex impulses to have much effect. It is in such a situation that education and availability of means may have a significant influence.

The existence of development plans serves to bring out an important qualification to the remarks made earlier on the limited influence of education and propaganda on the practice of birth control. In the West family limitation propaganda was unofficial and there were no official development plans comparable with those in India and other under-developed countries, and no organized international collaboration to further them. Family planning may now be introduced as part of a planned process of change (as in the Indian Five Year Plan, albeit cautiously). If a family limitation programme is introduced as a separate element even in a development plan, the chances of success are probably small, but the community projects, as already operating in India and Ceylon and under consideration in other countries, provide an unique opportunity to integrate family planning research, education and assistance, with other aspects of a 'multi-purpose' approach to agrarian betterment. By succeeding in promoting changes of other sorts which people want, encouraging technological consciousness and a greater propensity to change in general, and by emphasizing, with propriety, the health aspects of family planning, as they affect the mother and the child, the prospects of success are greatly enhanced.* This is consistent with the

* This was the view taken by the writer and his colleagues in a recent survey report: Horace Belshaw and John B. Grant, *Report of the Mission on Community Organization and Development in South and South-East Asia*, United Nations, New York, December, 1953, pp. 41–42. A joint project of the Government of India and the United Nations has been concerned for some time with research, mainly statistical, into attitudes towards and methods of family planning, but, as far as I know, this has not yet been tied in with the community projects.

general viewpoint of the Indian and Philippine authorities already cited.*

On balance, our expectation is one of qualified optimism as to the possibility of changing attitudes over a long period, but of qualified pessimism as to the possibility of a change in birth rates sufficient to offset prospective declines in mortality over the next few decades. Given the appropriate conditions, it is not entirely fantastic to expect the change in birth rates, as from now, to be more rapid than during the century or two of movement towards an industrial urban civilization in the West; for we have suggested that the dislocation resulting from western influence in the past is a part of the period of preparation and that the influence of western ideas and technology will become greater. But to expect it to be more rapid than in Japan seems over-optimistic, as few countries will have a tempo of economic change, with its desired effects on natality, as rapid as Japan's. These are among the reasons why special emphasis must be placed on non-demographic measures to increase national real income more rapidly than prospective population increases, not only so that consumption levels may be raised, but also so that the forces making for a retardation of population growth may be strengthened, thereby promoting further increases in income. It is especially true of economic development, that success breeds success, not only because higher incomes enable more to be set aside for future growth, but also because the process is likely to change demographic attitudes. So there is a circle to be broken. This raises the question of the viability of national development plans, and of the extent and nature of international assistance. But since, in any case, prospective rates of population growth are likely to be a deterrent to economic development in many, if not most, under-developed countries, we also conclude that family planning programmes should be included in development plans, and not simply included but integrated with them. This applies especially in rural areas where the 'multi-purpose' community project type of agency will normally offer the best prospect of success.

* _Supra_, Chapter II, pp. 36.

CHAPTER III

SOME CONCLUSIONS SUMMARILY STATED

We now summarize briefly the main relevant conclusions arising from the preceding discussion. The Malthusian Law of Population is concerned on the one hand with the procreative propensities of human beings, and on the other with the response of
nature to their productive efforts. This latter also boils down in
the last analysis substantially, though not absolutely, to a matter
of human behaviour as it affects innovations and capital formation.
Since behaviour as it is manifested in population change, is
affected by the whole complex of conditions influencing people's
lives, and those conditions are not uniform, we do not expect
absolute conformity to a simple uniform pattern. The question is
whether, by and large, and in broad outline, the Law provides a
useful description of reality in Asian countries.

Except for Japan, Asian countries have remained mainly
agrarian with the familial structure and attitudes towards perpetuation of the family characteristic of peasant communities. This
is true even of India, among the most advanced in industrial
development and urbanization. Even in Japan, where the urban-
industrial ratio has risen, peasant attitudes are still influential.
Except in Japan, preventive checks, such as delayed marriage or
the use of contraceptives, have been unimportant, but positive
checks have occured, especially in the form of disease, war and
shortage of the necessaries of life. While populations in these
countries do not uniformly press on subsistence in such a measure
that real incomes are the same in all at the bare survival level, the
margin over bare subsistence for large numbers is so small that
fluctuations in it tend to lead to corresponding fluctuations in
mortality. The deterioration in production of food per head in
under-developed areas as a whole by comparison with pre-war

levels must be noted. In the main it may be ascribed to war dislocation but, after all, war is one of the preventive checks, and it is a matter of some significance that it has not yet been possible to catch up with population increase, though this has been achieved in developed countries. Low and precarious levels of nutrition greatly increase susceptibility to disease. Hence, although birth rates are not uniform, nor absolutely steady, and fertility as well as mortality seems to be affected by changes in harvests and general health conditions, the major cause of fluctuations in population growth is fluctuations in mortality.

Increases in productive power have tended to be taken out in increased population rather than in improved consumption. In some countries improvements in levels of consumption have occurred, but these have been small so that the generalization of the preceding paragraph still substantially holds. Moreover, there may be phases over which productive power *temporarily* outstrips population growth to some degree. The biologically feasible rate of population growth (say a doubling in twenty-five years) has seldom taken place. The rate of growth of productive power has not been sufficient to permit it. Except to a small degree and precariously, it has not been possible in low income agrarian societies to promote innovations, or to generate a rate of capital formation, of such magnitudes as to enable productive power to grow more rapidly than population. Nor have economies of scale to population growth led to such an improvement. In the pre-war period especially, poverty and the low propensity to innovate or accept innovations in preventive health measures imposed a check on the rate of growth of population through mortality rates. This has been a factor in such small improvements in levels of consumption as have taken place. We have shown that a decline in mortality rates occurred in pre-war years but, had preventive health measures been *more* effective, it is unlikely that even the small improvements in levels of consumption, other than in health elements, would have occurred. They would have been largely absorbed in a higher rate of population increase.

This latter point, and the existence of a biological urge to increase population more rapidly, are evidenced by the reduction in mortality and the increase in rates of population growth of more recent years as preventive health measures have become more effective. The illustration of Ceylon in particular, where in the short space of a year or two the rate of population growth doubled (and conformed to Malthus' North American example) is highly significant in demonstrating the underlying pressure. The prospect which it opens up for an acceleration in the rate of population growth in under-developed countries in Asia, and probably elsewhere, raises a major issue. If the process occurred as a *concomitant or result of economic development* so that it was associated with rising levels of consumption, there would perhaps be no serious cause for concern. There would still arise the question of the desirability of retarding the rate of population growth to accelerate the improvement in levels of consumption; but a cumulative process would be possible. If, however, the more rapid increase in population is the result of comparatively cheap measures for the mass reduction of disease, which are antecedent to economic development, it may greatly retard, or even prevent, an improvement in levels of consumption, other than in health.

As will be shown later, there are important items on the credit side of improved health measures, and we do not suggest, even diffidently that they should be curtailed. But the prospective increase in population arising from this cause and the unlikelihood that preventive checks will be applied to offset the effects of health measures, imposes a real threat to the prospects of improving levels of consumption. It may well happen that inability to raise levels of consumption, especially of food, imposes a positive check, and prevents a cumulative increase in population. It is then no consolation if the actual rate of population increase is not great; for it has been controlled by inability to initiate a process of economic development. The situation in the countries under consideration is at least presumptive of diminishing returns, or at best, constant returns to population growth, *per se*, since otherwise, unless we assumed a deterioration in the *quality* of the means to work, an improvement of real income would be a concomitant of growing population. In general, however, such changes as have occurred have been in the direction of some technological improvements rather than deterioration, but these have not been sufficient to markedly offset the effects of population growth.

The law of returns is a major problem to be discussed in Chapter V. But we can anticipate by asserting that to rely on increasing returns to population growth is a very slender reed indeed, though there is a possibility of increasing returns if capital increases *pari passu* with population. We can then state the Malthusian dilemma in slightly different terms. If a population is already in a Malthusian situation, so that levels of consumption are close to the subsistence level, an amelioration of the over-all economic position is likely to be taken out, first in an increase in consumption levels, second in an increase in population. The necessary growth in capital formation to sustain an increase in consumption levels and set in motion a *cumulative* process, requires a corresponding increase in savings. These are most unlikely to occur. Indeed, in a situation where consumption levels are low, it is difficult to see what would motivate the necessary increase in savings among individuals. Historically the generating force must normally have been technological innovations, though there may have been other kinds of innovations such as the opening up of new markets. The key to the Malthusian dilemma is then technological stagnation.*

If it were possible to conceive of an increase in capital formation in under-developed countries in Asia, unaccompanied by innovations, it is virtually certain that any initial increase in income would be mopped up by growing numbers. Fortunately technological innovations are likely to be embodied in the increased capital; but this does not entirely solve the problem. First, an increase in the rate of capital formation will be most difficult to bring about. Second, for reasons given, the rate of increase in population is likely to accelerate. Third, the innovations embodied in the capital may be insufficient. For such reasons, although the need for more capital must be emphasized even more importance

---

* Somewhere I have come across a recent exposition of this point but the reference eludes me.

must be attached to promoting innovations ; for it is these which will prevent the effects of any initial increase in capital formation from being exhausted by population increase. Later* we emphasize that this is not simply a question of improving the economic arts through better capital and processes; but of changing attitudes and institutions, and improving the human productive agents. These arguments add strength to the case for international capital aid and technical assistance programmes; for a country with low income per head is poor in the means to accumulate capital and often in the means to innovate. In both it must overcome especially obstinate resistances.

* Chapters IX and X.

PART II

SOME FUNDAMENTAL RELATIONS

CHAPTER IV

A 'DEVELOPMENT' EQUATION

The total real income of a country will be a function of the size and efficiency of the labour force and the stock and quality of wealth.* If levels of consumption are to rise, national real income must in the long run grow faster than population.

We must distinguish between an increase in population and an increase in the effective supply of labour, or the labour actually engaged in work. The two will normally grow together but not necessarily at the same rate. If population increase is brought about by an increase in birth rates, the first result is likely to be an increase in the ratio of dependants to workers and there will be a lag in the increase in labour. If the increased population results from improved health measures, which reduce mortality and lost time through sickness, the ratio of labour supply to population may be improved or worsened according to the age groups affected by the decline in mortality, and whether or not fertility declines. The results will differ also, according to the time period considered.

The effective labour supply may be improved in relation to population by socio-economic measures which reduce unemployment or idle time.

An improvement in the ratio of effective labour supply to

* It will also be affected by changes in the barter terms of trade, which for simplicity we define as changes in the purchasing power of exports over imports. These changes may assist economic development or be a drag upon it, but I shall confine attention to major determinants within a country. For a discussion of alternative definitions, cf. Sir Dennis Robertson, 'The Terms of Trade,' *Problems of Long Term International Balance*, UNESCO International Social Science Bulletin, Vol. III, No. 1, 1951, pp. 28–33. See also articles by H. Staehle and Colin Clark in the same issue.

population may make an important contribution to levels of consumption for the population as a whole. Hence special consideration is given to the problem in Chapter VIII. Meanwhile, we shall assume a constant ratio.

Labour, of course, includes any type of activity directed to producing goods and services, and not merely manual labour. We shall simplify the discussion by assuming to begin with that an increase in labour in an industry means an increase in man-hours directed to production, similar in efficiency, kind and composition, (i.e., as between different kinds of labour) to existing man-hours.

Wealth includes natural resources as well as capital, i.e., it covers stocks of *all* concrete things directly or indirectly used to produce utility. But land and other natural resources are already there and, except in so far as they are exhausted, we regard the variable part of wealth as capital, even when it consists of man-made improvements to land. Bringing in new land will require labour and some capital in the form of machines and materials of various sorts.

Capital presents the same sort of difficulties as labour. It is a congeries of different kinds of concrete things. So also is the product created when labour uses wealth to produce goods and services.

We cannot avoid thinking of labour and capital as in some sense homogeneous, though in doing so we conceal a complex of sub-variables and set aside the conceptual difficulties referred to at the beginning of this essay. We shall try to remedy this so far as is possible and necessary, by separate discussion of some of the more important factors subsumed under the main categories, or set aside in the residuals in preliminary analysis. If, then, we can be so bold as to regard labour and capital as homogeneous quantities (e.g., by using standardized man-hours for labour and the convention of accountancy units corrected for price changes for capital) we should expect an increase in either the labour force or the stock of capital of a society to increase total productive power and aggregate real income.

The same result would follow from technological improvement, or more accurately from innovations. The term innovations will be used to cover any qualitative changes affecting the efficiency of labour and capital. Labour may become more efficient by better health, better training or changes in attitudes towards work resulting, for example, from more powerful incentives; and capital may become more efficient because of inventions. Both may become more efficient because of improvements in organization and administration, though in large measure these mean an improvement in one kind of labour. The above, of course, do not exhaust the list.

Economic development in the sense of a progressive increase in consumption levels requires that an increase in one or all of the variables (labour, capital and innovations) increases output more rapidly than population. There are then two other matters which affect the result.

The first is the law of factor returns, which is concerned with changes in the ratio of output to the input of a factor as its quantity is increased in relation to another factor, or factors: with whether the ratio remains constant, increases, or decreases. If, for example, labour increases by 1 per cent but capital and land in use remains constant, will the increase in output be equal to, or more or less than, 1 per cent? We are concerned with quantity relationships, and assume no change in the qualities of the factors used.*

The law of factor returns is of especial importance in relation to the effects of population growth, because it points up the question: what are the effects on production per head as population increases in relation to wealth? Consideration of the law of factor returns to labour increase is important if we are to distinguish between the effects of population growth *per se*, and the results when population increase is accompanied by an increase in capital or technological innovations. It may well be that levels of con-

---

* Changes in total output may make it economical to use technically more efficient kinds and qualities of factors. This, however, is a question of internal economies of scale or output discussed more fully in the next chapter.

sumption are rising, but they would increase faster if population growth were slower. If increasing factor returns apply to labour for an economy, all that is needed for levels of consumption to rise is for population to increase. If constant factor returns apply the same result will require an increase in capital or improvements in technology. If diminishing factor returns apply, the rate of increase in capital or improvements in technology must be greater still by an amount more than sufficient to offset the rate at which factor returns to labour decrease.

Of course the law of factor returns for capital is also important; for the higher the ratio of output to the input of capital as capital increases in relation to labour, the bigger the contribution which a given amount of capital will make to output per head. We may anticipate later discussion by stating that for both labour and capital as a whole diminishing factor returns are likely to apply: but this may not be the case at any time and place for a particular kind of labour or capital.

The second matter is the extent of *economies of scale or output.* These relate to the question whether an increase in output will increase production per head. More specifically they relate to the question: if *both* labour and capital increase by 1 per cent will the increase in output be equal to, greater than or less than 1 per cent? As is shown later, the result will be affected by the law of factor returns to the factors used. Economies of scale or output raise some of the most difficult aspects of the problem to get clear ideas about, more particularly as an increase in total output will usually be accompanied by changes in the proportions of the factors as their quantities increase. Growth may permit a better combination of factors, and it may promote other economies as well. Since our main concern is with the law of returns to population growth (with whether or not production per head increases as a result of population increase) we must compare the results according to whether or not the increase in population is accompanied by a corresponding increase in capital. The laws of factor returns to labour and capital, and the consequent economies of scale will affect the outcome.

We are concerned with the probable law of returns to population within a likely range of population increase in under-developed countries, especially in Asia, over the early future. If, as Colin Clark appears to believe,* increasing returns to population growth may be expected, we need not be unduly concerned over current rates of growth, or even over a prospective acceleration in the rate of growth. I hasten to add that I do not share this optimism.

In the light of our discussion so far, the variables to be considered are:

(a) Changes in the amount of labour.
(b) Changes in the amount of capital.
(c) Factor returns.
(d) Economies of scale or output.
(e) Innovations (broadly interpreted).

Strictly speaking, the law of factor returns and economies of scale are covered in changes in labour and capital, but it is useful to list them separately. Although, for convenience, we shall consider each variable separately, they will usually all be changing together and they are not independent. Population growth will normally be accompanied by some increase in capital. A change in labour supply may not only affect the demand for capital, but also the supply of new capital through its effect on income; similarly with a change in technology. New capital, whether it be in replacement, or a net investment, will frequently embody some technical improvements, or be associated with improvements in lay-out or organization. The inter-relationships are so close that it is not always helpful to be rigorous in isolating the factors for separate discussion.

We shall first consider, in general terms, some important relationships, then examine conditions likely to affect economies of scale, and follow this with a discussion of selected aspects of investment, savings, the effective supply of labour, and innovations.

It is convenient to begin with a 'development equation' which

* 'Population Growth and Living Standards,' *op. cit.*, pp. 101–2.

brings together the variables requiring consideration, and is reasonably appropriate to the problem of under-developed countries.

The well-known Cobb-Douglas 'production function' provides a convenient model to introduce the discussion (though we are using it for a purpose different from that for which it was constructed), because it takes specific cognizance of changes in labour supply, and provides a framework for considering laws of factor returns and economies of scale. We use it not as an *adequate* description of reality, but as a useful logical tool, or conceptual approach, more relevant to the problems of under-developed countries than the dynamic models commonly used to explain the behaviour of developed societies.*

---

* Dynamic equations of the types developed by Harrod, Domar and others (e.g., Evsey D. Domar, 'Expansion of Employment,' *American Economic Review*, March, 1947, p. 34, and 'The Problem of Capital Accumulation,' *American Economic Review*, December, 1948; and R. F. Harrod, *Towards a Dynamic Economics*, Macmillan, London, 1948) are sometimes used (though not as far as I know by their authors) to illustrate the problem of development in under-developed countries. Such models are usually concerned with the problem of the rate of economic growth required to sustain full employment; with the relationships between income, investment, and saving if this condition is to be achieved. Their analyses relate to developed economies in which the motives to save and invest are determined to a large extent by the economic calculus of a commercial society and in which unemployment through a shortage of effective demand is an ever-present possibility. Full employment is frequently an objective of government, and unemployment may again become a problem. But under-developed societies differ from this description in many ways, for example, in the smaller strength of the investment motive in saving and the smaller effect of changes in commercial yields on investment, and especially in the relatively small importance of unemployment due to a shortage of effective demand. In them the problem of full utilization of labour is related to the removal of seasonal unemployment and disguised unemployment rather than to increasing effective demand (in the sense this term usually has in western societies). We require a different approach, in which the problem of social organization looms large. More important, such dynamic equations often subsume changes in labour supply under other variables, or assume them away. So, while the dynamic models appropriate to western societies may be suggestive, they do not provide the sort of equation we are looking for.

The Cobb-Douglas equation is expressed*:—

$$P = b\, L^K\, C^J$$

where P = Index of Physical Volume of Produce
L = Index of Number of Workers
C = Index of Capital
b = a constant. This will be different for different
economies or industries, but it does not affect
the following argument.

K and J are exponents of labour and capital respectively and indicate the proportionate change in output (P) for a given proportionate change in the factor (L or C).

We may allow for the influence of innovations by writing the function in the extended form—

$$P = b\, L^K\, C^J\, e^{at}$$

and interpreting a as an exponent which will vary with innovations over time (t).

Unless the innovations are neutral, equally 'saving' labour and capital, they will affect the exponents of labour and capital. We find it more convenient to assume no innovations to begin with

I believe also that assumptions as to the behaviour of multipliers and accelerators deemed to be appropriate to developed societies are inappropriate to under-developed societies. These questions, however, are outside the frame of reference of the present discussion. I have touched on them very briefly in 'Economic Development in Asia: A Preliminary View,' *Economia Internazionale*, Vol. V, No. 4, Genoa, November, 1952. V. K. R. V. Rao deals with the question of the multiplier in under-developed countries more fully in 'Investment, Income and the Multiplier in an Under-Developed Economy,' *Indian Economic Review*, Vol. I, No. 1, February, 1952.

* Cf. Paul Douglas, *op. cit.*, pp. 131 *et seq.* See also Colin Clark, *The Conditions of Economic Progress*, Macmillan. Second Edition, 1951, pp. 514–20; G. Tintner, *Econometrics*, Wiley, New York, 1952, pp. 51–52, and pp. 134 *et seq.*; Tintner, *Econometrica*, Vol. XII, 1944, pp. 26–34; and a critique by H. Menderhauser, *Econometrica*, Vol. VI, 1938, p. 143. For an alternative formulation leading to much the same general conclusions, cf. Joseph J. Spengler, 'Economic Factors in the Development of Densely Populated Areas.' *Proceedings American Philosophical Society*, Vol. XCV, No. 1, February, 1951.

and so shall use the original Cobb-Douglas formulation in this chapter.*

Empirical enquiries in the United States seem to suggest that the following values fitted the data for manufacturing:—

$$P = b\ L^{0.75}\ C^{0.25}$$

Other investigations in different sectors and countries revealed different exponents and we might certainly expect them to be different in under-developed societies, where their empirical discovery might be of great practical importance. For example, Divatia and Trivedi found the following equation for manufacturing in India in 1938–39†:—

$$P = b\ L^{0.402}\ C^{0.598}$$

Our problem really calls for a function which applies to the economy as a whole. This is a more difficult task than finding similar equations for individual industries or sectors. If a Cobb-Douglas function holds for each sector there should also be a Cobb-Douglas function for the whole economy. But the values of the constants and exponents in this aggregate function must depend upon the precise way in which factors are distributed over the separate sectors. It would, that is, have to incorporate principles of allocation for factors over all the sectors as well as the separate technological relationships, and would, accordingly, change with changes in such allocation. While it may not be possible to discover such a 'production function' for a whole economy, it is possible to indicate some changes which affect it. Such changes are a part of the subject-matter of the following

* As mentioned in the Foreword, I am especially indebted to Professor C. G. F. Simkin for drawing my attention to the possible use of the Cobb-Douglas function in relation to problems of economic development, and for clarifying its interpretation. My indebtedness is particularly great in respect of Chapters IV–VIII where he has traversed the argument in detail, drawn attention to errors, inconsistencies and pitfalls, and made innumerable suggestions for applying the function and improving the exposition. Professor J. O. Shearer and Mr. J. V. T. Baker have also made valuable suggestions.

† M. V. Divatia and H. M. Trivedi, *Industrial Capital in India*, p. 9, N. M. Tripathi, Bombay, 1947, p. 9.

chapter. We do not deem it necessary to consider these formidable complications for the present sketch. Instead we shall make the assumption that

$$P = b\, L^{0.75}\, C^{0.25}$$

holds for an under-developed economy. It has to be clearly understood that no great significance attaches to the actual values of the exponents in this quantitative argument, and the tenor of the argument is not affected by this selection.

The sum of the exponents of labour and capital in this equation equals unity, which means that constant returns to scale apply over the range of data used, because a 1 per cent increase in both labour and capital brings about a 1 per cent increase in product.*

There are thus no net economies of scale or output from such a growth. Whether or not such economies are likely to result from a growth of the market in under-developed countries is a matter of considerable importance, and we shall suggest the possibility that in the long run it will differ according to the causes of growth. But we consider first the inferences to be drawn if constant returns to scale apply.

The meaning of a production function having the exponents used above, and in the absence of innovations, may be summarily stated as follows:—

(i) An increase of labour (L) of 1 per cent with capital (C) constant would increase product (P) by 0.75 per cent. An increase in the stock of capital (C) by 1 per cent with L constant would increase product by 0.25 per cent. An increase of both L and C by 1 per cent would increase P by 1 per cent.

(ii) In order to maintain real income per head with an increase in population (in which the ratio of workers to total population was unchanged) the capital stock would have to increase at the

* Douglas (*Theory of Wages*, pp. 20–25), concludes a theoretical argument in support of this empirically observed condition by stating that: 'The most probable of all assumptions seems, therefore, to be that production can be described as a simple homogeneous linear function of the first degree and that if all the factors are increased or decreased by a given per cent, product will increase or decrease by that per cent.'

same rate as population, i.e., the amount of capital per head would have to be kept constant.

(iii) If we take levels of consumption as including services such as health and education (as we should), investment in hospitals, schools and other 'social over-head' would have to increase at the same rate as population to maintain levels of consumption per head.

(iv) Properly, C in the equation should refer to wealth, i.e., it should include natural resources as well as concrete kinds of man-made capital. Unless the natural resources used (e.g., land in cultivation) can be increased *pari passu* with population, then man-made capital must increase at a faster rate than population to make up for the failure of natural resources to increase equally with population.

(v) The total increase in product resulting from a 1 per cent increase in labour would be 0·75 per cent of the existing product. If capital remains constant this means that the marginal increment due to labour, i.e., the increment due to employing each additional worker, will be falling: for the total product increases more slowly than the labour force. With an exponent of 0·25 for capital, the marginal productivity share going to labour will be three-quarters of the total product (i.e., its share if rewarded in proportion to its contribution to increased production as when labour and capital increase equally), and its share of the increment of product will be three-quarters of the ¾ per cent increment.* But we are really concerned with the change of income *per head* as the amount of the factors changes and this will be affected by the total increase in product and not simply the share attributed to labour and capital respectively.

(vi) Since an increase in labour with capital constant will yield a less than proportionate increase in product, the added product per additional person, and the average per head, must fall with increasing population, i.e., in the absence of a corresponding increase in capital. Suppose, to begin with, that the population is 1,000 and income is £100,000, or £100 per head. Suppose further

---

* Cf. *Theory of Wages*. Especially pp. 145 *et seq.*

that population increases by 2 per cent per annum compounded but capital remains unchanged, and that prices remain unchanged. The income will then increase by 1½ per cent per annum compounded, i.e., twice 0·75 per cent. The results (assumed to follow very quickly) would then be:

End of	Population	Total income	Increase per additional person	Average income per head
		£	£	£
	1,000	100,000 ⎫		100
1st year . .	1,020	101,500 ⎭	75	99·5
10th year . .	1,219	116,050 ⎫		95·2
11th year . .	1,243	117,795 ⎭	72·7	94·8

If the exponent of labour were lower, a not improbable event in under-developed countries, the decline in the increment contributed per additional person would be more rapid, as would be the decline in average income per head. Thus, if the exponent were 0·5 instead of 0·75, and other conditions were as assumed, the contributions to total income per additional person would decline from £50 in the first year to £46 in the eleventh, and by that time the income per head would be £89·9 instead of £94·8. It is, of course, highly improbable that population would increase without some increase in capital, but if capital stock increased at a slower rate than population, the contribution to total income per additional person and the average income per head, would still decline over the period.

(vii) Similarly, an increase in capital with labour constant will yield a less than proportionate increase in product, and the marginal product, i.e., the increment per added unit of capital, and the average product for all units of the capital stock will fall. But the income per head will rise. Merely to simplify the arithmetic we make the unreal supposition that the capital stock and national income, both measured in accountancy units called £. are both £100,000, and there are 1,000 people. Capital stock increases by 4 per cent per annum. This will increase income by 1 per cent per annum because the exponent of capital is assumed to be 0·25. Population, we suppose, remains unchanged. The results then (again assumed to follow very rapidly) are:—

End of	Capital stock (increasing 4 per cent per annum compounded)	Capital per head	Total income	Additional units of capital per added unit of income	Units of capital per unit of total income	Income per head
	£	£	£			£
	100,000	100	100,000 ⎫		1·0	100
1st year . .	104,000	104	101,000 ⎬ 4		1·03	101
10th year .	148,024	148	110,462 ⎫		1·35	110·5
11th year .	153,945	154	111,567 ⎭ 5·4		1·38	111·6

For the figures chosen, a 1 per cent increase in income requires a first investment of 4 per cent of the capital stock, which is also 4 per cent of current national income. But the rate of increase in income is slower than that of capital. Hence to sustain a geometric rate of increase of 1 per cent of income, investment must rise to 5·4 per cent. of income by the eleventh year. The product per additional unit of capital falls progressively, i.e., the ratio of total capital to total income rises, from 1 in zero year to 1·38 in the eleventh year.

We may express the position differently by saying that, to sustain a given geometric rate of increase in income per head, it will be necessary for an increasing proportion of national income to be set aside for the provision of capital, i.e., an increasing proportion of national income must be saved. This means that the marginal propensity to save (i.e., the proportion of each additional increment of income saved) must rise, and be higher than the average propensity to save. We may add that the lower the exponent of capital the greater the rate of decline in the marginal and average product of capital, and the greater the rate at which the proportion of income saved must increase for any given rate of increase in national income per head.

Alternatively, we may put it that out of a given percentage increase in capital stock, the more rapid the rate of population growth, the bigger the amount and proportion of the capital increment which is needed to maintain levels of consumption per head and hence the smaller the amount and proportion of the capital increment which is left *to promote an increase* in consumption per head.

We may vary the assumption and imagine that each of the exponents is below unity but their sum exceeds unity. If the exponent of labour is 0·80 and of capital 0·40, there would still be diminishing factor returns to both. If both labour and capital increase by 1 per cent the product would increase by 0·8 per cent plus 0·4 per cent, i.e., 1·2 per cent, and there would then be increasing returns to scale, or output. Increasing returns to population growth alone (still assuming a constant ratio of labour to population) would apply only if the exponent of labour exceeded unity. In this case there would be both increasing factor returns to labour and economies of scale. Since it is difficult to imagine a negative exponent for capital, or labour, the sum of the exponents would exceed unity if the exponent of either capital or labour exceeded unity. It is theoretically possible that the exponent of labour could exceed unity, but such a situation seems likely to be exceptional, so that increasing returns to population growth is also likely to be exceptional. We return to this question in the following chapter.

If the exponents were 0·8 and 0·4 per cent for labour and capital respectively, and labour increased by 1 per cent, capital would have to increase by $\frac{1}{2}$ per cent to maintain production per head; but if the exponent of capital were 0·2 instead of 0·4, capital would have to increase by 1 per cent. So the higher the exponents of labour, and capital, the smaller the increase in capital needed to maintain production per head for a given percentage increase in population.

The discussion so far leads to the conclusions that a rise in levels of consumption in a growing population would require one or more of the following conditions:

(1) A rate of increase in capital stock (i.e., rate of investment) exceeding both the rate of increase in population and that in national income.

(2) Economies of scale large enough to offset such diminishing

factor returns as might occur if the rate of growth of population exceeded that of capital stock.

(3) An improvement in the ratio of labour to population.

(4) Improvements in the efficiency of labour and/or capital. Except for the first, these conclusions might appear to be self-evident and not to require argument or demonstration; but there is a common belief in many countries* that an increase in population will itself increase productive power per head of population, without due weighing of the capital requirements and of the conditions which affect economies of scale. Opinions of this sort often derive support from the fact that population growth in the past has been accompanied by improvements in levels of consumption (often under very different socio-economic conditions). In fact these improvements may have been due rather to capital growth and technological improvements. As is shown in the following chapter, the view that population growth enjoys increasing returns is not confined to the general public. It must therefore be examined.

The conclusions of this chapter serve to bring out the importance of empirical investigations into production functions in order to assess the effects of population increase and facilitate estimates of investment needs. They lead into the whole process of economic development but we confine attention to selected main aspects.

* For example, among many in New Zealand at the present time.

CHAPTER V

ECONOMIES OF SCALE

It is useful to begin consideration of economies of scale or output by some general observations. Economies of scale are concerned with the effects of an increase in output consequent on
increased input of labour or capital or both. An increase in output
may also result from innovations, which may affect economies of
scale in the long run by influencing the exponents of labour and
capital, but we neglect them for the time being, except in so far as
the encouragement of innovations is one of the consequences of
an increase in output.

The effects are designated as internal and external economies
respectively. The distinction is rather loose, for internal economies to one industry, say transport, will be external economies to
another. Internal economies are the improvements in organization
within an enterprise which become possible because its output is
larger. These will result from the fuller use of a factor, or factors
of production, or from a greater degree of specialization within
the enterprise. They are especially likely to occur in industries
where either the product or the units of capital employed are
large, so that investment tends to be discontinuous, or where the
finished product is highly complex and production can be exten-
sively subdivided.* Growth may move discontinuously towards
different optima in terms of economies of scale, both because of
the large size of the units of input of capital, and because the
appropriate technologies (even if already known) may be different
for various scales of output. This is not so much a question of

* For a fuller discussion, c.f. G. F. Stigler, *Production and Distribution
Theories*, Macmillan, 1949, *passim*; E. A. G. Robinson, *The Structure of Com-
petitive Industry*, Cambridge U. P., 1931; Marshall, *Principles*, Book IV,
Chapters VIII–XIII.

technological innovations as of ability to take advantage of machines and processes having different degrees of technical efficiency at different outputs. So we include among internal economies the possibility of using better machines and processes already known, which it becomes profitable for an enterprise to use simply because its output is bigger. But even though such a substitution may not increase the ratio of capital to labour, it may result in earlier obsolescence which increases the need for capital formation, or for foreign exchange if the new types of capital have to be imported. The relative scope for internal economies will differ in different types of enterprise or sectors of an economy. For example, it will usually be much greater in manufacture than in agriculture, because of the greater scope for mechanization and operational and functional division of labour and specialization, and sometimes because of the greater size of the units of investment. This is an important matter, for the promotion of internal economies by a growth in the market will depend a great deal on how this growth alters the relative importance of agriculture, manufacture and other industries.

External economies, or more properly economies of scale for a country as a whole will be influenced, *inter alia*, by such conditions as the following:

(1) Individual production units may be already of optimum size so that further growth does not lead to internal economies in respect of the production units themselves. But growth in national output may promote greater specialization *among* production units and be conducive to greater efficiency in each separate unit, even though each unit is no larger than the previously undifferentiated units in terms of output. This may occur not only in respect of fabrication and the more effective use of by-products, but also in respect of ancillary services such as marketing, finance, advertising and research.

(2) Growth in the market may promote fuller utilization of *social overhead*, by which we mean investments and services making a general contribution to the operation of other industries producing marketable goods and services, as well as providing non-marketable services. Among these we include communica-

tions, transport, sewerage, water supply, education, law and order, research, health and general public administration. There may be a minimum size of investment, or size of agency below which it is hardly worthwhile to go, but which is not utilized to full capacity. Up to a point, increased demand cheapens the service, and this is reflected in the costs of individual enterprises. Once this point is passed there is an excess load, which raises costs, until a new investment is made and the process repeated. Indeed, one of the problems in under-developed countries is the discontinuity in investment in social overhead, and the large size of the dose which may be needed from time to time. External economies due to an expansion of the market may reflect back also in the sense that the cheapening of the service may extend the market to individual firms, and so increase the scale of operations which is profitable. This applies particularly to the effects of transport.

(3) The concentration of population in urban areas may enable many services to be provided more cheaply, though it seems possible to. provide most of these economically in towns of moderate size.* The rapid growth of large urban areas may involve heavy expenditure in necessary amenities and services and have prejudicial effects on welfare through overcrowding and the lack of amenities. There may be diminishing returns in terms of both economic cost and levels of living from concentrated urban growth. This would suggest a case for planned development of decentralized towns of moderate size.†

(4) There may be a more nebulous congeries of factors or conditions such as the cross-fertilization of ideas, and the stimulus which these give to the absorption of skills and other technological improvements.‡ Growth, especially if accompanied by

---

* Cf. Colin Clark, 'The Economic Functions of a City in Relation to its Size,' *Econometrica*, Vol. XIII, No. 2, April, 1945.

† This is being attempted in the urban-cum-rural community projects in India, which aim at the integrated development of small or moderate sized towns and the surrounding countryside.

‡ Cf., for example, the discussion of Marshall's views, Stigler, *op. cit.*, pp. 68 *et seq.*

industrialization and urbanization, may promote a sort of economic élan in a society.

The problem of deciding what will happen as output increases is rendered more difficult because we are concerned not simply with a static situation, but with longer period changes associated with growth or recession in levels of consumption. This is a highly complex matter which could be pursued much further in several directions than it is our present intention to go. In order to clear the ground, however, it is desirable to draw attention to certain concomitants of growth or recession which are important, but not necessarily related to factor returns, nor normally regarded as economies of scale. We mention only two by way of illustration.

In a developed society, which is susceptible to unemployment arising from a shortage of effective demand, a growing population may have an expansive effect on aggregate demand or output even if output per head would not be increased by population growth at full employment. It may therefore provide an incentive to investment, making it easier to approach a position of full employment or recover from depression. Expanding population becomes one important element in a rising trend of *aggregate* demand and output. A *change* in the rate of population growth may then affect the volume of employment, so that if it increases there is both more capital and a higher ratio of working labour to population. The decline in the rate of population growth in the 'twenties may have had a bearing on the intensity of the depression in the 'thirties, and on the difficulty in getting out of it.* It is possibly because attention has been directed so much of recent years to the factors affecting aggregate demand, investment, and employment, that population growth has been regarded as 'beneficial'. My own view is that the occasions when *population growth at full employment* would be beneficial in terms of output per head is much less general than tends to be implicitly assumed. Indeed, it may be the exception rather than the rule because it would require increasing factor returns to labour. The case for

* N. Kaldor, 'The Relation of Economic Growth and Cyclical Fluctuations,' *The Economic Journal*, March, 1954; footnote, p. 68, makes such a suggestion with special reference to the United States.

population growth in terms of the criterion of the rate of increase in consumption levels then rests on the failure to sustain full employment by other means.

This may be an important argument in support of population increase, for example, by immigration; but an increase in the rate of population growth when there is already full employment tends to increase inflationary pressures because of the increased investment demand which it induces.* This situation is currently illustrated, for example, in New Zealand.

In under-developed societies, however, the relatively small importance of unemployment due to a shortage of effective demand gives little support to a case for population increase based on these grounds. The essential requirements (as we shall argue) are to reduce institutional unemployment or under-employment by a direct attack, or by economic development in the sense of an increase in levels of consumption. Factor returns and economies of scale then become of primary importance. Consideration of population growth in these terms need be little qualified, if at all, in regard to its effects in stimulating investment. Buoyancy or economic lethargy—the degree of economic élan—are more likely to be correlated with changes in consumption levels *per head* than with *aggregate* output, more especially as these will affect the *relative* importance of the rural sector which is most susceptible to under-employment and seasonal unemployment.

The second concomitant to which attention must be given is a change in food supply and levels of nutrition. It is our conviction, argued later, that an improvement in nutritional levels (which by and large requires an increase in available food per head, either directly or through the purchase of imported food by expanding exports), is a primary necessity for economic development. It is required to improve the quality of labour.

An improvement in levels of nutrition depends a great deal on factor returns to labour and economies of scale (positive or negative) as population grows, but an improvement in the inherent

---

* Even in such a situation, the shortage of labour which results may stimulate technological innovations to economize in labour.

quality of labour would not normally be regarded as one of the economies of scale. In fact, however, the general drift of our argument is that in under-developed countries population growth *per se* reduces food output per head, so that the quantitative conclusions which follow in succeeding paragraphs are reinforced by the qualitative effects on labour and efficiency.

In an article already quoted* Colin Clark considers that 'probably the majority of industries in the modern community are quite specifically benefited by increasing population. These are the industries that work under the law of increasing returns rather than the law of diminishing returns. . . . The law of increasing returns prevails in any industry where, as a consequence of increased scale of output, we can expect to obtain increasing returns per unit of labour or other economic resources employed. . . . In fact most of the economic operations of a modern community are carried out in such a way that, if there were an increase in the population and the size of the market, organization would become more economical and productivity per head would increase, not decrease. Without the large and densely settled populations of North America and Western Europe, most modern industries would be working under great difficulties and at a very high cost—it is doubtful, indeed, whether they would have come into existence at all.' While the statement is not entirely free from ambiguity the general drift seems clear, especially in the setting of an attack on neo-Malthusians. It suggests a belief in increasing returns to population growth of itself, production per head being raised as a result of population increase. Previous discussions will have shown that even if economies of scale occur when population growth is accompanied by an increase in capital, this result will not follow from population growth unless there is increasing factor returns to labour.

Before discussing the matter further, two observations seem relevant, which may appear to be debating points, but are a little more.

(i) If increasing returns to population had applied, an increase in population in India and other under-developed countries might

* 'Population Growth and Living Standards,' *op. cit.*, pp. 101–2.

have been expected to lead to increasing income per head and the problem of economic development would have been solved already. In fact, production per head has increased little, if at all, in such countries despite some increase in capital and some technological improvement. This leads to a strong presumption of decreasing factor returns to population growth *per se*, and no economies of scale to population growth of itself. In this event production per head would have been higher with a slower rate of population increase. In any case it is apparent that the matter requires further examination.

(ii) The reference to the density of population in North America and Europe does not quite hit the target; some degree of population density in these areas would be necessary for optimum economies of scale; but beyond this diseconomies might well arise. While a large and dense population may be necessary for optimum economies a larger and denser population may bring no further advantages, and indeed bring disadvantages. Moreover, it may well be that the economies result not from the demographic situation but from this situation plus something else. Population in some under-developed countries is larger and denser than in some of the developed countries, and in terms of these demographic factors alone might derive economies of scale equivalent to those in the areas referred to; but the something else is lacking. The question at issue, however, is whether *further* increases in population would result in increasing returns in under-developed countries, i.e., whether output per head would be higher with a faster than with a slower rate of population increase. Here the analogy made does not help a great deal. Moreover, other opinions could be cited to the effect that populations in these *developed* areas have exceeded the optimum from the point of view of economies of scale. Thus, in dealing with the economies of specialization, which is one important aspect, J. J. Spengler considers: 'There is every reason to suppose, however, that we have long passed it (i.e., the point of optimum in terms of population size) in the United States and in the larger European economies.'*

* 'Population and Per Capita Income,' *Annals of American Academy of Political and Social Science*, January, 1945, p. 187.

I would lean to this view rather than Colin Clark's, especially if account be taken of congestion of social overhead, which tends to occur in transport, power and urban amenities.

Nor do such empirical enquiries as have been made lend unequivocal support to Clark's propositions, especially when it is noted that they apply to situations in which growth in the labour force has been accompanied by capital growth. Thus Douglas* finds a 'faint suggestion of diminishing returns (i.e., to scale) in three out of four time series 1899–1922, and in five out of six cross-sections of American manufactures.' In various series in different years over the period 1889–1919 he found 'an unmistakable indication of true diminishing returns so far as the size of individual plants is concerned.' He concluded that: 'While much more study is needed to develop and clarify this point it is suggested that quite possibly American plants during this period were in practice developed beyond the point of maximum efficiency.' Colin Clark† deduces from certain results obtained by Douglas and Bronfenbrenner for 1909 in the United States that in the industries covered 'largely constant returns prevailed at that date'. John M. Blair‡ also brings forward evidence suggesting that in many lines of enterprise technological innovations have tended of recent years to shift towards a smaller size the point at which internal economies of scale cease and diminishing returns to scale begin to operate. Tintner§ found some suggestions of decreasing returns to scale in Iowa farms other than dairying (where there was some tendency to increasing returns) but the factor of management was not included in the analyses and its inclusion might have shown constant or increasing returns. It will be noted that these findings relate to economies of scale in farming and not merely to what happens if other factors are more inten-

* Paul Douglas, 'Are there Laws of Production?' *American Economic Review*, Vol. XXXVII, March, 1948.

† *The Conditions of Economic Progress*, Macmillan, 2nd Edition, 1951, pp. 518–19.

‡ 'Does Large-scale Enterprise Result in Lower Costs? Technology and Size,' *American Economic Review*, Vol. XXXVIII, No. 2, May, 1948.

§ *Econometrica*, Vol. XII, 1944, pp. 26–34.

sively applied to land, for a larger enterprise in terms of output may result from cultivation of a larger area as well as from applying more labour and capital.

There may well be a minimum area of land in respect of a particular crop or farming situation, below which there is little scope for mechanization and capital intensification, or for specialization in management. Below this area an increase in the scale of output may require labour intensification, and there might be a substantial under-utilization of labour and of capital if the increased output resulted from any considerable increase in capital intensity. If it resulted from labour intensification there would be diminishing returns to labour. In such circumstances increasing returns to scale seems improbable. Above this size, the scope for mechanization and specialization of functions, including managerial functions, may enable output to be increased in such a way as to lead to increasing returns to output up to a point, at least if it results from an increase in both labour and capital. In under-developed countries with dense populations it is the former situation, with holdings of small size, which exists, and we have argued that it will continue. While comparatively simple improvements in techniques may lead to rapid substantial relative increases in output, these are in no way contingent on an increase in the labour force, though they may result in a fuller use of existing labour. When they have occurred, increased labour application would lead to diminishing returns to labour in the same way as before they occurred, and quite probably diminishing returns to scale, even if capital and labour increased *pari passu*. They do not indicate economies of scale so much as the significance of technological innovations.

In terms of our previous discussion it will be noted that the existence of either constant or diminishing returns to scale implies that there is diminishing factor returns to labour and capital, and that economies of scale will not occur if labour increases at a faster rate than capital, still less from an increase in labour alone.

The studies and conclusions referred to relate to different time series and economic sectors, and there is no *prima facie* reason why they should necessarily be consistent with each other. They are quoted to suggest that in respect of internal economies, economy of scale beyond a certain point is not necessarily and always one of the facts of life, and that the point where it stops has been passed in some of the examples cited; and that, further, technological improvements are tending in many industries to reduce the size of the optimum enterprise. Growth in the size of the market does not then bring further benefits by enabling size of enterprise to grow, and can be met by duplication of enterprises of optimum size. The responsibility for economy of scale to population growth is then thrown on the emergence of additional *external* economies, or more properly economies to the society as a whole.

The only evidence available to me at the time of writing as to economies of scale for an economy as a whole is the conclusion of Tintner* that in all probability there was increasing returns to scale in the American economy over the period 1921–41. This, however, appears to relate to total private net output,† and the result might be different if non-marketable output were included.‡ Moreover, economy of scale to an economy as a whole when both labour and capital increase is one thing. Economy of scale to population growth is quite another. Tintner's conclusion does, however, provide a hint of the complexity of the problem for a whole economy, because other evidence, some of which has been quoted, supports the existence of constant, or even a suspicion of diminishing returns to scale in both manufacture and agriculture. Tintner concludes with the cautious explanation: 'It is conceivable that the production functions for industry and agriculture separately are homogeneous functions of degree 1, but not a production function for the whole economy.'§ The latter would be more complex than the Cobb-Douglas function which we have

* *Econometrics*, p. 142.
† *Ibid.*, p. 134.
‡ As noted above, Spengler held the opinion that the American population was too large for optimum economies of scale. If account were taken of the large expansion of social overhead and non-marketable output, there need not necessarily be any inconsistency between the two views.
§ *Econometrics*, pp. 142–3.

used for purposes of exposition. Other economic sectors would have to be included besides agriculture and manufacture, and allowance would have to be made for *social overhead*. There may also be other factors or influences more difficult to isolate, such as the transmission of skills, or changes in the propensity to innovate, or change in industrial morale, affected by growth in output, and about which we know little or nothing.*

For such reasons something more than summation or averaging of the position in different sectors is required. Nevertheless, it would seem reasonable that the exponents in different sectors and the relative importance of different sectors, including those concerned with social overhead and non-marketable outlay, would have a bearing on the function for the economy as a whole. Changes in the relative importance of different sectors would then affect this function and have a significant influence on the results to be expected from an increase in population, or capital, or both.

Here we cannot generalize too closely from empirical studies in developed societies. Empirical studies based on historical series have been made over a period during which the economies were already industrialized. They have been in process of continued change, but we may expect much more striking changes in underdeveloped societies if the development process succeeds, and they move towards the pattern of industrialized societies. There will then be a movement into a different technological category so to speak—from handicrafts to factory production, or bullock dray to motor lorry.† Similarly there will be more striking differences

* On the complicated nature of some intangible factors within enterprises cf. Wroe Alderson, 'Social Adjustments in Business Management,' *Explorations in Entrepreneural History*, Vol. VI, No. 1, 1953–54, p. 20.

† S. Tinbergen ('Capital Formation and the Five Year Plan,' *Indian Economic Journal*, Vol. I, No. 1, July, 1953), illustrates the point; a transition from hand-looms to power-looms may enable a worker to handle four looms instead of one. Not only would the optimum size change, giving scope for specialization in management, accounting, servicing or buying and selling, but also most probably the exponents of labour and capital would be different. It seems unlikely that such an innovation would be strictly neutral as between labour and capital.

in structure and the degree of development of different sectors in developed and under-developed countries respectively, especially between farming and factory industries, or rural and urban areas. So it seems likely that the changes in structure and in the relative importance of different industries, would have bigger effects in altering the 'total' production function of under-developed than of developed economies. In the nature of things, this can be little more than a hunch, and relevant information as to production functions is so meagre that we have to rely on a general discussion of probable effects supported to only a small extent by empirical studies. The conclusions reached cannot then be entirely convincing, but they may help in forming a judgment on what is likely under different assumptions as to how growth occurs.

In considering quantitative aspects as affected by factor returns and economies of scale we ask first: given the existing function of an economy, what will be the effect on output per head according as the total increase in output results from a proportionate increase in labour in excess of the proportionate increase in capital, or from a similar proportionate increase in both, or from an increase in labour proportionately less than that of capital? Second, in each case, will the initial effect lead to changes in the structure of the economy such that the effects of any subsequent inputs of factors will be different? In large measure this will depend on the initial effects in terms of income per head; for these will affect the structure of demand and so the relative importance of different sectors of an economy. To recapitulate, while we do not suggest that the production function for an economy is merely a summation or averaging of the functions of the separate sectors, yet if we include social overhead and services as well as manufacture and agriculture, changes in their relative importance must exercise an important, perhaps a dominant, influence. We are saying, in other words, that it is unrealistic to suppose the production function of an under-developed economy remains unchanged with growth or recession in real income per head, and more realistic to consider the possibility that change in structure opens up different possibilities for economies of scale. As already mentioned, we do not attempt to derive a production function for an economy, but think it legitimate to draw attention to changes in structure likely to affect such a function.

Since the demand side of the equation is of considerable importance, it is useful here to make some general observations about it, as in part conditioning what follows. At low levels of income and of nutrition, the demand for food is intense and the consumption functions for manufactures and personal services, i.e., the proportions of increases in income spent on these, are relatively low. Empirical evidence indicates the probability that as production and consumption per head increase, the relative importance of manufactured goods and personal services increases. As real income increases further a point will come when the demand for these goods is likely to rise faster than for food. But by comparison with developed countries such goods are still relatively less important as elements in consumption patterns. From these conditions we can conclude that manufacturing and servicing industries will increase in relative importance if growth in aggregate income is accompanied by rising levels of output per head and of consumption, though not otherwise. If output per head falls there will be greater resistance to reducing food consumption than consumption of manufactured products or services. In the early stages of an improvement, the change in the pattern of demand will not be great, so that the change in economic structure may not be great. This is not to say that it will be unimportant.

Within such a framework, then, the initial situation is of some importance. One can imagine conditions in which increasing factor returns to labour would apply, in which case economies of scale would also apply. One man using capital in the form of a crowbar might be quite unable to shift a rock; two could do it, and four people with two crowbars could shift more than twice as many rocks as two. A low intensity of personnel in the community projects in India may have little effect in improving agricultural production, health and other social services. The effort is spread too thin and, up to a point, increasing returns might apply as the size of staff increased. On the other hand, there is a minimum size of population to be covered for economical operation if the administrative overhead is to be spread sufficiently and capital is to be used to capacity. In this case, up to a certain size of population and a certain intensity of staffing there may well be increasing factor returns to labour, and economies of scale.* In pioneer societies also, the same may apply for the community as a whole. An increase in the ratio of labour to capital through an increase in population might not only enable more land to be cultivated, but also social overhead to be more fully used.

In sparsely settled under-developed countries the sort of circumstances outlined may still apply, in the sense that an increase in population in excess of capital will be associated with a larger output per head as both are applied to readily available land. In more densely populated areas we cannot rule out the same sort of possibility entirely, in the absence of empirical evidence concerning exponents; but it is most unlikely that this will occur. The normal situation seems likely to be one in which there is rather marked decreasing factor returns to labour in the main industries. Otherwise we reiterate, it is difficult to understand why past population growth in under-developed areas has raised levels of consumption little if at all, even though accompanied by some increase in capital and some innovations. Moreover, those who discuss the problem, although they do not pose it in the terms now under discussion, do so, universally, as far as I know, in terms which implicitly assume falling output per head from population increase by itself; for they either emphasize the importance of innovations, or estimate the additional *capital* required to sustain or somewhat increase income per head—or they argue that both innovations and more capital are needed. They do not pose the problem in the terms that population growth will lead to such and such an increase in output per head, or sustain output, and indicate the requirements for *further* growth. Thus Colin Clark himself takes a capital : output ratio of 4·1 and deduces a simple rule that, to cover an increase in

* For a discussion in relation to economy in the provision of services in such projects, cf. United Nations, *Report on Community Organization and Development in South and South-East Asia.*

labour force of 1 per cent, a capital investment of 4 per cent of national income is needed.* All the authorities may be relying on false intuition but this seems hardly likely. The only reason for what may appear to be flogging this point is to underline the importance of more clearly isolating the effects of population growth from these or other changes.

Whether or not increasing returns to scale would apply if labour and capital increased in the same proportions so that capital per head remained unchanged is a more difficult question. The only evidence available at the time of writing is from India (quoted earlier) where, in 1938–39, a production function was estimated for manufacture which gave exponents of 0·402 for labour and 0·598 for capital, i.e., there was constant returns with a low labour exponent so that there were steeply diminishing factor returns to labour. There seems no *prima facie* reason why, for the economy as a whole, the labour exponent should be raised a great deal, nor why the sum of the exponent should be much, if at all, above unity. In a country where labour is redundant and capital is scarce we should expect the structure of economic organization to be such that the exponent of labour would be lower, and that of capital higher, than in economically more advanced countries where capital intensity is greater.† But this would be modified by other factors such as the technical quality of the capital and labour, and in particular the extent to which there is an abundant supply of land or other natural resources yielding a high return to the application of labour and capital.

It is not very satisfying to argue on the basis of one piece of evidence; but there are other conditions to take account of. In under-developed countries the ratio of farming to secondary and tertiary industries is high, and the farming sector consists of small holdings. As we have pointed out, it is virtually certain on such holdings that diminishing factor returns would apply to both labour and capital, and most unlikely that economies of scale would result.

* 'Population Growth and Living Standards,' *op. cit.*, p. 116.
† M. V. Divatia and H. M. Trivedi, *op. cit.*, pp. 65–67 and p. 90.

In farming industries, such evidence as is available points to the existence of diminishing factor returns to labour and decreasing returns to scale. Thus Colin Clark,* quoting statistics from Wickiser and Bennett (*The Rice Economy of Monsoon Asia*), states: 'Though increasing yields per acre through improved techniques do occur in some countries, decreasing returns as a consequence of pressure of population seems to be the general rule,' i.e., in Monsoon Asia. A recent study by the Indian Council of Agricultural Research shows that, by and large, the yield per acre has tended to remain stationary during the past few decades. 'All the attempts at agricultural improvement . . . have served merely to postpone the diminishing returns which inevitably follow increasing pressure on the land.'† We draw attention also to the evidence of diminishing returns quoted earlier from the Indian Census Report.‡ We are not concerned here with the historical process, but with the fact that when two periods are compared, in one of which there is more labour, capital and some technological improvement, there is virtually no difference in output per head. Where additional land is available, the onset of diminishing returns to labour may be delayed; but the size of the new holdings will be determined largely by the area which a family can manage with existing techniques and capital, and there is small likelihood of economies of scale from larger enterprises based on larger land areas.

We conclude, then, that in the major sector of the economy there will be diminishing factor returns to population growth, and the probability of diminishing returns to scale even if capital increases *pari passu*. The responsibility for increased production per head, even if capital increases *pari passu*, must be thrown on innovations or economies of scale for the country as a whole. The actual volume of output from the agricultural sector will usually be sufficient to permit effective organization in marketing and finance. There may be some economies from growth, but the

---

* *The Conditions of Economic Progress*, p. 227.

† Dr. S. R. Sen, *op. cit.*, pp. 448–449, cf. *supra*, Chapter I, p. 11. But see, also, *supra*, Chapter I, p. 11, for an opinion that output per head has fallen.

‡ *Supra*, Chapter I, p. 13.

main scope for lowering costs is in the reform of marketing and financial institutions. Some economies are also possible in the fuller use of social overhead, in urban growth, and in the intangible elements in economies of scale. But these must offset diminishing returns in agriculture, the main industry, if production per head is to increase. Hence it is asking a great deal for economies of scale to offset diminishing returns to labour. Apart from innovations it is unlikely that income per head will rise unless there is at least an equal increase in capital, and it is safer to assume that a somewhat more rapid increase in capital than in population would normally be needed.

We now consider the effects further on different assumptions as to the causes of the initial increase in output. The first case is where there is an increase in population with a smaller proportionate increase in capital. As indicated earlier, economies of scale will not result, even if the sum of the exponents in a sector exceeds unity, unless the proportionate increase in capital is more than sufficient to offset diminishing factor returns to labour. Here again the relative importance of peasant farming affects the outcome; for an increase in population greater than in capital will require an increased application of labour to land. This is precisely the situation in which diminishing factor returns applies to labour in a sector in which economies of scale are prevented by the institutional set-up. So a decline in output per head would seem unavoidable except for innovations. To maintain food production per head the proportion engaged in farming would have to rise so that there would be a declining proportion engaged in manufacture and tertiary industries. It is in these that internal economies of scale are most likely. But such economies would appear to be contingent not only on an expansion of output but also on availability of capital for larger units with greater capital intensity, providing scope for greater mechanization, division of labour and production specialization. If expansion of demand for manufactured products occurred, it would be more likely to be met by an increase in the number of small, labour intensive units than by a growth in the size of units, and in these optimum size would be quickly reached. Hence, as far as internal economies are concerned, there is little ground for expecting economy of scale or an over-all increase in production per head from population growth not accompanied by an equivalent increase in capital. Where there is new land to settle, the position would be somewhat better because it would reduce the extent to which a more intensive application of labour was required on existing holdings. But normally this would need capital for roads, irrigation, drainage and other communal services, which would reduce the capital available for other purposes.

Substantially, in the circumstances assumed, the increase in income per head would have to come from economies external to agriculture and manufacture. Some social overhead, such as transport, would no doubt be more fully used. There might also be some economics in marketing and ancillary services; but in largely subsistence economies the growth of rural population would reduce the proportion of the increased output marketed and transported. In any case, we have suggested that, in respect of marketing, there is usually already sufficient bulk for effective marketing organizations and the problem is one of institutional changes, rather than of too small a marketable surplus. We cannot expect a great deal from urbanization, because the main growth would be concentrated in agriculture.* Nor, bearing in mind these conditions, is there reason to suppose that cross-fertilization of ideas and similar intangible 'external' economies would be markedly stimulated. The general conclusion seems inescapable that, apart from innovations, a proportionate increase in population in excess of the proportionate increase in capital will be

---

* The problem of offsetting diminishing returns in agriculture by economies of scale in the economy as a whole will not be easy, as Indian experience shows. We have mentioned that for India, Dr. S. R. Sen draws attention to the fact that percentage engaged in agriculture was about the same in 1951 and in 1900, but the total number was much larger, despite innovations and capital growth. He adds: 'This only proves that all the industrialization and urbanization during the last fifty years has not really been able to reduce the pressure on the land in the slightest degree, although it must be admitted that the situation might have been worse but for the secondary and tertiary employment which was thus created,' *op. cit.*, pp. 448–449.

accompanied by declining productivity per head and declining levels of consumption. In short, increasing returns to population growth are most improbable.

The position is more favourable if capital increases *pari passu* with population. Economies of scale would have less work to do in order to raise levels of consumption, and in addition they would be somewhat more likely to occur. For the production function initially to show constant returns for an economy, such economies of scale as occurred in manufacture and tertiary industries, including social overhead, together with 'nebulous' improvements, would just balance diminishing production per head in agriculture, but there would be no increase in income per head if capital grew *pari passu* with population. For the production function of a whole economy to display the characteristics of increasing returns to scale would require that with growth, economies in manufacture and tertiary industries, including social overhead, would more than offset diminishing production per head in agriculture. It is well to remember also, that although, for convenience, we have been discussing the relationship between labour and capital, the significant relationship is between labour and wealth. If, therefore, land cannot be increased proportionately with labour, capital must be increased more than proportionately.

If the sum of the exponents exceeded unity in the initial situation, and capital and labour increased equally, there would be an increase in income per head. This would lead to an increase in the relative importance of manufacture in which economies of scale are more likely. Since population is growing we would still expect diminishing returns to labour as it increased in relation to land; but for a given population increase the effect would be less than in the previous cases because more capital was available to offset it, and more people were drawn into manufacture. The greater availability of capital would also make it easier to meet the expansion in manufacture by developing forms of organization which use more capital, and facilitating a greater degree of mechanization, division of labour and specialization, i.e., to move into a situation where growth was now possible toward a larger optimum size and where superior techniques could be used. The increase in the demand for tertiary services would also be greater, and with the qualification made about the possible need for discontinuity in investment, increase the degree of utilization of capital already invested in social overhead and of agencies providing social services. A bigger proportion of the increased product would be marketed and transported. Similarly, urban growth would also be stimulated to a greater extent, and provided it occurred, through small or moderate sized towns, rather than through an increase in the congestion of larger cities, it would encourage further economies.

So, if the initial situation is conducive to economies of scale, an expansion of capital comparable with the growth in the labour force, would make it easier for the economy to move into a position still more favourable to economies of scale. We should not expect these effects for the economy to be very great, for, as has been mentioned earlier, the structural changes on which the effects largely depend occur within a range circumscribed by the not-very-high marginal propensity to consume non-food products. Moreover, in so far as internal economies are concerned, managerial ability imposes a limit to the optimum size of production unit or enterprise. To take full advantage of the possibilities a managerial evolution might have to accompany growth in output. This is one reason why, later, we draw attention to the more limited potentialities of entrepreneurs in under-developed than in developed countries, to differences in the location and rôle of leadership, and to the necessity for emphasizing better management of the production flow, as well as innovations, among the functions of leadership.

The situation is still more favourable if the rate of capital growth exceeds the rate of population growth, or there are substantial innovations. For then, even if the initial production function were to indicate constant returns (or probably even some diminishing returns to scale), either more capital or innovations might enable expansion of total production to keep ahead of population increase.

The consumption function still imposes a limit on the rate of growth of manufactures and tertiary products. But the proportions of manufacturing and tertiary products in total consumption and national output, as well as the absolute amounts, are likely to grow more than in the other cases discussed. We now have a greater decline in the relative importance of agriculture, a greater increase in the relative importance of manufacture, greater scope for specialization among production units, and a faster increase in the use of social overhead.* *Ex hypothesi*, there is more capital to finance types of enterprise more conducive to economies of scale than those existing, and utilizing a higher level of technology. Such an improved potentiality we have suggested as being properly regarded as an economy of scale. Managerial problems still impose a limitation, but there is a higher income out of which to finance facilities for training in management, administration and the various crafts, and for research. In short, for these and other reasons *growth* as distinct from size, may stimulate innovations. If output expands without an increase in real income per head, these possibilities are much less.

The fuller utilization of labour now unemployed or underemployed may prove of considerable importance. Under-utilization is inherent in the economy of peasant farming and is relatively more important in farming than in other sectors. The extent to which labour is more fully utilized will depend a great deal, therefore, on changes in the relative importance of the sectors. Where relatively more people must be engaged in agriculture, the degree of under-utilization will be increased rather than decreased, thereby contributing to decreasing returns to population growth. The smaller relative importance of farming, when growth is accompanied by an increase in income per head, brings a further benefit in the relatively fuller utilization of labour. When capital increases *pari passu* with labour there will be smaller relative change in the degree of utilization of labour than when it increases more rapidly than labour.

Provided that we can increase income per head by more capital

---

* There may be complications because the point at which substantial lumps of new investment are required are reached more quickly.

and by innovations, we can then draw comfort from the Biblical formulation of the principle of distributive injustice: 'To him that hath shall be given.' The result follows, however, not from population growth, but from other causes leading to an increase in income per head, which promotes structural changes. The direct benefits of having more capital to work with then have a cumulative influence through the structural changes they induce as well as the capacity to create more capital out of the increased income.

While we cannot affirm with certainty that economies of scale from population increase will not occur, we can be reasonably confident that they are unlikely in under-developed countries except those which have abundant unused resources and are sparsely settled. If this is so, it is seldom likely that levels of consumption will rise, exclusive of innovations, if the rate of capital growth is less than the rate of population growth. The benefit resulting from innovations and more capital would normally be greater if the rate of population growth were slower.

There is one further point which may or may not prove important. In so far as the generalization proves true that technological change is reducing the optimum size of the enterprise,* the point is reached more quickly in the growth of the market when under-developed countries can establish enterprises or industries on competitive terms. But, of course, optimum internal economies are also reached more quickly. Moreover, this is only one of many factors affecting absorptive capacity on a competitive basis.

* *Supra*, Chapter V, p. 74.

CHAPTER VI

INVESTMENT

In under-developed countries it is necessary progressively to increase the rate of capital formation so that capital per head of population continues to grow, and to apply appropriate investment criteria so that the capital available goes as far as possible in generating income. Previous discussion indicates that in an economy subject to constant returns to scale, apart from innovations, a cumulative rate of increase in output per head requires a faster rate of increase in capital than of output per head. If increasing returns apply, there will be an increase in *per capita* output if population and capital grow at the same rate, but the requirement just mentioned is necessary for any cumulative increase in *per capita* output beyond this. In many, if not most under-developed countries it is safest to assume constant or at best slightly increasing returns to scale in the early stages of the development process, so that apart from innovations a progressive improvement in output and consumption levels will require that savings become an increasing proportion of national income. The marginal propensity to save must be rising at a rate fast enough to provide the new capital, or the rate of increase in output per head will slow down. If savings increase more rapidly than voluntary investment there may be a shortage of effective demand, and unemployment. As suggested earlier, this may be a problem in developed societies, but it is not a serious problem, as yet, in under-developed societies. In these the problem is rather to increase the rate of savings and capital formation so that capital grows more rapidly than population. Attitudes towards savings and investment then become primary elements in growth, because the marginal propensity to save has to rise.

The process cannot go on for ever, because there must be a

percentage of income beyond which people and societies are not prepared to save and invest; but this need hardly concern us in present circumstances. In a society which saves and invests a high proportion of national income, innovations are likely to come to the rescue in preventing the growth in income per head from petering out. In under-developed societies the problem is progressively to raise savings and net investment from perhaps 5 per cent of national income to, say, 20 per cent. The direct effects of a progressive improvement in capital and output per head may well be reinforced by economies of scale as the structure of the economy changes, in the manner discussed earlier. They are likely also to induce innovations, not only by bringing about changes in attitudes but also by providing the means with which to innovate. The promotion of innovations is a major requirement for initiating a cumulative process of growth. But poverty is itself an obstacle to innovations, so that the growth of capital and output per head may be expected to accelerate innovations, many of which will be embodied in the new capital. An increase in the proportion of income invested, therefore, becomes all the more important.

Although we discuss savings and investments as amounts or percentages of national income, investments are embodied in concrete things, and not all of them equally increase productive power. Hence, much will depend on the wisdom used in formulating and applying investment criteria.

So far we have discussed the contribution of capital to production in terms of the exponent of capital; but the central problem of the effects of population growth on investment needs can be approached somewhat more conveniently by means of the capital coefficient, by which is meant the ratio of added value to capital in an existing situation. Thus if it requires four units of capital to generate one unit of income, the coefficient is 0·25. A higher coefficient in our terms will mean that each unit of capital generates more income, e.g., if the coefficient rises from 0·25 to 0·33 three units of capital will generate a unit of income instead of four units of capital.

The capital coefficient is not the same thing as the exponent of capital or the marginal net product of capital. The exponent is a ratio between a percentage increase in capital and a percentage increase in product, in the absence of innovations and with 'labour' held constant. It isolates the effects of the increment in capital. The marginal net product of capital is the increment in product resulting from an increment in capital, similarly isolated; i.e., with other factors remaining constant. We have pointed out that this will fall as more capital is used by labour even though the exponent is constant.

The capital coefficient, on the other hand, is a ratio between the amount of product and the input of capital, when the capital is combined with all the other factors in the circumstances of the time. It does not isolate the contributions of capital and labour but considers the two together. Similarly, the marginal coefficient is the ratio between an increment of product and an increment of capital (i.e., between quantities, not percentage changes), again in combination with all the other factors at the time. There is, however, a relationship between the exponent of capital and the marginal net product, and the coefficient. In general, the higher the exponent and the marginal product, the higher the coefficient, i.e., the ratio of output to capital. Earlier it was shown that the exponent of capital in Indian Manufacturing was about 0·6 as against 0·25 in the United States, which would be a factor contributing to a higher coefficient in Indian manufacture; but there are other factors affecting the coefficient, and it would be rash to generalize from this example that a unit of capital would contribute more income in India for the economy as a whole.

The significance of other conditions can be illustrated by the Cobb-Douglas function extended to take care of innovations:

$$P = b\,L^k\,C^j\,e^a$$

If C remains constant, P will be increased and therefore the coefficient will be improved if L (labour), k (the exponent of labour) and j (the exponent of capital) are improved, or e^a (the effect of innovations) is larger. Since we are concerned with improving production per head, it will be small consolation if the ratio P : C is improved *simply* because labour is increased, for this is likely to be accompanied by a reduction in income per head.

Changes in the exponents of labour and capital will be the result of innovations, or of changes in the structure of an economy consequent on growth or recession in real income per head, but in this process many other factors will have changed (such as capital intensity or the level of technology) and have affected the coefficient. Innovations, or technological improvements affecting labour and capital, provide direct means of improving the capital coefficient. The complex effects of all the variables mentioned and of others to be referred to, suggest that it is hazardous to generalize from one country about the results of additional investments in another.

The capital coefficient at any time indicates what will happen from investment which results in capital broadening: from more or less duplicating investments of the existing degree of capital intensity. If, however, the investment leads to capital intensification, or an increase in the amount of capital per worker, this will probably lower the coefficient, except in so far as offset by technological improvements embodied in the intensification of capital. Capital intensification will no doubt occur as economic development proceeds in under-developed countries, income per head rises and capital formation grows as a percentage of national income. But, as a general rule, the next step in under-developed countries will seldom result in any great degree of capital intensification on the average, and the existing capital coefficient would provide a useful guide to over-all capital needs.

Unfortunately, there is not a great deal of information about capital coefficients in under-developed countries, nor in developed countries for that matter. There are, moreover, wide differences in existing estimates. This is to be expected, but it is not at all clear whether various coefficients are strictly comparable. They will differ according as gross or net figures are used, or as the coefficients are average, or marginal. They will be affected by the appropriate amount to be set aside for depreciation, the extent to which capital is not fully utilized, or the coverage of the coefficients. Comparability is affected especially by the extent to which social overhead is included. For the United States, Fellner* found a marginal capital : output ratio of 3·31 : 1 over the period 1919–28, or a marginal coefficient of about 0·3, but the coefficient for *all physical assets*, including those for health, education, transport and other services not sold for a price, would appear to have been 0·20 to 0·25 in 1929.† In 1953 it was estimated that $4,000–$5,000 of capital investment of all sorts was required to sustain production of all goods and services for one person in the United States, as against $300 in Pakistan,‡ which would imply a lower coefficient for Pakistan: perhaps roughly 0·2 as against 0·3. In New Zealand in 1951–52 capital to meet all requirements was estimated at £2,000 per head, income being about £310 per head. The amount of capital per head is higher and the coefficient lower (less than 0·2) than in the United States. In part this may be accounted for by a different coverage and a higher relative cost of national social overhead such as transport, schools, hospitals, and housing, but it is probably due also to the margin of error in rough and ready estimates.

Estimates for under-developed countries are just as conjectural. A United Nations report§ estimates that $19 billion of capital is needed to produce 2½ per cent of an estimated national income in under-developed countries of $97 billion. The assumed capital : output ratio is then about 8 : 1 or a capital coefficient of 0·125. This is undoubtedly so much too low as to be quite unrealistic. It would require a degree of capital intensification neither possible nor appropriate. For India the Planning Commission assumes a coefficient of 0·33‖ but the coverage is not clear and may possibly take insufficient account of national social overhead

* William Fellner, 'The Capital-Output Ratio in Dynamic Economies,' *Money Trade and Economic Growth*. Essays in honour of John Henry Williams, Macmillan, 1951.

† J. J. Spengler, 'Economic Factors in the Development of Densely Populated Areas,' *op. cit.*, pp. 26–27.

‡ Samuel W. Anderson in *U.S. Foreign Commerce Weekly*, October 12, 1953.

§ *Measures for the Economic Development of Under-Developed Countries*, United Nations, New York, 1951.

‖ *The First Five Year Plan. A Summary*, Planning Commission, New Delhi, 1952, p. 4.

and private non-income earning investment such as housing. Pazos* quotes post-war figures for Columbia and Chile which suggest a coefficient of 0·39, higher than in the United States, but points out that the average productivity of capital was raised by improvements in the terms of trade and a more intensive utilization of productive equipment in the war and post-war years. He interprets the results as a rough indication that the capital coefficient had an order of magnitude comparable with that found by Fellner for the United States, or about 0·3. By the same token, allowance for 'non-income' producing social overhead would lower the coefficient. Colin Clark† works on a capital coefficient for under-developed countries of 0·25. A similar coefficient has been used between *gross capital* formation and *gross income* in Ceylon.‡ Both of these estimates are educated guesses, which seem probably not unreasonable for most under-developed countries if we take account of the need for social overhead. We shall use them simply for purposes of illustration, because we really know very little about average or marginal capital coefficients in such countries. These are matters which would repay empirical investigation both in respect of different sectors and for the economy as a whole. They would facilitate estimates of investment needs, provide guidance in the formulation of investment criteria, and reduce the need for generalizing on the basis of data from developed countries, with their very different structures and levels of technology.

The importance of the size of the coefficient may be illustrated in the case of India, which also reflects the precariousness of the prospects of improving levels of consumption if we have to rely on domestic capital formation alone. The Planning Commission has estimated savings in India at 5 per cent of national income, and based the financial requirements for the first Five Year Plan on the assumption of a population increase of 1¼ per cent annually.

* Felipe Pazos, 'Economic Development and Financial Stability,' *International Monetary Fund*, Staff Papers, Vol. III, No. 2, October, 1953.

† 'Population Growth and Living Standards,' *op. cit.*, p. 116.

‡ *The Economic Development of Ceylon*, International Bank for Reconstruction and Development, and John Hopkins Press, Baltimore, 1953, p. 104.

With a capital coefficient of 0·25, the estimated savings would enable national income to be raised by 1¼ per cent (i.e., quarter of 5 per cent) so that income per head would be maintained. If savings were 6 per cent, then 1 per cent of national income would be available for growth in income per head, and it would increase national income by one quarter per cent over that needed to maintain income per head. But with a smaller capital coefficient of 0·20, savings of 5 per cent of national income could only take care of a 1 per cent increase in population and savings would have to be raised to 6¼ per cent to maintain income per head. Given the coefficient of 0·33 used by the Planning Commission, the growth in population of 1¼ per cent would require savings equal to 3¾ per cent of national income, and 1¼ per cent would be left for growth in income per head, but this would make less than a ½ per cent increase in national income available to increase income per head.

This approach serves also to bring out the effects of population increase. In Ceylon, as we have stated, the rate of population increase was doubled from 1·5 per cent to 3 per cent over a period of a few years. If malaria control programmes and other health measures such as improved village sanitation under the community projects in India were to raise the rate of population increase to 2 per cent (surely by no means out of the question) current savings would be inadequate to sustain consumption levels on any one of the above assumptions about capital coefficients, had we to rely entirely on new capital formation financed out of domestic money savings. With money savings of 5 per cent of national income, a 2 per cent population increase, and constant returns to output, the position to maintain existing real income per head would be:—

Capital coefficient	Savings needed as per cent of national income	Deficit in savings as per cent of national income
0·33	6	—1
0·25	8	—3
0·20	10	—5

Fortunately it is not necessary to rely entirely on capital formation out of domestic money savings, and there are credit items to be allowed for if population increases as the result of improved health measures. But, together with the arguments advanced in previous chapters, the illustrations show that population growth cannot be regarded with equanimity.

Especially because the volume of savings is small, it is necessary to formulate and apply investment criteria which ensure that the additional capital will generate the maximum additional income. There is a complex of criteria (some of which may conflict), and many aspects of the problem are outside the range of the present discussion. This applies, for example, to important considerations relating to the balance of payments.*

For the economy as a whole, preference for types of investment with a low ratio of capital to labour is a useful rule of thumb, for the capital coefficient will normally be higher in such cases. This would give support to the sequence light consumer industries → medium industries → heavy industries, where the resources permit. But many issues are raised by a rule of this kind, and important qualifications have to be made. We shall refer to some of these in summary fashion without attempting a blue print for investment.

One issue which immediately suggests itself is the possible conflict between production per head of the labour engaged in an industry or sector, and output per unit of capital. Because the objective is to increase production per head, it is easy to slip into the argument that a capital structure should be preferred which yields the highest output per person employed. Normally output is positively correlated with capital per head, and the greater efficiency of western industries, where this amount is large, is taken as evidence that a similar structure should be attempted in under-developed countries. The following table, showing the relationship between capital and output in the cotton industry in India, serves to illumine the problem.

* Among the many discussions which deal, *inter alia*, with this aspect, note may be taken of Hollis B. Chenery, 'The Application of Investment Criteria,' *Quarterly Journal of Economics*, Vol. XVII, No. 1, Feb., 1953.

Capital and Output in Cotton Weaving in India

Type	Capital per worker	Output per worker	Ratio of capital to output	Labour employed per unit of capital
	(Rupees)	(Rupees)		
Modern Mill (Large Scale) .	1,200	650	1·9	1
Power Loom (Small Scale) .	300	200	1·5	4
Automatic Loom (Cottage Industry)	90	80	1·1	13
Handloom (Cottage Industry) .	35	45	0·8	34

(P. S. Lokanathan, 'Cottage Industries and the Plan,' *Eastern Economist*, July 23rd, 1943. Quoted, *Economic Background of Social Policy, including Problems of Industrialization*, I.L.O., 1947, p. 15.)

The table demonstrates the importance of having more capital, because output per head is greatly increased as capital per head is increased, but this is inversely correlated with output per unit of capital. So the illustration brings into relief the conflict between two possible tests.

The superiority of the modern mill in financial terms is shown by the necessity of protecting less intensive forms, especially hand-loom weaving, by cesses on factory output, reservation of certain markets, subsidies and other types of assistance. If the difference were expressed as the cost of subsidization in money by a government, this would provide a measure of the amount which could be used for capital formation which would be an offset to the high capitalization in the modern factory.* But this far from demonstrates the superiority of more capital intensive structures for industry as a whole, and as a general rule. Weaving is a type of industry in which skills are readily learned, and the size of the market is such that, with a low wage cost it has been possible to compete, not only with less capital intensive types but also with older established cotton industries in Europe. Against these advantages there are concealed benefits in decen-

---

* Since writing this essay I have enjoyed reading a stimulating essay by Maurice Zinkin on *Problems of Economic Development in Asia* (International Secretariat Institute of Pacific Relations, 1953) in which he makes a similar point. But our general conclusions differ in some other respects.

tralized, less intensive types, for example in the utilization of labour which would otherwise be idle. But these do not express themselves in competitive financial costs and they are insufficient, in a free market, to offset financially the superior technology of the modern mill.

The conflict between the two criteria requires further examination. The test of low capital intensity must first be qualified in at least three respects. In some cases the technologies embodied in greater capital intensity are so superior as to outweigh the advantage of investments in less intensive forms. Other industries, such as railways or electric power, make so important a long-run contribution to the economy that they must be undertaken even if the capital coefficient is low. In certain districts in China before the war, carrier coolie charges were twenty times and carter's or barrowman's charges ten times as high as those of the railways.* It would be a dubious advantage to prefer porters or bullock drays because of a higher capital coefficient. On the other hand, in the reclamation works after the Yangtse flood in 1947, bullocks and wheelbarrows were found to be cheaper than bulldozers, and the bullocks could later be used as draught animals on the re-established farms. In some cases also an industry or capital structure with a lower ratio of output to capital might be preferable to one with a higher because it made a bigger contribution to the balance of payments. For example, the large textile mill might find a better market for its products because its output was more uniform in quality, and more adjustable to changes in market demands than the output of hand-looms, and because it could more readily use existing marketing organizations.

In a recent article Walter Galenson† advances formidable arguments of a more general character in support of capital-intensive

* Ching-Chao Wu, *Plan for China's Industrialization*, China Paper, No. 2, Ninth Conference Institute of Pacific Relations, January, 1945, p. 18. See also R. H. Tawney, *Land and Labour in China*, Harcourt Brace, New York, 1932, p. 87. (George Allen & Unwin, London.)

† 'The Problem of Industrial Productivity in Backward Areas,' in *Labour, Management and Economic Growth*, Institute of International Industrial and Labor Relations, Cornell University, Ithaca, 1954, pp. 34–57.

types of investment. Galenson accepts as incontrovertible the view that in the very short run a unit of investment in a labour-intensive industry or process will yield a greater amount of employment than a unit in capital intensive types. He advances arguments in support of capital-intensive types in terms of long-run advantages. Over the longer period, he concludes, these will generate a greater surplus for capital formation, and so make a bigger contribution to employment and national income. In addition: 'Efficiency breeds efficiency, inefficiency is self-perpetuating. A single modern manufacturing establishment in a backward area may serve as a focus from which skills and techniques radiate.'*

Using for illustrative purposes the table of capital and output in cotton weaving in India quoted above he deduces the following hypothetical results:

Hypothetical Employment provided by a Uniform Investment in Various Types of Cotton Textile Machinery†

Year (t + 1)	Modern mill large scale	Power loom small scale	Automatic loom cottage industry	Hand loom cottage industry
5	5	15	13	35
10	34	83	13	35
15	242	444	13	35
20	1,718	2,390	13	35
25	12,200	12,860	13	35

* *Ibid.*, p. 48.

† The assumptions of the model are represented by the following equation (Galenson, p. 46):

$$E_{t+1} = E_1 \left(1 + \frac{p-ew}{c}\right)^t$$ where E_{t+1} represents employment in the $t + 1$ year, E_1 employment in the initial year, p the output per machine, e the number of workers per machine, w the wage rate, and c the cost of a machine, If E_1, p and e are assumed to be parametric constants, then the value of E_{t+1} will depend on the relationship between c and w.'

The model might be modified by providing for a constant increase in real wages and in consumption out of profits, but this would reduce the rate of capital formation. The same applies on these assumptions whatever the rate of capita lintensity.

These deductions assume that the total product, less labour cost, is re-invested each year, and for simplicity no allowance is made for capital replacement. This would slow up the process of net capital formation and of employment and income growth.

We use the model as a convenient means of introducing a number of considerations and do not traverse in detail all of Galenson's arguments, to which the reader is referred, as expressing an interesting exposition of a particular viewpoint.

(1) The higher the real wage rate, the greater the relative importance of the capital-intensive types. Contrariwise, the lower the wage rate the smaller the relative disadvantage in Galenson's terms, of types of investment with low capital intensity. The further the process of growth in levels of consumption, the stronger the case for capital-intensive types, provided that workers share in the increase.

(2) Since for a given volume of output the more intensive type uses more capital, the scarce resource, and less labour, the abundant resource, more capital is drawn from other uses, and the reduced output in capital starved sectors must be subtracted to determine any net advantage. As is illustrated below in the case of Etawah this deduction might be substantial.*

(3) Capital-intensive industries are usually located in the larger urban centres, and there are capital and other costs in economic and social amenities which the enterprise does not fully meet. In rural areas the amenities required are fewer, and underemployed labour can be used to produce them at small *financial* cost. Where, as in India, large urban centres already exist, many of these amenities may already be established, and redundant labour is available to man the factories. But further industrial concentration does not entirely remove the necessity for additional investments in economic, and especially social, amenities, since additional employment opportunities are very likely to draw in additional labour. Industrial development in India does not appear to have relieved urban congestion, even apart from large refugee populations.

* p. 106, this chapter.

(4) Unless the greater part of the investment is in heavy construction industries with a deliberate deferring of consumption, the model is based on an inherent contradiction. The whole of the excess over wages is assumed to go to capital formation. Given the large redundancy of labour, competition for jobs is not likely to lead to an appreciable increase in wages except over a long period of time. This must be qualified by the extent to which strong trade unions emerge and force up wages; but the aggregate of capital formation will then be correspondingly reduced. Apart from this contingency, contradiction arises because the model assumes a high income elasticity for the product, but denies the increase in income for consumption out of which the goods are to be bought. Even apart from this, the relatively low consumption function for manufactured products referred to earlier, imposes a limit on the profitable expansion of manufactures, in which, by comparison with agriculture, there is greater scope for capital-intensive types. So, undue emphasis on capital-intensive investment, where this is possible, may promote an unbalance by starving other industries of capital.

(5) There is a similar market limitation on the economic rate of growth of heavy, capital producing industries. In large measure the consumers of their products must eventually be industries producing consumers' goods.

Expressed more generally, the capital coefficient is not simply a technical phenomenon but a matter of the value of the output per unit of capital investment. The income generated by an investment depends on demand. This changes with income available for consumption. For production to create its own demand requires a balanced growth corresponding to such a changing pattern. Unless investment is to go to waste there is a limitation on the amount of increased income which can be diverted to capital formation. There is also the necessity for attention to the sequence: new light consumer industries through medium to heavy industries, so that each provides a market for the next. These considerations further restrict the validity of the model.

(6) Even in its technical aspects the capital coefficient is a creature of its environment. For this reason, as well as because of

differences in the volume and structure of demand, we cannot expect the income generating power from identical firms or industries to be the same in different countries. In a country in which technical efficiency is high, managerial skills are well developed, educational and training facilities are adequate, and social overhead in the form of power, transport, and monetary and marketing institutions is also well developed, the coefficient will be higher than for enterprises similar in size and with similar capital structure in countries where these facilities are less fully established. What in a developed society might be a technically less efficient type yielding a lower product per worker employed might prove more advantageous in less developed economies. This, again, gives point to the undesirability of generalizing too slavishly on the basis of western experience and economic structure.

Galenson does not use a western example for his model, and chooses the textile industry in India for illustrative purposes. But, as pointed out, this is a type of industry in which the relative disadvantages in under-developed countries appear less than in many other types. Any generalization on the basis of the example selected would have to be seriously qualified by differences in the economic environment due to conditions such as those listed above.* The essence of the matter is that concrete forms of capital must be considered in relation to existing technical skills and administrative competence, and to early prospects of improvement in these. Simpler forms will often increase income more than technically advanced forms because for the latter these prospects are inadequate.

(7) As mentioned in the introduction, we cannot assume that investment criteria are politically neutral, or that political and

---

* Galenson, *op. cit.*, p. 50, recognizes limitations imposed by professional and technical personnel, but discounts them. He refers also to other institutional obstacles to investments with high capital intensity, including the low cost of labour which reduces the incentive to modernize, the pressure of radical trade unions to raise wages, so that increased output goes to consumption instead of investment, and the resistance of labour to the adoption of new machinery.

social reactions have no bearing on the development process. Russia might force the pace of capital-intensive investment by restricting consumption. The democratic approach rules out this solution to any degree, and Galenson's model then requires voluntary investment by those in whose hands property is increasingly concentrated.* Some part of the added income of this group would undoubtedly escape into conspicuous consumption, thereby bringing more sharply into relief the growing inequality of incomes, if improvements in consumption levels of wage-earners (and peasants and others who are *ex hypothesi* capital starved) were held back. Having regard to the growing demands for improved economic conditions, and to the pervasiveness of communist influence, it is unlikely that this situation would be passively accepted. Resistance to the process might well defeat it.† After the revolution, capital intensive investment might be forced, but this is unattractive to those who regard economic development as a contribution to democratic evolution.‡

---

* By the extent to which there is direct taxation on companies of individuals, especially if graduated, the model provides greater scope for capital formation by government because of the greater income concentration.

† Galenson considers that his 'high-productivity' solution 'with its counterpart of fewer and better paid workers will tend to mitigate the almost inevitable upsurge of labour protest', and that the 'low-productivity solution will yield such small results in terms of higher living standards as to have little mollifying effect upon the degree of labour protest' (p. 51). This argument is difficult to follow. In the earlier period the latter approach will cause investment to generate more income. The longer run case for capital-intensive forms depends on the failure of consumption levels to rise at all substantially. Moreover, one supposes that it is relative rather than absolute poverty which breeds revolutionary forces, and the capital-intensive approach increases relative poverty even if workers in the capital-intensive industries gain some increased real wages.

‡ In the same volume in which Galenson's exposition appears, Yale Brozen ('The Effect of Technique Choices on Labor Attitudes and Productivity') argues that decentralized investment of low capital intensity and a wider distribution of property ownership would contribute to an increase in the number and dispersal of those exercising initiative and making decisions, and so contribute to a democratic solution. In criticizing this view Simon Rottenberg (*op. cit.*, pp. 74–76) draws attention to the fact that decision making in

In weighing such indirect effects we cannot neglect the time factor in investment returns. Since economic development is a continuing process, the long run effects must be considered. Sometimes, as in large public works, a low contribution to income now may have to be put up with for a larger contribution later. Nevertheless, there are a number of reasons why such austerity is often less virtuous in poor than in rich countries. In the present world political context more emphasis must be placed on the shorter run than is consistent with the logic of a mathematical equation.

A part of the problem of increasing labour efficiency is to change attitudes and cause people to work harder, longer or better; and one necessary condition for this is to produce incentive goods, i.e., consumer goods which the people want. In short, a break through fairly soon is of some importance, and the considerations raised weight the arguments somewhat in favour of industries which yield an early return to assist in this. They also support, as a rule of thumb, the sequence light consumer goods→medium→heavy industries, and have a bearing on the appropriate balance between investment in agriculture and industry.

More income is needed to provide more savings to provide more income. An early return has something to be said for it, as providing an earlier capacity to create more income and savings for more capital, and to finance expenditure of various sorts which would increase labour efficiency. In perhaps fifteen years the Galenson effect appears to possess advantages; for it concentrates the additional income in the hands of those presumed more likely to invest it. But we have suggested reasons why the advantages of this in terms of capital formation may prove illusory.

Less capital-intensive decentralized industries, even if less

under-developed countries is, in fact, widely dispersed, and has led neither to democracy nor to economic development. My own views, as implicit in later chapters in this essay, and explicitly formulated in 'Social Aspects of Economic Development' are in strong support of Brozen's thesis. But the results will not follow unless effective leadership is exercised by governments in promoting widespread centres of smaller-scale leadership and change, through programmes, procedures and agencies which emphasize active participation of the people. The *Community Projects* described in outline in Appendix II are potentially significant in these and other ways.

efficient in financial terms than urban industries, will spread the increase in income more widely; but in the earlier years they are likely to generate more income, and be more in conformity with the socio-political requirements for development referred to. They may bring indirect benefits, not only in the use of idle labour power *in situ*, and a lower cost of amenities, but also in the stimulus to dispersed centres of leadership.* In addition they may strengthen the investment motive in rural savings, because concrete investments are there to be seen. The wealthier villagers, or groups of villagers, might not be tempted by 10 per cent to invest in the capital market in Bombay or Calcutta, even if the facilities existed to do so, but might be more disposed to establish a small private or co-operative enterprise in the village. The Galenson approach does, however, give point to the necessity for special efforts to encourage savings, and mobilize the smaller units of savings which *ex hypothesi* are likely to result, and divert income to capital formation through taxation.

While Galenson's line of argument presents a strong case for moving progressively toward more capital-intensive types, as development gathers way, it is concerned too little with the short run and intermediate effects, and largely abstracts away the complex of human reactions to continued austerity and deferred consumption for the majority, and to their concomitants of concentration of wealth and economic power.

One general line of approach suggested by the discussion so far is to organize innovations so that the technology of less intensive types of investment is improved, and output per head is increased even while the capital coefficient remains high. There is very considerable scope here for simple improvements in farm processes and implements, and for designing small-scale industrial plants which can operate at low financial cost on a small scale,

---

* There is a point in Galenson's suggestion that urban industries are centres which radiate change, though there does not appear to be strong historical support for the contention in under-developed countries. Our argument is for a deliberate attempt to develop dispersed centres of change and leadership. It will be noted that Japan followed this course and integrated small-scale decentralized units into larger enterprises.

provided that economies of scale can be organized in marketing and finance. This problem is discussed further in the chapter dealing with labour utilization but some reference is warranted here because of the importance of the possibilities opened up.* The emphasis, of course, is on innovations, but of a type directed to improving investments with low capital intensity.

As an outstanding example of the potentialities in agriculture, we quote the results at Etawah in the United Provinces, a project which is a prototype of the community projects under the Indian Five Year Plan. The project was begun in 1948 to cover about ninety-seven villages with a population of 80,000 and later extended to include another 100,000 people. Over a period of four years the average yield of wheat from the area was increased from 820 lb. to 2,175 lb. per acre, of potatoes from 8,200 lb. to 18,200 lb., and of peas from 1,375 lb. to 1,970 lb. These, and other improvements, followed from improved techniques associated with *comparatively simple and inexpensive capital investments* in machinery, wells, hand pumps, fertilizers, and improved seeds.†

* Support for the general thesis that special attention should be given to small-scale decentralized industries with low capital intensity is given in a recent report by Mr. D. A. Morse, Director-General of I.L.O., to delegates to the International Labour Organization's Asian Regional Conference in Tokyo (September, 1953):

'The methods of production based on high capital investment per unit of labour which prevail in the advanced countries would surely be uneconomic for countries of Asia to-day. In Asia, labour is plentiful and cheap, and it is capital which has to be economized. This is a new economic problem and demands new technical methods for its solution.'

The report added: 'More specifically, the problem will be to develop a new type of industry—radically different both from the present cottage and handicraft industries and from the present large-scale factory industries—which for the same amount of capital investment, can at the same time produce more than the former and provide more employment than the latter.' (*I.L.O. News*, Vol. VI, No. 6, September, 1953.)

† The writer can vouch from personal observation in Etawah and other places of the value of comparatively simple investments of low capital intensity when associated with appropriate innovations in this way, but the above information is taken from S. K. Jain, 'An Indian Experiment in Rural Development,' *International Labour Review*, Vol. LXVIII, Nos. 4-5, Oct.-Nov., 1953, pp. 393 *et seq.*

They were associated with the development of co-operatives, literacy classes, and the organization of the people for capital formation by the utilization of voluntary labour. In short, they were part of an integrated programme.

A similar application of technological improvements with investments of low capital intensity in small-scale industries is more difficult, since it involves a greater measure of invention, as well as planning in a field where much less experience can be drawn on than in agriculture. There are some indications of the potentialities. Thus, in one area in Madras, a few hand looms were replaced by power looms, each driven by a one-horse motor. The monthly income per operator increased from Rs. 30 to Rs. 120. A co-operative spinning mill, with primary weavers' societies as members has been established to supply yarn to these looms and to hand looms.* Of course, there are financial, marketing, and other problems raised by this approach and one swallow doesn't make a summer. During UNRRA days in China the Agricultural Industries Service was also engaged in designing improved implements and machines for farmers and small industries, in the experimental development of small industries† (some of which were able to compete with larger scale industries), and in the integration of small with large-scale industries. Unfortunately, these highly promising experiments were given no chance of fruition: but the success of Japan in integrating small industries into the pattern of larger scale industries is well known, and suggests an alternative to Galenson's model. The trend in industrialized countries towards technological improvements which make for a smaller optimum size, and the extension of electric power, or improvements in small internal combustion engines or other sources of power, may possibly facilitate inno-

---

* *Report on Working of Co-operative Societies in the State of Madras*, Government Press, Madras, 1951, pp. 71–73.

† For a recent discussion of the rôle of small industries, cf. Joseph E. Stepanek and Charles H. Prien, 'The Rôle of Small Industries' in *Approaches to Community Development*, Editor P. Ruopp, W. van Hoeve, The Hague, 1953. See also *Training Rural Leaders*, Food and Agricultural Organization of the United Nations, Washington, 1949.

vations increasing the competitive capacity of small industries of low capital intensity.

Our analysis prompts certain further observations. Whatever degree of capital intensity is preferred, success requires that investments embody or are used with improved technologies. To support these, resources must be diverted to education and training so that absorptive capacity for better types of capital is improved. In addition, social overhead in the form of transport systems, power, and ancillary financial, marketing and other services is needed if other capital is to make its full contribution to output. The capital investment in educational and training facilities, and in 'economic' social overhead, may lower the average capital coefficient for an economy while it is occurring. It may well be that the first stage is one in which existing social overhead, e.g., in the form of main roads, is more fully used, and the coefficient is improved; but a time comes when a lump of investment is needed, and the coefficient is lowered until improved by fuller utilization. Hence, although investment in social overhead is necessary to provide external economies for other industries, there may be phases in economic development when the ratio of income generated to capital invested is lowered because of it. The same may apply when investment in heavy industries is needed, until such time as they work to full capacity in helping the rest of the economy to produce income. To be realistic, we cannot discuss the coefficient in terms of the full use of capital in enterprises of optimum size.

The necessity for investments in social overhead is one reason why earlier we used a coefficient of o·25 instead of the coefficient of o·33 used by the government of India in its estimates for the Five Year Plan.

Expenditure on education and training may not appear in capital estimates, but the process of developing these services to an adequate level competes with capital formation and reduces the growth in capital stock as normally conceived. Nevertheless investments in social capital and expenditures on such services are necessary to growth and to improving the coefficient in industries directly producing income. Capital has no generating power of its own but only when combined with labour. Hence investment in people is usually a pre-requisite for the efficient use of new kinds of capital, and though for the time being it may reduce the amount of capital formation or lower the capital coefficient, it will often be a mistake to defer it until more growth has made it easier to 'afford' it. We may add that the shortage of capital in under-developed countries does not necessarily warrant the assumption of a high marginal net product unless expenditure in social capital and services is adequate.

It is sometimes considered that balance will be achieved and the effects of investment will be maximized, if the marginal net products of all new investments are the same. But here we run into the familiar problem that some investments, such as in harbour works, or roads, create benefits for which they cannot be fully credited, while others require investments and create costs which are not assessable against them in financial terms. This might apply, for example, in the case of investments in large concerns or industries located in cities which might have a higher marginal net product than smaller decentralized industries, but the former necessitate a bigger investment in social overhead of various sorts. The contribution to output per unit of capital is not then necessarily higher in the former case. These disparities between individual and social net products are difficult to assess, but call for judgment.

There are also other indirect effects to be considered which may be even more intangible: indeed much of our previous discussion is concerned with intangibles which not only affect individual marginal net products but also cause them to diverge from social marginal net products. This is especially the case in respect of the manner in which investments, capital structure and organization influence income distribution, the gap between standards and levels of consumption and the opportunities for self-expression, and through these affect social coherence and economic élan. Somewhat less nebulous but still difficult to assess in financial terms is the contribution which investment to produce material consumer goods may make to labour efficiency. We have touched on this aspect in stressing the need for incentive goods to stimulate effort. The same applies particularly to food. Thus, the direct financial return from export industries may be large, but more may be gained even in terms of development, from improvements in domestic food production which raise nutritional levels and improve the human agent in production, even though the *direct* comparative advantages appear to rest with the export industry. The retort that food could be imported is unconvincing, since there is no automatic mechanism to ensure that food would in fact be imported or go to the under-fed.

The balance between agriculture and industry is a further case in point. It is common to emphasize industrialization, giving it priority over agriculture. But on the one hand, agricultural expansion is necessary to improve nutritional levels, provide a surplus over rural requirements to feed industrial workers and those engaged in capital formation, and increase the income of rural populations, so that they can buy industrial products. On the other hand, as we have stressed, the economical growth of industry and its contribution to income is limited by the consumption function for industrial products.

Our general line of argument suggests a pattern of growth *towards* the economic structure of the West, but also the danger of a forced growth. In the early stage particularly, it indicates that financial criteria must be qualified by divergencies between social and individual net products, which are likely to be both greater and (often) different in character from those in developed societies. It stresses the necessity for services and social overhead to increase the marginal net product in the production of marketable goods. While recognizing the necessity for important qualifications we conclude in favour of investments of low capital intensity as a rule of thumb, and progression towards investments of greater capital intensity as the rate of capital formation increases, markets expand and the technological climate becomes more congenial.

The large supply of low wage labour not only has a bearing on the capital structure most appropriate within an industry, but also may be used to advantage in capital formation. The first possibility is avoiding use of machinery and other capital in the process of capital creation, especially in respect of public works; for example, in using buffalo carts and dirt in erecting barrages instead of bulldozers, concrete, concrete mixers and cement plants.* The main point is in part the negative one of avoiding the use of western methods expensive in terms of capital required *simply* because they are technically more efficient.

The second possibility arises from the existence of unemployed or under-employed labour, and its use either in capital formation or in small-scale decentralized industry. In the former case capital may be created with the use of a small volume of financial savings, at low social cost, because the labour is otherwise idle or near idle. In the latter a comparatively small amount of capital may put to work a resource otherwise idle, or near idle. From the produce, other than in respect of the capital employed, we then need subtract little or nothing to allow for the result of the operations from which labour has been diverted. What is substituted for is idleness, or near idleness.†

* The scarcity of capital and the redundancy of labour suggest that in capital formation as well as in other production, more may often be achieved by innovations which make labour more effective through improvements in simple tools and machines, than by expenditure on expensive machinery. As an illustration, it is stated that only recently American engineers evolved techniques of earth dam construction to a height of 70 feet, but that the Gangapur dam in India has a height of 125 feet and was undertaken entirely without the help of heavy earth-moving machinery. *Approaches to Community Development, op. cit.*, p. 51. On the other hand, it would be interesting to have a census of derelict tractors, jeeps and other mechanized wonders throughout Asia which have been abandoned on the score of relative costs, or because of faulty maintenance. Comment on this problem is made in a recent *I.L.O. News* (Vol. VI, No. 6, September, 1953) as follows:

'Seventy per cent of the motor vehicles in Asia are sent prematurely to the junk heap due to lack of proper care, according to J. H. Hartzenbusch, technical assistance expert on motor maintenance at the International Labour Organization's Field Office.'

'It is not a question of normal wear and tear but of innocent neglect because the driver and motor mechanics do not know any better.'

† Cf. below, Chapter VIII. On the use of under-employed labour for capital formation, cf. Ragnar Nurske, *op. cit.*, Chapter II. This book will repay reading for a fuller exposition of many of the problems referred to in this section. I have touched on the utilization of labour for capital formation and

There is a further possibility of considerable importance in some under-developed countries in bringing into use large areas of land by controlling malaria. In effect this consists in a substantial increase in wealth in proportion to the capital and labour utilized. Stimulated by the joint work of W.H.O. and F.A.O., a number of countries are already engaged in projects of this kind. The visitor to the so-called dry zone in Ceylon will see ruined cities and irrigation works, and many other evidences of the advanced civilization which flourished there some 2,000 years ago. Wars and malaria decimated the population so that now the area is sparsely settled. A major technical assistance project in Ceylon is to control malaria, re-establish the irrigation works, develop a system of agriculture suitable to the topography and climate of the area, and resettle the people on it.* It is said that in India in the foothills of the Eastern and Western Ghats and the sub-Himalayan belt, there are areas totalling 60,000 square miles which are either not cultivated or are lightly populated by shifting-cultivators because of the anopheles mosquito. The first stage in bringing in such lands is likely to require a saturation attack on malaria, organized and conducted by governments; and settlement cannot be undertaken without some capital expenditure. But with the carefully organized use of redundant labour, and of pioneer peasants, this need not necessarily be great in relation to the asset created. Continuance of malaria control on an economical basis requires organized self-help activities among those settled.†

the rôle of small industries in: *Agricultural Reconstruction in the Far East*, Institute of Pacific Relations, 1947; in 'Observations on Industrialization for Higher Incomes,' *Economic Journal*, September, 1947; and in 'Economic Development in Asia,' *Economia Internazionale*, November, 1952.

* Cf. *The Economic Development of Ceylon, op. cit.*, Chapter II, pp. 737 et seq.

† In further reference to the utilization of idle labour for capital formation, see note to this Chapter in Appendix I.

CHAPTER VII

SAVINGS

Wise judgments on the kinds of capital to create, and their economical use, are one side of the picture. The other is to provide the necessary resources through savings. The use of idle or semi-idle labour will help a great deal but there still isn't a large volume of savings to go round. Even the wide margin of error in estimates of national savings leaves no doubt on this.

The United Nations experts* estimated that domestic savings in under-developed countries throughout the world were $5,240 million in 1949, say 5½ per cent of the estimated national incomes of $97,000 million. In Asia, including Egypt, but excluding Japan, the savings are put at $2,530 million out of national incomes of $59,400 million, or about 4·3 per cent. In more developed countries at the present time savings are seldom below 10 per cent of national income and are usually much higher. With a capital coefficient of 0·25 the rate of savings in Asia, on these estimates, would maintain levels of income for a population of 1 per cent, or of just under 1½ per cent with a coefficient of 0·33. To promote a 2 per cent increase in income per head (used as a basis of calculation by the experts) at the latter rate of growth would mean deficits in savings to start with roughly equal to 9½ per cent and 6 per cent of national incomes respectively for coefficients of 0·25 and 0·33. These would amount to $5,600 million and $3,500 million respectively, much less than the experts' estimate of $11,700 million for a smaller population growth, but still sizable. We attach no great importance to the precise figures but use them to illustrate the order of size of the gap.

* *Measures for the Economic Development of Under-Developed Countries*, *op. cit.*, p. 76.

The paucity of the domestic savings available for new investment may be brought home by comparison with those in a small developed country. In 1949–50 net savings in New Zealand were £90 million ($250 million), or just under 19 per cent of a net national income of £480 million ($1,344 million). For a population of two million, savings of $125 per head greatly exceeded total income per head in countries such as India. With a population 1/600th of that of Asia, domestic savings were about 1/10th of those estimated for Asia. Savings in under-developed countries are a much smaller percentage of a much smaller income per head. On the estimates quoted they would be a little over $2 per head per year on the average for Asia, as against $125 for New Zealand.

The Five Year Plan of the government of India further illustrates the problem of finding sufficient savings. The national income in 1950–51 was estimated at Rs. 9,000 crore* of which 5 per cent, Rs. 450 crore, was saved. With a population of some 362 million income would be about Rs. 250 per head ($50), and savings Rs. 12·50 ($2½) per head. The cost of the plan in the *public sector* is Rs. 2,069 crore, or an average of Rs. 414 crore a year, or say Rs. 11 per head (a little over $2); but a great deal of importance is attached to capital formation in rural areas by voluntary efforts, and to improving efficiency by agricultural extension and other means. The aim is to raise national income by 2 per cent annually, of which one-fifth would be ploughed back through additional savings and taxation to sustain the plan, thus raising savings to Rs. 675 crores in 1955–56. The amount left would sustain a growth of 1·6 per cent of national income for an expected increase of 1·25 per cent in population. So the improvement in levels of consumption per head would be very small to begin with. As mentioned earlier, the estimates are based on a capital coefficient of 0·33. If this proved too optimistic, or if population improved more rapidly, the plan could not be sustained without an increase in foreign borrowing.†

* 1 Crore = 10 million ; 1 Lakh = 100 thousand.
† Since writing this chapter I have come across a careful assessment of the Indian Five Year Plan, viz.: 'Economic Development with Stability,' E. M. Bernstein, R. M. Goode, M. Friedberg and I. G. Patel, in *Staff Papers*,

The illustrations used point to the necessity for increasing the savings available for capital formation. This may be approached by the familiar routes of promoting, mobilizing and more effectively disbursing voluntary savings, and of increasing forced savings through taxation or the more hazardous expedient of inflation*; and of ensuring an adequate supply of foreign exchange for imported capital goods.† We shall touch on one or two points only.

As indicated earlier, when once income per head begins to rise the problem may be posed in terms of raising the marginal propensity to save, or rather of this plus forced savings through taxation, so that an increasing proportion of national income is skimmed off. There are difficulties in achieving this, not only because of low income and prevailing attitudes, but also because it is little use producing more goods unless they can be bought. In the case of heavy industries and capital works, production of consumer goods is deferred in the nature of things. But savings are required to produce capital to produce goods for consumption. It serves no purpose to increase the means to produce goods not wanted, or which the people have not the means to buy. So

I.M. Fund, Vol. III, No. 3, Feb. 1954. The general tenor of this report is that even on the assumptions made in the Five Year Plan, capital formation has been inadequate during the first two years of the Plan and is likely to prove inadequate. This assessment, however, appears to me to take insufficient account of the possibilities (discussed in the next chapter) of utilizing idle or near-idle labour for capital formation.

* For fuller discussion, note the United Nations' Reports on *Domestic Financing of Economic Development, 1950,* and *Mobilization of Domestic Capital,* United Nations, 1952; I have touched on some aspects of the problem of domestic capital formation in *The Mobilization and Use of Domestic Capital in Relation to Agricultural Improvement,* and in other papers in *Proceedings of International Conference on Agricultural and Co-operative Credit.* University of California (in co-operation with Department of State (Technical Co-operation Administration), Department of Agriculture and Mutual Security Administration), August-October, 1952.

† One of the best discussions on this problem, but with special reference to exchange control, is E. R. Schlesinger, *Multiple Exchange Rates and Economic Development,* Princeton Studies in International Finance, May, 1952.

spendable income must grow with the increased flow of goods coming on the market. Moreover, the incentive of more goods is needed to encourage people to earn more income. For these reasons it is expecting too much for a rapid increase in the propensity to save among individuals, and even more for the withdrawal of the whole of any increase in income per head to capital formation. There is a problem of balance here as well as in respect of the distribution of investment.

The critical question, however, is not so much how to save a bigger proportion of *growing* income per head as how to bring about more savings so as to start the process. Savings among large sections of the people are not primarily determined by the investment motive, in the sense of a desire for more current income from the investment, but express themselves a great deal in bunched ceremonial expenditure which is high in relation to income, in hoarding as a security reserve, and in land which is the main economic foundation for the perpetuation of the family. As a corollary, investment is not so markedly affected by judgments on the financial rate of return. Much of the additional income of wealthier groups escapes through high ostentatious consumption, or is invested in buildings or land, or in foreign currencies. In using funds to earn more income there is a preference for trade or finance rather than investment in concrete capital for industrial or agricultural production. So a great deal of saving is not used in such a way as to generate real national income. In these observations we are not suggesting a purely material definition of production, but arguing that over-emphasis on buildings, trade and finance (of existing kinds) leads to a smaller increase in the capacity to increase the total production of goods and services. Anticipated marginal net products in financial terms are not only less influential in determining the direction of investment than in developed, commercialized societies, but also (as was argued in the previous chapter) less appropriate. Changes in motivations and attitudes, through education and appropriate incentives, as well as an improvement in financial agencies are necessary, therefore, to increase the volume of savings directed to income generating capital formation. The problem is both to increase the means to save and change the cultural environment, and improve the institutional arrangements so that the aggregate of savings is increased and investment has a better balance.

As development proceeds such changes are likely to occur in any case; but the governing phrase is 'as it proceeds'. Some attempt must be made to get the process started. This is not impossible but it will be difficult; and spectacular results must not be expected.

An important aspect in any approach is to demonstrate the possibility of income-earning investments for purposes in which the people are interested. This is one reason why we have stressed the rôle of small-scale decentralized industries, and of small improvements in machines and implements for farm and small industries. Another aspect is to bring home the possibility of achieving something worthwhile by aggregating the small units of savings of individuals into larger sums which can be applied effectively. This requires organization as well as education and propaganda. If such investment savings are to be substituted for hoards, the small saver must have confidence in the institutions established, there must be sufficient liquidity to enable him to withdraw his savings when the need arises, and the institutions must be conveniently located. Credit instruments must be similarly designed to meet the tests of security, convertibility into cash, and convenience.

In rural areas, co-operative societies, savings banks, and branches of commerical banks are among the sorts of organizations which may serve these purposes and promote the geographical flow of funds. Co-operative societies in particular may also be of great value as educative and propaganda agencies, for example, in restricting ceremonial expenditure. The 'multipurpose' community projects may be powerful agencies in changing attitudes toward savings and investment, and in organizing and strengthening institutions for small savings and investment.

In urban areas an effective company law, and the eventual establishment of stock exchanges and other agencies commonly found in a well-developed money market may provide investment opportunities with greater convenience and security; but their premature growth opens up possibilities for fraud, and the misapplication or misdirection of funds until the appropriate tradition and experience have been established and enforcement is effective. Government must exercise much greater responsibility than in the West, not only in establishing the required conditions to encourage private investment, but also in developing specialized financial institutions. Moreover, most of the investment in public utilities must be undertaken by government, and specialized facilities and institutions are often needed to promote sufficient private lending of the right types for these and other purposes.

The obstacles to an expansion of private savings, the large investment responsibilities of government and the necessity for developing health, educational and other services, increase the importance of taxation as a means of extracting more from the flow of production. Not all of the responsibility rests with central governments, and the reform and strengthening of local government is a necessary part of the process. That it is possible to increase forced savings through taxation is shown by the achievement of Japan where, between 1887 and 1925, a large proportion of capital formation resulted from using land taxes to siphon off much of the increase in agricultural income.* But in most Asian countries the difficulties in such a procedure are quite substantial. Low income limits the amount which can be raised without hardship. The relative importance of subsistence production, the small use of accounting, and often immature or inadequate fiscal administrations usually make direct taxes relatively unimportant, and reliance has to be placed in taxing objects which can be seen, or transactions which can be intercepted.† This reduces the resiliency of tax systems and is conducive to regression in tax

* Bruce F. Johnston, 'Agricultural Productivity and Economic Development in Japan,' *Quarterly Journal of Economics*, Vol. LIX, No. 6, December, 1951.

† For example, in Iraq in 1949–50 direct taxes were 13 per cent of budget receipts and indirect taxes 87 per cent. The corresponding figures for Egypt were 18 per cent and 82 per cent. United Nations *Public Finance and Information Papers* for Iraq and Egypt respectively, 1951 and 1950.

distribution so that a large share of increased taxation is likely to be borne by those with low income.

An increase in the relative importance of direct taxes seems clearly desirable both on distributional grounds and to tap the larger incomes, but this is often difficult both for political and administrative reasons. Higher taxation, moreover, may reduce incentives, including incentives to invest. Private investment may be encouraged by some exemptions in the early years of a new enterprise, higher rates of depreciation for new machinery, lower rates of tax on profits ploughed back, exemption from import duties of capital imports, and in other ways.* But the immediate effect is to reduce sources of revenue for government services and investment and again there is a problem of balance. On the other hand, more revenue may often be obtained by stopping leakages within the existing tax structure. One authority estimates tax leakages in India at 15 per cent of taxes due, and India is a country in which administration is relatively efficient.†

There remains the highly controversial question of obtaining forced savings through inflation. W. A. Lewis,‡ arguing from the experience of industrialized countries, considers it highly unlikely that the necessary increase in capital formation can be brought about by the voluntary savings of individuals, and that in the private sector the increase must come mainly from undistributed profits in business enterprises as their income grows. The main sources of the increased income have been foreign trade, new inventions and the profits of inflation. Experiences of the United

* The Government of Pakistan has adopted such devices. Cf. Maurice Zinkin, *Problems of Economic Development in Asia*, op. cit., p. 17. E. B. Nortcliffe, 'Tax Incentives in Under-developed Countries,' *The Accountant*, February 20, 1954, gives an interesting analysis of a variety of fiscal measures to encourage private investment in a number of countries. On the stimulus to private investment in Mexico by liberal tax concessions, cf. R. Richard Wohl, 'The Formation of Entrepreneurial Groups in Under-developed Countries,' in *Labor, Management and Economic Growth*, p. 103.

† Quoted by Paul H. Appleby in *Report of a Survey on Public Administration in India*, Cabinet Secretariat, Delhi, 1953, p. 49.

‡ *Aspects of Industrialization*, National Bank of Egypt, Cairo, 1953, pp. 15, et seq.

Kingdom cause him to place main emphasis on inflation which provided the incentive to invest as well as the means.* But it would be rash to apply these generalizations to under-developed countries as arguments in favour of inflation.

If inflation is induced from without by an increase in export receipts, as resulted from the Korean war, it may provide an opportunity to divert a part of the additional real income to capital formation, unless imported commodities rise equally in price. As taxable capacity grows with inflation it may be possible to extract more for public purposes through *ad valorem* sales, taxes or customs duties, or through income tax; but, again, the high relative importance of fixed taxes on land and other property is a limiting factor, and such price increases as occur affect costs. Public borrowing directed to purchasing imported capital goods plus exchange control might help. Export taxes might also be used, but a system could not be set up overnight, and would have to be already in existence or improvised in a hurry. So a great deal of the increased real income seems very likely to escape in higher consumption.

In any case we are concerned mainly with domestic inflation as an aid to capital formation rather than with seizing on conjunctural export gains.

The generally high propensity to consume, and in particular leakages into consumer goods (including imports) from the income of the more wealthy, and a greater propensity to invest in real estate, foreign currency, and commercial† or financial types of enterprise, suggest that inflation induced investment in productive enterprises of the type suggested by Lewis may not be large.

There might be something to say, as a long-run policy, for matching purchasing power withdrawn into hoards by credit

---

* J. A. Schumpeter, *Theory of Economic Development*, expresses a view which is consistent with this in that he argues that innovations, which are the generating force in economic development (discontinuous in his model), have been financed by withdrawing resources from the circular flow through credit creation.

† For example, in building up inventories, at least in the early stages of inflation.

creation, if indeed the amount of this could be discovered, though, in the first instance, this would not mean that inflationary effects were entirely avoided. Nor could the release of existing hoards avoid them, unless the hoards were used to finance imports (i.e., if they were gold or jewels). The use of additional purchasing power to put idle resources to work is not likely entirely to avoid inflation either. In developed economies unutilized labour and capital due to a shortage of effective demand are matched and *in situ*. The position is very different where the capital has to be *created* to put seasonally idle or otherwise unutilized labour to work. The labour would have to be organized, there would be some lag before the investment was reflected in more goods, and meanwhile inflationary pressures would occur. The case for creating additional purchasing as a means of forced savings would be stronger for investments in fertilizers or tube wells, which increased production within a growing season, or in light consumer goods industries, especially of low capital intensity which quickly increased the flow of consumer goods, than for the financial element in the cost of public works or heavy industries, the returns for which are delayed.

The main inflationary device is likely to be deficit financing for public investment. The resources must then come from reduced consumption by somebody. It will not be evenly spread and so will affect income distribution through price increases. Peasants may benefit, and if occupying owners their debts may be reduced. But in part their gains will be absorbed in higher prices for consumer goods not produced on the farm. Profit receivers in the business sector may also benefit. Wage and salary earners are the ones most likely to be squeezed, and they are smaller in relative numbers than in developed countries, and the aggregate of squeezability, so to speak, is limited as a source of capital formation.*

* I suspect that models which place emphasis on wage-cost-price spirals, by analogy with developed societies, over-emphasize the relative importance of the wage economy group and their capacity to bargain effectively for wage increases. This observation is less valid where industrialization and urbanization have already proceeded a substantial distance, and trade unions are well organized.

In countries where levels of consumption are already low, the social consequences of a further reduction through inflation may well be grave, and their effect in promoting unrest may actually impede development. If an attempt is made to suppress these effects by price control and rationing, the consequent inflexibility in prices and production may impede the smooth transfer of resources to where they can bring most benefit in the form of an increase in productive power.* Moreover, the price increase will distort the pattern of investment in the private sector, and whether or not there is a net addition to capital formation depends a great deal on what the more fortunate do with the larger money incomes. The redistribution in favour of corporate enterprises and the relatively well to do provides an opportunity for capital formation. But corporations which could avoid distributing profit increases by ploughing them back as investment are relatively much less important than in the West, and we have already drawn attention to the pattern of consumption and investment behaviour which is often common among the more affluent. So the investment pattern to which Lewis refers is not likely to follow in the countries under consideration, at least until their economies become more like those of developed countries. Moreover, the relatively smaller emphasis on graduated income or corporation taxes than in developed societies means that less of the increase in purchasing power is tapped for tax financed capital formation.

For a mild inflation, the additional public investment might possibly represent a net gain, but one would expect it to be quickly offset with any increase in the rate of inflation, through the decline in the real income left, and eventually disincentives to save and a rush into consumer goods such as has occurred in cases of hyperinflation, for example in Germany and China.† We might

* Assuming that the great administrative difficulties are overcome, so that controls are not evaded in black markets.

† Pazos, *op. cit.*, pp. 235 *et seq.*, compares capital formation in Chile, Colombia and Cuba in post-war years and finds the percentage of national income invested to vary inversely as the degree of inflation. He concludes ... 'the figures seem to suggest that "forced savings" do not force, but instead weaken, capital formation; the volume of spontaneous savings discouraged

add, further, that the distributional effects may well be more serious than in developed societies because of the weaker bargaining power of the poorer groups, and inflation is more likely to get out of hand because fiscal and monetary agencies of control are less efficient.

My own summing up would be that a mild inflation is likely to help a little, but that such inflation is likely to occur in any case from development plans even if inflationary methods are not deliberately pursued, while any beneficial effects are likely to be felt in the early stages. It may well be difficult to keep such inflation within bounds, and to deliberately use methods of deficit finance increases the hazards which must be weighed against any possible gain.

The considerations raised in this chapter indicate the difficulties involved in finding sufficient finance for capital formation to raise levels of consumption in a growing population. They increase the importance to be attached to the use of idle labour in capital formation. But we have yet to consider improving the labour component, and the rôle of innovations in the development equation. We may anticipate, however, by observing that even when these are allowed for, to start a cumulative process will usually be a matter of extreme difficulty, and that the availability of capital will remain a matter of major importance. They do not remove the necessity for international capital assistance. Indeed, they give added point to proposals to provide some of this by way of grants or cheap loans for social overhead. Investments in these, we have argued, for the time being lower the marginal capital coefficient, but they are necessary to provide services for other industries and improve the economic quality of the people. The arguments advanced give point also to the importance of designing technical assistance programmes so as to increase absorptive capacity for imported capital.

is greater than the volume of savings forced.' The same might result from too high a rate of taxation through its discentive effects. The Latin-American evidence is not conclusive but it is indicative.

CHAPTER VIII

POPULATION AND THE EFFECTIVE
SUPPLY OF LABOUR

A. Introduction

Earlier we identified changes in population with similar proportionate changes in labour, and assumed that the effective labour
supply would grow at the same rate as population. It was implicit
that countries with the same population would have the same
number of man hours of labour to apply. Such assumptions have
been convenient, but they obscure important differences between
societies, effects of changes in population growth, and means by
which effective labour supply may be increased in relation to
capital.

Quantitatively, differences in the ratio of effective labour
supply to population are determined by demographic structure
as it affects the ratio of potential workers to dependants, and by
a variety of non-demographic conditions influencing the extent
to which the potential labour force is in fact employed. Qualitative differences influencing efficiency carry us into many aspects
of economic development: for example, education, training, technology, organization, incentives and occupational mobility and
distribution. In this chapter consideration of the quality of the
labour force is limited to reference to the effects of improved
health and nutrition. Clearly quantitative and qualitative conditions interact on each other, and both may be affected by the same
conditions. Improved health may not only reduce the amount of
lost time but also increase efficiency per man hour. By promoting
an increase in output per head of total population, an improvement in efficiency of labour may be conducive to industrialization
and for reasons discussed earlier,* increase the ratio of man hours

* Chapter V, p. 72.

worked to population through the reduction in the proportion of workers subject to under-employment and seasonal unemployment.

The following list of determinants of the effective supply of labour provides a schematic framework for a fuller discussion than is attempted here.* From it we select certain factors for consideration:

I. QUANTITATIVE
    A. Demographic Aspects.
        1. Size of population.
        2. Age structure of population.
        3. Sex composition.
        4. Occupational distribution as affecting participation in gainful employment.
        5. Level of fertility as affecting family responsibilities.
    B. Non-Demographic Aspects.
        1. Variations in the proportion of each age group working (as affected by custom, law, income and social stratification or grouping).
        2. Institutional factors affecting hours of work, holidays.
        3. Time lost through ill-health.
        4. Unemployment and under-employment.
        5. Technology and economic structure as affecting participation by sex and age.†

II. QUALITATIVE ASPECT. For example:
        1. Age and sex composition of the working force.
        2. Health and nutrition.
        3. Education and training.
        4. Quality and quantity of capital and technology.
        5. Occupational distribution and urbanization.
        6. Incentives and other factors affecting economic élan.

---

* For a fuller consideration, cf. *The Determinants and Consequences of Population Trends*, United Nations, New York, 1953, especially Chapter XI.

† For example, the increased mechanization on dairy farms in New Zealand has been a factor in reducing the labour of women and children in farm occupations.

Our main concern is with the effects of demographic changes resulting from improved health measures and better nutrition, and the utilization of unemployed or under-employed labour. Other aspects are lightly touched on.

B. Health and Labour Supply

Before considering the effects of improved health and nutrition on labour supply it is convenient to compare certain demographic conditions in under-developed and developed countries.

The first important difference is in age composition. Regional differences are estimated by the United Nations as follows:

*Estimated Age Distribution of World Population by Regions, 1947**

Regions	Under 15 years	15–59 years	60 years and over
World Total	36	57	7
Africa	40	55	5
America:			
Northern America [1] . .	25	64	11
Latin-America [1] . .	40	55	5
Asia:			
Near East	40	54	6
South-Central Asia . .	40	56	4
Japan	37	55	8
Remaining Far East [2] . .	40	55	5
Europe:			
North-West-Central Europe.	24	62	14
Southern Europe . .	30	59	11
Eastern Europe [3] . .	34	59	7
Oceania	28	62	10

[1] Northern America, countries north of Rio Grande. Latin-America remaining countries including Caribbean countries.
[2] Excluding Asiatic U S S R.
[3] Including Asiatic U S S R.

* After United Nations *Demographic Year Book*, 1950, p. 15. Quoted United Nations *The Determinants and Consequences of Population Trends*, p. 144.

The identity of the figures for Africa, Latin-America and 'Remaining Far East' hints at inadequacy in the data and an element of conjecture in some of the estimates. Moreover, the percentage distribution would differ in different countries, as affected by migration and changes in birth rates as well as by the age distribution of mortality. But the comparisons are broadly typical and probably close enough to bring out the order of difference.

A different breakdown is given as follows:

Percentage of Populations in Various Age Groups

Country	Infants	Infants and children under five	Under 15	55 and over
Europe	2·0	9·8	26·9	17·2
North America . .	2·2	10·9	27·6	16·5
Oceania	2·5	10·5	26·0	17·8
South-East Asia . .	3·3	15·1	40·9	7·3
South-West Asia . .	3·1	16·7	40·6	9·5
South and Central America	3·1	14·6	40·1	7·4
Africa	2·9	13·7	39·1	8·5

(After *Census of India*, 1951, Vol. I, Part 1. A Report, pp. 68–69.)

In the first table the selection of the age grouping is presumably based on the supposition that those aged 15–59 cover the productive classes.* On this assumption it gives the relative order of size of the potential labour force expressed as a percentage of population. In North America, Europe and Oceania this force comprises 59–62 per cent of the population, as against 54–56 per cent in the rest of the world. If the working-age group were taken as 15–65,

* As Frank Lorimer points out, this is somewhat arbitrary, and the selection of the age grouping influences the result; but it provides a uniform base for comparison. 'Demographic Trends and Labor Force Characteristics prior to and during Early Industrialization,' in *Labor, Management and Economic Growth*. Institute of International Industrial and Labor Relations, Cornell University, 1954, p. 11.

the comparison would be even more favourable to developed countries. Dependants 60 years of age and over are a higher percentage in developed countries, but those under 15 years are much lower. So net dependency is higher in under-developed countries.

The second table shows that the percentage of those too young to contribute to production is very much greater in under-developed regions: between 13·7 per cent and 16·7 per cent are under 5 years as against 9·8–10·9 per cent in developed areas. Those who reach 5 years but die before the age of 15 years are a bigger proportion in under-developed countries.

The comparisons made are broadly confirmed by the following more detailed figures for an under-developed and developed country using census data:

Age Composition of Population in Thailand and United Kingdom

Age group	Thailand (Census, 1947) Per cent		United Kingdom (1950) Per cent	
Under 1 year . .	3·5		1·6	
1–4 . . .	11·6		6·9	
5–9 . . .	14·2		7·0	
10–14 . . .	13·0	42·3	6·5	22·0
15–19 . . .	11·1		6·2	
20–24 . . .	8·9		6·8	
25–29 . . .	7·2		7·7	
30–34 . . .	6·6		7·0	
35–39 . . .	5·8		7·8	
40–44 . . .	4·8		7·8	
45–49 . . .	4·0		7·2	
50–54 . . .	2·9		6·3	
55–59 . . .	2·3		5·5	
60–64 . . .	1·6	55·2	4·9	67·2
65 and over . .		2·7		10·9

(United Nations *Demographic Year Book*, 1951, Table 4.)

If the labour force be regarded as those between 15 and 65 years of age, they comprise 12 per cent more of the population in the United Kingdom than in Thailand. There is a much more rapid decline at each five-year period in the latter country, so that between the ages of 20 and 65 years the advantage of the United Kingdom is even greater: 61 per cent as against 44·1 per cent. If those below 10 years are considered as fully dependent and making no contribution to production, the advantage is again heavily with the United Kingdom: 15·5 per cent as against 29·3 per cent. These much more than offset the higher old-age dependency in the United Kingdom.

Certain factors modify the effects of age distribution. In under-developed countries young people will begin to work at an earlier age. But as has just been shown, the percentage of them so young as to make at most a trivial contribution to production is much higher. Moreover, the partial offset of those who make some contribution is more than balanced by superior training made possible in developed countries by a longer period of preparation, and fuller provision for health and all forms of education and training. As the United Nations report puts it*: 'Thus the under-developed countries continually resort to wasteful exploitation of the oncoming generation of workers in the effort to achieve a more nearly adequate current standard of consumption. Their position is rather like that of peasants compelled by hunger to harvest their wheat every year before it has ripened.'

Older people also tend to work longer in under-developed countries. But again there are counterbalancing factors, since those who do work are likely to enjoy better health and have greater vigour in the more economically advanced societies.

The normal assumption based on census returns is that a smaller proportion of women engage in gainful employment in under-developed countries. But there are wide differences in census definitions and their interpretation.* The assistance which women give on the farm or in the cottage handicrafts, or in petty trades, may not be fully recorded in census returns, since occupa-

* United Nations *The Determinants and Consequences of Population Trends*, p. 265.

tions in under-developed countries are less clearly differentiated.* It is highly probable that the greater proportion of women assisting in farm operations and cottage handicrafts would suffer even more from under-employment than would male workers.

The United Nations Report gives an instructive table comparing the economically active males grouped according to age. This provides a useful indication of the extent to which the potential male labour force is used. The table is reproduced below†:

Economically Active Males as a Percentage of Total Males in Each Age Group in Selected Countries

Country and year	All ages	10–14 years	15–19 years	20–64 years	65 years and over
United States, 1940 .	60·5	1·2	40·4	91·8	41·8
Sweden, 1940. . .	69·3	1·9	82·2	94·5	42·6
Australia, 1933 . .	63·7	3·1	73·4	95·8	34·3
New Zealand, 1936 . .	66·8	3·7	80·3	96·3	40·4
Jamaica, 1943 . . .	53·8	4·0	56·6	93·0	62·3
British West Indies, 1946.	57·0	9·0	77·4	97·0	60·7
Japan, 1930 . . .	58·8	14·1	78·5	95·3	63·0
Panama, 1940. . .	59·5	19·7	77·6	97·5	82·9
Peru, 1940 . : .	53·3	22·8	63·0	95·9	82·6
Portugal, 1940 . .	63·9	26·2	75·4	96·4	88·1
Turkey, 1945 . .	58·8	48·7	79·9	92·4	79·0

The percentage who are active in the age group 10–14 years is very much higher in the under-developed countries listed. So also is the percentage 65 years and over. In the two remaining age groups there are considerable variations from country to country but there is no marked contrast according to economic development. The greater activity ratio in the under-developed countries is in the age groups where, by and large, productive efficiency is

* On this point, cf. P. T. Bauer and B. S. Yamey, 'Economic Progress and Occupational Distribution,' *Economic Journal*, Vol. LXI, No. 244, December, 1951, pp. 741 *et seq.*

† *The Determinants and Consequences of Population Trends*, p. 195.

likely to be lowest. Moreover, because of the greater relative numbers in the more active age groups, the developed countries have a decided over-all advantage if the United States and Portugal be excluded.*

The greater dependency and a lower ratio of effective labour supply are due not so much to rapid rates of population growth as to high birth rates, together with high mortality, and the age distribution of mortality. India has a much lower rate of population growth than New Zealand but a smaller proportion in the working age group because of heavier mortality before the working age is reached, and a shorter working life of those who enter it.† The conditions referred to have other consequences which warrant some attention.

Earlier we compared crude death rates in developed and under-developed countries to the great disadvantage of the latter. Because improvements in health and in economic and social conditions usually have a bigger impact on infantile mortality than on mortality in higher age groups, infantile mortality is a better indicator of these conditions. As a rule, the higher the crude death rates, the higher the proportion due to infantile mortality.

The wide disparity in infantile mortality rates is well known and the following table is given simply as a reminder of the order of difference:

Deaths of Infants under One Year per 1,000 Births

New Zealand			Thailand	.	. 62·4 (1950)
(European)	.	. 21·8 (1952)	Ceylon .	.	. 81·6 (1950)
Netherlands	.	. 22·5 (1952)	Philippines	.	. 104·2 (1951)
U.S.A.	.	. 28·5 (1952)	India	.	. 115·9 (1951)
Japan	.	. 57·5 (1951)	Egypt	.	. 129·6 (1950)

(After United Nations *Demographic Year Book*, 1953, Table 11.)

* The position in the United States would be affected by the exceptional proportion between the ages of 15 and 19 years enjoying the benefits of a higher education.

† This is partly, but not entirely, accounted for in New Zealand by greater immigration. Immigrants have a somewhat more favourable age composition.

Contrasts of expectations of life at birth provide an equally striking commentary on health hazards:

Country and Year	Males	Females	Country and Year	Males	Females
United States (1950) .	66·6	72·4	Taiwan (1936–40) .	41·08	45·73
United Kingdom (1951)	65·8	70·9	India* (1921–31) .	26·91	26·56
Netherlands (1947–49)	69·4	71·5	Thailand (1947–48)	48·7	51·9
New Zealand (1950–52)	68·29	72·43			

(After United Nations *Demographic Year Book*, 1953, Table 19. New Zealand figures are from *New Zealand Life Table*, 1950–52, Census and Statistics Dept., 1953. Indian figures are before partition and include Burma. United States figures are for white population.)

These contrasts are greatly, though not, of course, exclusively, influenced by high juvenile (i.e. up to 15 years) and especially infantile mortality.

High birth rates make their contribution to the high juvenile dependency. High juvenile death rates reduce the proportion of these who enter the working age group, while high mortality rates among the latter also reduce the ratio of potential workers to total population.

High mortality rates, especially among juveniles lead to great economic and social wastage.

A general indication of wastage due to high mortality, though not specifically of juvenile mortality, is given by differences in gross and net reproduction rates:

* The *Indian Census Report*, 1951, *op. cit.*, p. 187, shows some improvement, as follows:

Expectation of Life

Year	At birth	At age 10 years
1921–30	26 years 11 months	36 years 5 months
1941–50	32 years 5 months	39 years
Increase	5 years 6 months	2 years 7 months

Country	Date	Reproduction rates	
		Gross	Net
India	1941	2·76	1·30
Egypt	1937	3·11	1·44
Japan	1937	2·14	1·44
U.S.A. (White) . . .	1942	1·27	1·19
England and Wales . .	1940	0·85	0·75
New Zealand . . .	1942	1·30	1·21

(New Zealand figures, *New Zealand Official Year Book*, 1953, p. 19. Remaining figures, Kingsley Davis, *Population of India and Pakistan*, p. 87.)

A much larger number of people would have to be born per 100,000 people in India or Egypt than in New Zealand, or the United States, to maintain population or promote a given percentage rate of increase.

The economic cost of this wastage is difficult to estimate. It would be higher for those who died before making a contribution to production, i.e., by the extent to which juvenile mortality was responsible for the gap. If mortality occurred during the first year the direct economic wastage would be small; but juvenile mortality is higher at all ages in under-developed countries. Moreover, allowance must be made for a reduction in the working time and energy of mothers during child bearing, and the attention which must be given to children in their early years. There are few estimates of the economic loss due to juvenile mortality, but in 1946 Dr. D. Ghosh compared it for India and for England and Wales.* He estimated that before the war 45 per cent of India's population died before reaching the age of 15. Some 22½ per cent of national income was required to rear young people who died making little or no contribution to it, corresponding figure for England and Wales being 6½ per cent. Without attaching special importance to the precise estimates, they may be used to indicate the contribution which might be

* *Op cit.*, p. 22.

made to levels of consumption if the current rate of population growth were achieved in India with a mortality rate up to the age of 15 years comparable with that in England and Wales.

But it is not only at birth that expectation of life is lower in under-developed societies. It applies in each age group. This means that, having reached the age of entry into production, the worker will contribute to production for a shorter period. The ratio of working to total life is less. The following figures dramatically bring out the contrast between India and New Zealand:

Number surviving to Various Ages from Each 100,000 Males born in India and New Zealand

Age	India 1921–31	New Zealand 1934–38
5 years . . .	60,161	95,212
10 years . . .	56,467	94,576
15 years . . .	54,112	94,069
20 years . . .	51,203	93,217
30 years . . .	43,931	91,084
40 years . . .	34,563	88,365
50 years . . .	24,348	83,328
60 years . . .	14,933	73,472
70 years . . .	7,036	54,184

(United Nations *Demographic Year Book*, Table 28, 1951. Figures for India are pre-partition and include Burma. Figures for New Zealand exclude Maoris.)

Roughly the same proportion in New Zealand reached age 70 as reached age 15 in India. Out of 100,000 males born in New Zealand, some *40,000 more survived to enter the labour force*. Of the 54,000 aged 15 years in India, under 15,000 would still be living at age 60. Of 94,000 in New Zealand 73,000 would still be alive at age 60. Quite apart from differences in efficiency the typical New Zealand worker would make a much bigger contribution to production during his lifetime. His working life would be longer in relation to his period of dependency. In 1921–31 an Indian boy of 15 might expect to live a further thirty-three years and a girl thirty years. In 1935–38 a New Zealand boy of similar age might expect to live more than fifty-four years and a girl fifty-seven years. Using 1931 figures, Ghosh* makes a similar comparison between India, and England and Wales. He estimates the average contribution to productive work at thirty years in India and forty years in England and Wales.

Disease, ill-health and under-nourishment, of which the conditions described are a reflection, have other damaging effects. For every one who dies from disease large numbers suffer from it but survive. Some 3,000,000 people are believed to die every year from malaria, but 300,000,000 suffer from it.† This causes a loss of twenty to forty working days per year for each person affected‡ between 6,000,000,000 and 12,000,000,000 days in all. It is not unknown for the greater part of the working force in a village to be laid low at critical periods of planting and harvesting. A single seasonal anti-malarial campaign in the East Bengal area of Pakistan is reported to have increased the yield of rice by 15 per cent.§ 'Surveys conducted in the Philippines in 1946 revealed that in that year absenteeism caused by malaria among primary and secondary school pupils ranged from 40 to 50 per cent.; in 1949, following a DDT campaign, daily absenteeism was reduced to about 3 per cent. In 1946 the managers of a number of enterprises had reported an absenteeism of 35 per cent for which malaria was largely responsible. The 1949 survey, which followed the anti-malaria campaign, showed that daily absenteeism for any reason represented not more than 2 to 4 per cent of the total complement. The survey showed that only 75 to 80 per cent as many

* *Op. cit.*, p. 22.

† I cannot trace my information on deaths, but the estimate of the total affected is from United Nations *Preliminary Report on World Social Situation*, E/CN.5/267, 1952, p. 46.

‡ United Nations *The Determinants and Consequences of Population Trends*, p. 266.

§ *Ibid.*, p. 266, quoting C. E. A. Winslow, *The Cost of Sickness and the Price of Health*, World Health Organization Monograph Series, No. 7, Geneva, 1951, p. 23.

workers were needed for a job in 1949 as were needed in 1946.'*

These estimates provide a rough indication of the economic cost of malaria, even among those who survive. In addition, account must be taken of the reduction in land areas which can be farmed because of it.†

Other debilitating diseases such as schistosomiasis, filariasis, yaws, hookworm and other intestinal afflictions, syphilis, gonorrhœa, trachoma and leishmaniasis also take their toll and affect hundreds of millions.‡

In my view, equally if not more important than lost time are the effects of inadequate nutrition and disease in reducing energy, and inducing lethargy and low receptivity to new ideas. But the effects can hardly be measured quantitatively.

The effect of reduced mortality on age composition and the ratio of workers to total population are complex and much work on the problem still needs to be done, especially in respect of the sequence of changes under various assumptions. If fertility declined with mortality in such a way that the rate of population growth remained substantially the same, the reduction in wastage would bring benefits which might well be decisive in promoting a break through. But the probable trend is for mortality to decline before fertility, so that the rate of population growth will accelerate. A uniform reduction in mortality at all ages, unaccompanied by a decline in fertility would increase the rate of natural increase and therefore the size of the new generations; but it would also increase the expectation of life and the numbers surviving in successive age groups to advanced years. The United Nations Report concludes that the net effect of these tendencies on the average age might be in either direction, and requires further investigation.§

---

* *Ibid.*, p. 266, quoting *Report on Philippine Public Health Rehabilitation Programme, July 4, 1946, June 30, 1950*, United States Public Health Service, 1950.

† Cf. *supra*, Chapter VI, p. 112.

‡ United Nations *The Determinants and Consequences of Population Trends*, p. 266.

§ *The Determinants and Consequences of Population Trends*, p. 143.

But the probable result of improved health measures in under-developed countries will be a greater reduction in juvenile mortality, and especially in infantile mortality, (i.e., up to fifteen years) than mortality in higher age groups. This will increase the proportion in the early age groups and so increase dependency. But the number who survive and enter the working group will also increase. The secondary effect is then to reduce relative dependency below the high figure resulting from the decline in juvenile mortality, and somewhat restore the labour-population ratio. Moreover, there will be some reduction in mortality in the higher age groups and an extension of the working life. The net effects on the labour population ratio will therefore depend on the period of time under consideration and the relative improvement in mortality in the various age groups. The longer the period of time the more favourable is the ratio likely to become.

The net disadvantage of population increase in terms of the ratio seem likely to be much less than is often supposed, because of the combined effects of the reduction in wastage and the larger number who enter the working age group, and of the lengthening of the period of working life in relation to total life. Eventually, we should expect these offsets to the lowering of infantile mortality to be substantial. But during the first critical decade or two they seem unlikely to be sufficient of themselves to balance the higher dependency ratio and maintain output and consumption per head of population.

But this by no means disposes of the matter. In the first place, improved health is itself a very important element in consumption levels, and must be pursued for humanitarian reasons. But even the consequences in terms of productive power need not necessarily be cause for pessimism. The direct economic loss due to disease among workers would be reduced. Even more important, the quality of the labour force would be improved. It is to this aspect that major importance should be attached; for a population which is disease ridden and under-nourished, and in consequence suffers from 'a listlessness of the spirit'* cannot be expected to

---

* Cf. quotation from S. K. Dey, *supra*, Chapter II, p. 36.

carry forward a process of active development. As long as these conditions persist, the cumulative growth of innovations will be greatly retarded, if not inhibited. The net result on *per capita* production of the complex of effects following from improved health and nutrition can hardly be estimated quantitatively in advance. But we regard the reduction of lethargy and inertia, and an increase in the propensity to innovate and accept innovations, as such vital elements in the development process that health and nutrition measures warrant high priority in development plans. This article of faith is emphasized because of the natural tendency to stress the conflict between health and other elements in material welfare, even to the extent of doubting the wisdom of health measures till a break through has occurred and consumption levels have begun to rise.

The difficulties they raise through their effect on the rate of population growth do however pose a dilemma; but this must be resolved by other measures than deferred nutritional or health programmes. The difficulties reinforce the need for family limitation programmes which would enable the beneficial effects to be fully realized. But in the early critical period such programmes will not prevent population growth from accelerating. Hence, while we regard better health and nutrition as necessary conditions for economic development, we emphasize that to take full advantage of them requires an increase in the rate of capital formation and the organized acceleration of technological improvements. The minimum objective in terms of net investment should be to increase it to match the population increase. This would increase the ratio of capital to workers, and with innovations and improved labour efficiency, offer a solution to the dilemma. In particular, as in the rural programmes in India and Ceylon, a solution may be sought in the *integration* of health measures with measures designed to increase technological consciousness and provide technical help, promote education and training, and generally utilize the labour force more effectively in current production and capital formation. This last requirement is considered in the concluding section to this chapter.

The dilemma also reinforces the need for international capital aid and technical assistance. The very proper emphasis on health and nutrition in technical assistance programmes carries with it some responsibility to give help in offsetting the additional needs engendered by the effects of population increase, so that the beneficial effects of better health may be fully capitalized upon.

If such programmes were pursued there need be little fear that job opportunities for a growing population would be reduced.

C. Idle Time and Labour Supply

There remains the question of increasing the labour-population ratio through a reduction in unemployment and under-employment. The distinction between unemployment and under-employment is blurred and there is no clearly marked boundary between them. But for our present purposes we need not spend much time on refinements of definition. Chiang Hsieh* classifies under-employment into (a) visible, (b) disguised, and (c) potential. To these might be added idleness or under-employment resulting from disease as already touched upon. Visible under-employment occurs when the actual amount of time devoted to work is less than that which the labour force is able to supply. Substantially this is unemployment, and becomes significant in under-developed countries in respect of casual, part-time and, especially, seasonal unemployment. Disguised unemployment occurs when the workers are using their full labour time on their tasks, as determined by existing laws and customs, but not their full time or energy in effective work. It would be reduced, for example, if cultural practices already known, such as dibbling or transplanting paddy instead of broadcasting took more time but increased yield, or if the substitution of larger retail stores for hawkers or small shops reduced the time in idling and gossiping (because there were no customers) and increased the time in selling.

Visible under-employment (which is more properly regarded as unemployment) implies that for a day or more the worker is

---

* He makes a useful preliminary attempt at differentiation in 'Under-employment in Asia,' *International Labour Review*, Vol. LXV, June, 1952. I have somewhat modified his definitions.

completely idle, and has his full time free to devote to a job if there is one offering. Sometimes he may be doing something, but the net product is so low that by a slight liberty in the use of words we can regard him as idle. This applies, for example, to much seasonal engagement in handicrafts. The worker suffering from disguised under-employment may have to be on the job all the time but only a part of it is spent in work: or he must spend only a part of the day in actual work but he is unable to take employment elsewhere for the rest.

Disguised unemployment broadens into Chiang Hsieh's 'potential under-employment' which exists when the effectiveness of labour could be increased by increasing the amount of capital and by technological and institutional changes, so that the same or more produce might be obtained while at the same time labour was released for other purposes. Since, to remove potential unemployment is a major objective of economic development as a whole we do not consider it at length. It is, however, important to observe that general development measures would also reduce the relative importance of the other types of unemployment or under-employment, so that when once the process of economic development begins there is a secondary effect in improving the ratio of labour to population. Thus potential unemployment in agriculture would be reduced by the withdrawal of labour through the combined effect of industrialization, substantial changes in the amount of capital and in the technology of farming, an increase in the size of holdings, and a reduction in the subsistence element in farming. The removal of disguised unemployment also in the main requires general measures which increase opportunities and reduce the proportion engaged in the tasks affected. But to some extent it may be directly reduced by technological changes (such as the dibbling and transplanting referred to a moment ago), or making the worker technically conscious of the opportunities for using up spare time, in farm or home improvement, or improved and more economic cottage industries. But the processes by which this would be achieved are so similar to those designed to reduce visible under-employment (i.e., unemployment) that there is no need to consider them separately.

The most striking unutilized reservoir of labour is in the seasonal unemployment generated by the rhythm of the seasons. As a very rough estimate I have put this at the huge total of 30,000 million working days a year for Asia, about one-third of the total existing days worked.* The estimate is subject to a very wide margin of error, but even if 50 per cent out, it indicates the importance of the potential contribution to development by a direct attack on it. But in rural areas where land is inadequate, landless labourers may suffer from casual unemployment as well as from the seasonal rhythm, and there will be casual unemployment in urban areas. The overall process of development might reduce this, as also might labour exchanges and attempts at 'decasualization' in some urban employments such as stevedoring. It might also be alleviated, especially in rural areas, by the sort of direct measures discussed below.

We must notice also specifically institutional factors affecting the propensity to work. These are illustrated by the effects of the caste system in India and the attitude of many pre-communist landlords in China.† In large measure the use of the labour of such people awaits the gradual transformation of attitudes, but in part it is a matter of providing employment opportunities, especially of the small entrepreneur or professional type which

---

* 'Economic Development in Asia,' *Economia Internazionale*, Vol. V, No. 4, November, 1952. The assumptions were: Population 1,000 million, proportion working one-third, proportion engaged in agriculture and related pursuits 60 per cent, idle or near idle days, 150 a year. For estimates in certain individual countries, cf. Chiang Hsieh, *op. cit.*

† Note, for example, the medicant castes or sub-castes in India and the attitude towards manual labour of some groups of Brahmins. Recently the writer visited a village in West Bengal where the Brahmin small-scale peasant proprietors did not work in the fields but hired members of other castes to do this. This attitude persisted even after thirty years of operation of a rural betterment project. In *Earth Bound China* (University of Chicago Press, 1945), Chih-i-Chang and Tsaio-Tung Fei draw attention to the fact that many landlords lived lives of leisure, contemplation and opium smoking, with consumption levels not much higher than the peasants, rather than toil on the land (p. 43). In India, Egypt and other places also many landlords live lives of idleness or near idleness as absentees in the towns.

commend themselves to such groups, or of forcing them to work by removing the economic foundation of idleness through land reform, and improved credit and marketing services. Landlords frequently provide credit and marketing services—often under exploitative conditions—and the reform of tenure and alternative provision of these services might force them into economically more desirable occupations. It seems unlikely that this problem is of great *relative* importance in terms of labour supply; but it arises out of conditions which may be of considerable psychological and political importance in that it is deemed to be associated with economic privilege and exploitation.

The problem of seasonal unemployment is not only more massive, but different in character. If our earlier analysis is correct, the farming structure will for a long time be comparatively unaffected by economic development. Technological developments might reduce the labour force needed on the peasant holdings, and enable peasant families to dispense with hired labour at peak seasons. The proportion of total population subjected to seasonal unemployment would fall and this would bring a net gain in improving the labour-population ratio. But the seasonal peaks at times of planting and harvesting will continue, and so will the need for a direct attack on seasonal unemployment. There would be little or no social-economic cost in the utilization of such labour because, *ex hypothesi*, it is idle. There is some social cost by the extent to which capital formation financed out of money savings is needed and diverted from other uses, and also in the increased demand for consumer goods which might arise. This last cost would not occur by the extent to which other idle labour was used to produce the goods demanded. Nor would it occur if there were no payments to the workers: for they would not then buy more consumer goods except out of increased income resulting from the use of the capital, which would have added to the national product.

The approach to the utilization of seasonally idle labour and to a lesser degree to casual unemployment and 'institutional' idleness, may be attempted on three main lines. The first approach is to extend the farming season by new crop practices which keep the farm family more fully occupied over a longer period. Frequently, though not universally, this will require irrigation or drainage so that there will be demands on net capital investment except by the extent to which idle labour is utilized for the purpose.

The second approach is to utilize the idle labour for capital formation either individually or collectively. While the process may be applied in urban areas, collective capital formation in them will usually be in the form of public works requiring financial outgoings for wages, and so is similar to the problem of putting idle labour to work in economically developed societies: but in rural areas not only are the opportunities greater, but also the motivation is different, since with the greater social integration in the villages, it is easier to demonstrate the element of common advantage, and promote the necessary social organization to do the work. Individual capital formation consists in putting the farmer or artisan in the position to improve the farm or home, or make improved machines and implements. Collective capital formation may be applied for a wide variety of purposes: roads, ponds, wells, irrigation ditches, contouring and other soil conservation practices, as well as the improvement in amenities through the construction of communal buildings, village sanitation and so on.

It is worth briefly illustrating the potentialities of this approach from selected achievements in the community projects of Ceylon and India. The information is merely illustrative. We list 'social overhead' as well as other forms of capital but make no reference to a wide range of activities other than in capital formation.* By 1951, after a period of about four years, there were 5,118 Rural Development Societies established in Ceylon to promote 'self-help' activities. The following table gives the value of capital formation during 1951 and of government financial assistance to stimulate it.

---

* For example, improvements in farm production, settlement of disputes, establishment of co-operatives, or increases in literacy, all of which have a bearing on economic efficiency.

Projects	Number	Value of local effort (Rupees) (000)	Government financial assistance (Rupees) (000)
Halls and community centres.	915	509 ⎫	
Schools	467	328 ⎪	18·5
Industrial centres . .	300	115 ⎬	
Other buildings . . .	30	25 ⎭	
Roads (miles) new . .	1,870	694 ⎫	50·5
Roads improvements . .	610	151 ⎭	
Latrines	5,781	313 ⎫	262·6
Wells	1,750	391 ⎭	
Total . . .	—	2,526	331·7

To these should be added other works such as irrigation ditches, contouring and bunds not tabulated. Reports on the Firka Development Scheme in Madras give a similar indication of possibilites.* In 1951 villages contributed Rs. 3,348,000 in cash, kind, or labour towards works costing Rs. 6,733,000 and undertook many other works. During the first five years of operation 1,076 wells were constructed (and 732 were repaired or improved) as well as 11 ponds, dams, and hundreds of miles of roads. Nearly 200 minor irrigation tanks, lakes and ponds were repaired. Over a million trees were planted and 6,230 acres of land brought under cultivation. Works included 228 schools, 73 reading rooms, 3,060 latrines, 1,154 cesspits, and 22 miles of village drains.

The examples of Ceylon and the Firkas were chosen because information is available in convenient form, but there have been impressive achievements elsewhere including those at Etawah in the United Provinces and the recently established community projects in the various Indian states. While the actual value of the

* The information is drawn from United Nations *Report of Mission on Community Organization and Development in South and South-East Asia*, pp. 26 *et seq.*

works undertaken is small in relation to needs, it is indicative of what may be hoped for as the community project approach extends over the Indian sub-continent. A similar achievement to that of the Firkas over the whole of India might mean 'voluntary' capital formation worth Rs. 2,000 million as a very rough estimate, or the equivalent of, say, $2\frac{1}{4}$ per cent national income. But with time and experience and the fuller organization and integration of national services, a much bigger result is possible, especially if the effects on current production are taken into account. There would be contributions to production and welfare other than those covered by the estimated value of net contribution to capital formation, and a general encouragement of innovations raising the efficiency of labour and capital. From their monetary value would have to be deducted the costs of the services provided by government.

The whole problem is linked with that of innovations discussed in the next two chapters, where we consider *organizing to innovate*. Remembering that encouragement of capital formation is best achieved as part of a composite process, it is nevertheless useful, even at the expense of some repetition, to summarily list some of the ways in which it may be stimulated. The people must want the products for which the capital is used or be persuaded to want them. This is a matter of incentives and has a bearing on the problem of investment criteria discussed earlier. Given the incentives, the first step is the awakening of technical consciousness and the recognition that the capital formation is worth the effort. Associated with this is promotion of the recognition that potentialities for self-help exist. One of the major achievements at Etawah, and of the Firkas, and similar agencies, is that the stimulation of village works such as the construction of roads (especially if given an element of the dramatic and of inter-village rivalry) has for the first time made villages really aware of the potentialities for betterment in the reservoir of idle labour power. The labour power was already there and the road might be wanted, but it never occurred to the villagers that the means were to hand. Secondly, technical advice may sometimes be required and necessary supplies of material outside the village may have to be organized. Sometimes villages may be able to pay for supplies, but often credit must be given. Third, some works may require the help of technicians (as distinct from advice), or the use of heavy equipment: for example, in surveying irrigation ditches or excavating wells. Fourth, effective self-help usually requires leadership from without the village, at least in the beginning, and organizing of the villagers.* Finally, for works not entirely within the compass of the village endeavour, grants in aid of one form or another may be necessary. It is a matter of experience, as is illustrated by the examples quoted in previous paragraphs, that a combination of these methods has often been successful in promoting a considerable amount of capital formation, both individual and collective, and in improving production and amenities.

The third major approach is through small-scale decentralized industry, which by the nature of things is likely to be of low capital intensity. Industries processing agricultural products will often be seasonal in character. Even where the seasonal character is not determined by the nature of supply, the designing and establishment of units with low capital intensity may make it possible to operate them seasonally because the loss through idle plants is small. In any case, small-scale decentralized industry may provide all the year employment for other redundant rural labour.

Decentralized industry possesses the advantage that it caters for relatively immobile labour *in situ*, reduces the economic costs and social disintegration which might result from movement to urban areas, and avoids much of the social overhead which would be required in large urban areas. In many ways the establishment of small-scale decentralized industries presents a more difficult problem than the other approaches to full labour utilization touched upon: for such industries must often compete with urban factories more efficient in terms of financial cost. There is here a complicated theoretical and applied problem, with important social and political aspects, which requires further attention. In

---

* E.g., into panchayats or other forms of local government, rural development councils, women's and young people's groups, or co-operatives.

view of the advantages touched upon, we have raised the question,* whether financial investment criteria are entirely satisfactory, especially if, to the benefits mentioned, we add the possibility of stimulating dispersed centres of leadership and change, through the impact of a somewhat more advanced technology.

Very commonly the approach to the problem of fuller utilization of rural labour is through the encouragement of handicrafts. Personal observations in a number of countries confirm in my mind the *prima facie* doubt as to whether these can be successful on any scale, and as to whether their encouragement by subventions and penalties on factory production are justifiable, save in support of a rearguard action while plans are prepared and put into effect to established small power-motivated concerns in replacement of handicrafts. Some handicrafts may be so strengthened as to compete without subsidization; but it would seem important to explore more fully the alternative approach just mentioned. This would require research and assistance in designing and developing types of mechanized concerns which could be economically competitive while of small size, and in improving facilities for designing products, and organizing finance and marketing to give greater economies of scale in these particular aspects.†

* *Supra*, Chapter VI.
† For a fuller, but still summary, discussion, cf. United Nations *Report on Community Organization and Development in South and South-East Asia*, pp. 37–39.

CHAPTER IX

INNOVATIONS: SOCIAL COSTS AND OBSTACLES

'Technology,' writes Arnold Toynbee, 'is, of course, only a long Greek word for a bag of Tools. . . . But all tools are not of the material kind: there are spiritual tools as well, and these are the most potent that man has made.'* More specifically, techniques, the subject-matter of technology, are 'clearly designed and transmissible processes intended to produce certain results thought useful.'† Friedman paraphrases this passage in defining a technique as 'a means to an end that has been determined without reference to that technique.'‡ This separation of ends and means is no doubt formally correct, especially in reference to 'final' or near final ends such as good health or the avoidance of hunger, but it may divert attention from important aspects of the applied problem. Very frequently people may not want a thing in any sense which has real meaning (which implies a willingness to do something about it), because the technical means to acquire it do not exist, or are beyond the capacity or knowledge of the actor, or because the means are repugnant. Existing techniques or processes may possess values of themselves, so that people are not willing to give them up for techniques or processes more efficient in terms of ends but themselves less satisfying.§ Perhaps it is

* Arnold Toynbee, *The World and the West*, Oxford University Press, 1953, p. 11.
† Lalande, *Vocabulaire Historique et Critique de la Philosophie*, quoted Georges Friedman in *Social Implications of Technical Change*, International Social Science Bulletin (UNESCO), Vol. IV, No. 2, 1952, p. 244.
‡ *Op cit., loc. cit.*
§ For an elaboration of this point, cf. Cyril S. Belshaw, *Changing Melanesia. Social Economics of Culture Contact*, Oxford University Press, 1954, pp. 137 *et seq.*

possible to reach a goal with existing techniques, but not worth the effort. It is a commonplace that improved technology has stimulated an extension of the range of wants. And, of course, an end is usually a means towards something else. Villagers want better health, but pure water is not an end of activity, even though a necessary means to health. They do not see any connection between water and health, and might not know how to purify the water if they did. So a part of the process of economic development is to promote a technical awareness of how to satisfy existing wants by (*inter alia*) making new techniques available, persuading them to adopt the new techniques, revealing the significance of immediate wants or ends as a means towards more remote, or final goals, and generating new wants by persuasion and making it possible to satisfy them.

Economists sometimes give a narrower connotation to technology than in the passages quoted, and think of it as embracing the arts directly applied to the production of goods and services. To indicate a wider meaning, we speak of innovations, and regard technological innovations as changes affecting behaviour especially related to economic processes. Innovations cover all aspects of life and not simply economic aspects. But, except where the context indicates otherwise, we shall be concerned with changes in human behaviour (such as deciding to save more, or transplant paddy instead of broadcasting the seed), or the results of human behaviour embodied in concrete things, such as better machines, which raise levels of consumption. Of course innovations which are primarily motivated by other than economic ends, such as changes in religious beliefs, may have profound economic results.

By technical progress we shall mean the process by which the adoption of innovations leads to an improvement in levels of consumption; but we are far from claiming that this is Progress with a capital P. Nevertheless, in concentrating on the effects of innovations on levels of consumption we must perforce give scant attention, or neglect altogether other results of great importance. Economic innovations embodied in machines and production processes affect not merely levels of *consumption* but also the level, or content, of *living*. This, as we have noted, includes immaterial as well as material elements. Such innovations initiate changes in the *standard* of living and may have disruptive effects because they enlarge the gap between what is and what is aspired to. They require, or result in, changes in motivation, social institutions and organizations, and in the whole complex of relationships between people. This applies particularly to the introduction of innovations from a foreign culture, not merely to economic technology but also to other innovations such as enforcement of a different code of law, or a different system of administration. Such innovations have proved of great importance historically through the impact of the west on underdeveloped countries in Asia and elsewhere. It is hardly possible to absorb a new element from outside without bringing about other changes, often neither anticipated nor desired, and the result in Asia has been to create considerable dislocation and disturbance to traditional ways of life. This is well enough known though the seriousness of the effects is often not fully appreciated.* The dislocation is currently illustrated in the Philippines. The demonstration effect of American levels of consumption and those of of the wealthier classes, the increase in literacy and other consequences of the impact of the culture of the United States, and the effects of war, have generated aspirations which cannot yet be satisfied,† and contributed to the prevailing unrest and 'dissidence'.

Outstanding characteristics of the post-war era are the endea-

---

* Among the many discussions note may be taken of Arnold Toynbee, *op. cit.*, Guy Wint, *The British in India;* J. F. Furnivall, *Colonial Policy and Practice;* M. Zinkin, *Asia and the West*, Chatto and Windus (London) and Institute of Pacific Relations (New York), 1951; R. H. Tawney, *Land and Labour in China;* F. S. C. Northrop, *The Meeting of East and West*, Macmillan, New York, 1946; Sol Tax 'Selective Culture Change'; *American Economic Review. Proceedings*, Vol XLI, May, 1951; UNESCO, *Social Implications of Technical Change;* and Ernest Beaglehole, 'Cultural Factors in Economic and Social Change,' *International Labour Review*, Vol. LXIX, No. 5, May, 1954.

† Cf. Thomas R. McHale, 'Problems of Economic Development in the Philippines,' *Pacific Affairs*, Vol. XXV, No. 2, June, 1952.

vour by under-developed countries to speed technological progress, and international collaboration to assist them in this endeavour. Success requires, not merely the introduction of new machines and production processes, but also changes in attitudes, in economic and other social relationships, in institutions and forms of organizations: in short, a wide range of innovations. Even by the extent to which such changes are necessary for levels of consumption to rise, they are among the costs of economic development. But it may be difficult to avoid social dislocation which is not necessary to economic development. What is being attempted is to absorb some elements of the culture of the West. What cannot be done is to *confine* the process to the assimilation of these elements.

Gandhi saw this with great clarity,* and it is fear of the consequences to Indian society of the absorption of the machine technology of an acquisitive, 'violent' society, which causes his followers not to fully co-operate with the Indian Government in its current Five Year Plan; for they expect to have to accept the acquisitive violence with the machines. But if the aspirations of under-developed countries to close the gap between their consumption levels and those of developed societies are to be satisfied, they cannot avoid a closer approximation not only to western economic technology, but also to many western economic attitudes. This is quite a different matter from insisting, which we do not, that economic and social forms be *patterned* on the West, though some existing institutions, such as caste, may have to be substantially changed, and even existing primary units such as the family weakened.† In some cases the acculturation process

---

* Cf. Toynbee, *op. cit.*, p. 79.

† We are not thereby proposing to join the flock of anonymous neo-Malthusian sheep against whose religious iconoclasm Colin Clark, as a modern Don Quixote, lunges fiercely when he ascribes to them the opinion: 'As material advancement and the selling of more goods are our basic objective (these writers state) it is clear that we must do our best to discredit and destroy such religious beliefs' ('Population Growth and Living Standards,' *op. cit.*, p. 100). We argue, not that material welfare is of 'such transcendent importance that any belief which conflicts with it has to go by the board'

may occur by acceptance of both the ideas, or principles, and the mechanism. In others the ideas may be adopted, but the suitable method of application may be quite different.*

It is not necessary to our purpose to speculate on the form of the inevitable secondary changes. It may be useful, however, to sketch in what appear to be some of the main obstacles to innovations—some of the reasons why the propensity to innovate for material ends is low—before attempting to analyse some of the requirements for technical progress.

Three or four centuries ago, the civilizations of India and China were more closely comparable with those in the West in economic forms and achievement than they are to-day. The capacity to create capital was probably no less than in the Occident; but the urge to seek material advancement and ability to promote changes to that end proved much weaker. Had the advantage of the West been merely an early superiority in capital accumulation, rather than in the ability to develop significant innovations such as the use of steam power, the joint stock company, or an efficient civil service, the process of improvement in levels of consumption would have slowed down. The progressive widening of the gap in wealth and levels of consumption are primarily attributable to the greater propensity to innovate in the West. In particular they are due to the emergence of the social phenomenon of planned innovations; more recently, to organized research as a part of the

(*ibid*), but that *if* material advancement is to be achieved, much that is of value in a culture will be destroyed and that there will be a gap until, eventually, something equally appropriate, but to the new situation, is substituted. D. R. Gadgil, in a suggestive article on 'Some Requirements for Technical Progress in Asia, *Pacific Affairs*, Vol. XXIV, No. 2, June, 1951, is a little more blunt in speaking of his own and other Asian countries when he ascribes to nationalism the task of completing the work of destruction of the older institutional and class forms, and establishing a new synthesis. He would seem to go further than I, as an outsider, would think necessary, or possible, except gradually, other than by totalitarian ruthlessness.

* Cf. A. L. Kroeber, *Anthropology*, Harcourt Brace & Co., New York, 1948, p. 425, where he defines acculturation as comprising 'those changes produced in a culture by the influence of another culture which results in an increased similarity between the two.'

planning,* and at a rather late stage to innovation in the form of family limitation. These made it possible to increase investment faster than population increase.

The cumulative effects of past change, and in particular the accumulation of scientific knowledge, the expanding mastery of scientific techniques, and the progressive extension of the scientific attitude through society, and its concomitant, the weakening of tradition in its bearing on economic activity, have also widened the gap in the propensity to innovate. So the gulf in capacity to promote material advancement is wider than ever by virtue of the historical process of accumulation, not merely of material things, but also of types of knowledge and experience relevant to economic growth. We do not, of course, attribute the gap entirely to the conditions referred to. Differences in the ratio of population to resources would have resulted in some differences in levels of per capital output and consumption even if propensities to innovate had been identical. But while accidental differences such as geographical location and the amount and types of national resources have played their part, the main determinants have been differences in the degree of change in value systems embodying the accumulations referred to and, expressed in general terms, in a greater eagerness to seek material advancement.

No society remains static, but the change in oriental societies has been much slower than in the West. More recently, as contact with the West has become increasingly close—in commerce, technology, politics, ideas and war—the tempo of change has increased enormously, especially since the war. This has prepared the ground for a technological revolution which might be of momentous world importance; but in great measure, though not

* As Kroeber points out, deliberate planning of invention is nearly lacking in most of the history of civilization. 'It began timidly to come up in Europe around 1300 or 1400, increased in the 1600's, but did not become systematic and important until the nineteenth century. It is therefore an exceptional feature of our own civilization. In fact it would have been extremely difficult to plan much invention until both theoretical science and practical technology reached a development, about the seventeenth century, such as had never before been attained,' *op. cit.*, p. 352.

entirely, the effects so far have been negative. They have con-
sisted largely in weakening the hold of traditional culture. This is
a necessary prelude to a positive, innovatory phase which might
initiate the technological revolution; but disruption does not
necessarily lead to growth. Japan has successfully passed through
this phase. In some countries, such as Ceylon, China and India,
the problem of starting the development process is being firmly
tackled. In nearly all there are at least fumbling attempts to make
a beginning. In all there are obstacles resulting partly because the
historical socio-economic causes of a low capacity to innovate
have not been fully removed, partly because of the dislocating
effect of such changes as have in fact occurred, including the
sudden transfer of responsibility to politically independent
governments. The frustration of peasants and workers resulting
from the disappointment of nebulous aspirations for betterment
are not the least among the difficulties in providing positive
leadership; and indirect aggression is playing its part. The
obstacles referred to will naturally differ in kind and degree from
country to country; and all that we can attempt is a generalized
summary of the more important of them, recognizing that some
of the conditions described are even now in process of change,
and that to generalize leads to over-simplification, and conveys
an undue impression of rigidity and uniformity even within
countries.

The first obstacle is poverty and the conditions associated with
it. If traditional methods are followed, the results can be tolerably
well forecasted, apart from natural hazards and other events
beyond individual control. Adoption of new methods involves
risk. The occidental farmer is more disposed to try a new crop or
buy a new machine, or the manufacturer to handle a new line, not
only because the whole economic system is geared to risk-taking,
but also because he anticipates, usually with some reason, that
loss does not mean catastrophe. The farmer or the manufacturer
expects his resources to be large enough to absorb possible losses.
In any case, the western manufacturers' customers are more
disposed to like change for its own sake, and be attracted to something new. The income of the oriental peasant, handicraftman, or

shopkeeper is so small and precarious that losses may mean all the difference between existence and starvation, or involve debt from which recovery is extremely difficult. So the results must be more convincingly demonstrated.

Poverty also affects the *ability* to innovate. A technological improvement will usually involve some additional outlay, be it in buying fertilizer, a better plough or a small power-driven loom. Trivial savings are often inadequate and credit is so very expensive that a larger relative increment in income than in the West would be required in order to justify the investment. Even if the superiority of a new technique is apparent, the economic cost may be too great. This presents a problem for a community as well as for an individual, because of the shortage of savings to meet individual and collective investments which embody innovations. A pre-requisite to increasing the acceptance of technological improvements by individuals may be innovations in the form of changed attitudes to saving and investment, and of improved financial systems.

Among the conditions associated with poverty we have already mentioned disease and insufficient nutrition which sap energy and induce lethargy and inertia. One who thus suffers is hardly likely to be alert in seizing new technological opportunities. To this add widespread illiteracy. Literacy is not synonymous with wisdom, and an excessively scholastic educational tradition such as existed in China may be conducive to a veneration of the classics and contemplative aloofness from mundane affairs rather than to material advancement.* But properly oriented, literacy extends the mental horizons and increases receptivity to new ideas. The fatalism which is ascribed to peasant communities may be due as much to existing poverty and consequent inability to provide against natural hazards, including disease, and to illiteracy, as to religious beliefs.

But poverty, of course, is not an independent variable. The

* Chih-i-Chang and Tsaio-Tung Fei write, 'In the middle class, opium and education appear to have had an equally stultifying effect,' *Earthbound China*, p. 225.

institutions through which individuals express themselves, and indeed the whole complex of culture affect the propensity to innovate. We touch lightly on some important aspects. The cultures with which we are concerned are still predominantly those of peasant societies. There is an abundance of literature testifying to the importance of the family as the primary unit in such societies, and, beyond the biological family, of the extended family or clan, and of the village.*

Perhaps the most powerful contribution of the family system to poverty is in its effect on population increase already discussed. Because the security and perpetuation of the family is a central concern, it largely determines also the motivation for saving and the uses to which savings are put; for example, in investment in land which seems the best foundation for security and family perpetuation. There is a psychic element in land ownership which causes farming to be much more a way of life than is usual in the West. The effects go further. The family system, including the extended family, increases the dependence of its members, and to it their primary loyalty is given. The demands made by the family reduce both the scope for and the incentive towards the exercise of individual initiative.†

Family and clan loyalties and responsibilities are reflected in the working relations in small enterprises. At this level of intimacy and entrepreneurship, when relations within the enterprise are in any case personal, because it is small, there is much to be said for

* Cf., for example, Chih-i-Chang and Tsaio-Tung Fei, *op. cit.*; Olga Lang, *The Chinese Family*, Yale University Press, 1946; J. H. Boeke, *Oriental Economics*, Institute of Pacific Relations, New York, 1947; R. Firth, *Elements of Social Organization*, Watts & Co., London, 1951; Martin Yang, *A Chinese Village*, Columbia University Press, 1945, F. S. Northrop, *op. cit.*

† Some years ago during a survey of economic conditions among the Maori people in New Zealand, the writer noticed that no orchards were planted on the recently established dairy farms. The reason given was that when the fruits were ripe there would be an influx of relatives to share them. So it was not worth the trouble to establish orchards. But in societies which are too poor, or too poorly organized to establish a system of social security, the family and the clan exercise a valuable protective function. Demands by the young for independence come as a disorganizing force.

this type of arrangement, just as there is for the small family business in the West. But a corollary to the strength of family loyalty and responsibility is that wider loyalties are weaker, and this has a bearing on the successful conduct of larger enterprises. Thus Northrop writes of pre-Communist China,* 'The tendency is to regard it as expecting too much of human nature to hope that a determinate social relationship beyond that guaranteed by the family will maintain itself. As a consequence the traditional governments were family or royal governments. And in between the family, which provided the sovereigns and the local individual families making up the community, there tended to be a vast no-man's-land. In this . . . the soldiers and the bandits had their sway.' Nepotism, graft and squeeze are in large measures attributable to the pressure of responsibility towards the family or clan which has precedence over other responsibilities. Even beyond the family, or clan, relationships tend to be personalized or particularist rather than universalist, and to be affected by status, friendship, caste, or other characteristics unrelated to ability to perform a task. They are dependent on who a person is, rather than what he can do.†

Such characteristics of a culture are significant from the point of view of economic organization and government administration. They make it much more difficult to establish and maintain the bureaucracies needed to manage large-scale enterprises, or plan and implement development programmes. In these, the professional application of specialized functions in an impersonal way, with primary loyalty given to the enterprise and its purposes, are essential to success.‡ Whether or not our explanation be adequate,

* *The Meeting of East and West*, p. 391.

† Cf. Talcott Parsons, *The Structure of Social Action*, Free Press, Glencoe, Illinois, 1949, pp. 550–1, in contrasting the Confucian and Christian ethic, and S. Herbert Frankel, *The Economic Impact on Under-developed Societies*, pp. 170–1, in respect of occupational selection.

‡ For an exposition of the characteristics of bureaucracy as examined by Max Weber (*Religion and Modern Capitalism*), cf. Talcott Parsons, *op. cit.*, pp. 506 *et seq.*, and Max Weber, *The Theory of Social and Economic Organization* (translated by Talcott Parsons and A. R. Henderson), Hodge, London, 1947, pp. 302–13.

the effects in terms of entrepreneurship, management and public administration are well enough known. Thus, speaking of Chinese business in Indonesia, Lea E. Williams writes,* 'Chinese business organization was singularly unsuited to the operation of large industrial and commercial enterprises. The attainment of entrepreneurship, made difficult by the inaccessibility of the capital market, was further discouraged by the ties of kinship and friendship by which Chinese businessmen were bound.' But, of course, there will be loss as well as gain if relations become more universalist and impersonal, especially in the weakening of support to the individual as stresses result from economic and social change. Indeed, resistance to innovations which patently seem likely to bring specific advantages arises in part because accustomed ways of life spell adjustment and security and their disturbance may appear to threaten a society with confusion and disorganization.†

The 'representative' citizen in the West is an urban dweller. As we have suggested in other connections, the anonymity of relations in modern cities, the faster tempo of movement, their attractiveness to those most venturesome and unwilling to conform to tradition and the discipline of the small group, have been conducive to innovations. Towns provide openings for the middle class with its sturdy acquisitive 'virtues'. The majority of citizens in under-developed countries live in villages the size of which is very generally determined by the sustenance area conveniently reached by prevailing transport methods. In these there is much sharing of tasks and responsibilities. But the value of material help and responsibility to the village community is often offset by

* 'Chinese Entrepreneurs in Indonesia,' *Exploration in Entrepreneurial History*, Vol. V, No. 1, Oct. 15, 1952. See also Northrop, *op. cit.*, p. 327; Olga Lang, *op. cit.*, p. 184; Martin Yang, *op. cit.*, p. 235; Guy Wint, *op. cit.*, pp. 43 *et seq*. The writer came across an illustration in a small Chinese town some years ago. A Chinese engineer in charge of a CNRRA project employed his relations in the enterprise, used the petty cash for speculating in cotton and let the project truck for hire to local merchants, all greatly to the distress of UNRRA officials.

† For a discussion of this and other barriers to innovations, cf. Kroeber, *op. cit.*, p. 363.

intolerance of economic difference and, meritorious though it be, even by the compulsion of public opinion to care for the needy.* Compulsion is also exercised towards conformity with conservative tradition. Leadership is usually vested in elders who are traditional and conservative. Habits of collective action and material aid, and existing relations and institutions may sometimes pave the way towards village organization for economic development, though this will usually require a new type of leadership.

But this picture of a compact village community devoted to mutual aid and collective action for the common good savours overmuch of Shang-ri-la. Division and dissension arise out of religious, caste, clan and other conflicts, and rival factions weaken or shatter village solidarity. The amelioration or removal of factional differences may be one of the main problems to be overcome in promoting participation by the villagers in programmes for rural betterment.† In addition to their effects on village solidarity, caste and other institutional divisions reduce the functional and occupational division of labour and often lead to exploitation.‡

* In an informative survey (shortly to be published) of an urban native community near Port Moresby (*The Great Village: The Social and Economic Welfare of Hanuabada*), Dr. Cyril S. Belshaw describes the effects of many of these compulsions among a group only partially oriented to the life of a European town. Consumption noticeably above the general level is frowned upon and is the focus of jealousy and adverse comment. So a native who received a gift of a refrigerator from a European felt impelled to remove the motor. Among references to the rôle of the village in Asian countries, cf. Boeke, *Oriental Economies* and his *Structure of the Netherlands Indies Economy;* Institute of Pacific Relations, New York, 1946; Martin Yang, *op. cit.*; Chih-i-Chang and Tsiao-Tung Fei, *op. cit.*; and M. Zinkin, *Asia and the West.*

† Among the most interesting of the many valuable projects undertaken by the Ford Foundation in its Technical Assistance Programme in India is a study of factions and leadership in an Indian Village. 'The crucial factors which give village social organization its distinctive character are the importance of kinship, caste, factions and inter-village networks.' Ford Foundation Programme Letter Report, No. 26, April 29, 1953.

‡ On effects of Caste, cf. K. G. Sivaswamy, *Caste and Standard of Living versus Farms, Rents and Wages*, Servants of India Society, Madras, 1947.

To these impediments to the exercise of economic initiative should be added institutional arrangements such as systems of land tenure, credit and marketing. It is a commonplace that, although the high economic cost of the two latter is not entirely due to exploitation of the peasant, and though landlords, money lenders and merchants perform economic services, yet there is very commonly an exploitative element in the reward of all three. In consequence, the small proportionate returns to the peasant both discourage enterprise and reduce the margin available for improving farm or handicraft production. These aspects of the rural economy are well known, and the small space devoted to them is no index of their importance.*

To round off the picture we touch on other attitudes, beliefs and prejudices which often have important economic effects. Many of these have a religious origin but it is never easy to know where religious influences end and others begin, if indeed there is a beginning and ending. So we shall not attempt to differentiate very closely.† Without going into detail it can be said that the major religions of the Orient are a deterrent to worldly pursuits or, at most, give little positive inducement to thrift, hard work and the accumulation of wealth. Contrariwise there can be no doubt that the Protestant ethic, by commending these virtues, has contributed to the growth of capitalism. The Confucian emphasis on contentment and contemplation, and the Hindu emphasis on mysticism and other-worldliness are reminiscent of some Christian sects or orders, but hardly of Christianity as a whole over the past two or three centuries. Certainly over the past 2,000 years the

---

* Again there is a voluminous literature on the subject and we refer only to the following recent publications: United Nations *Land Reform: Aspects of Agrarian Structure as Obstacles to Economic Development*, New York, 1951; *Philippine Land Reform*, U.S. Special Technical and Economic Mission, Mutual Security Administration, U.S.A., Manila, 1952; V. Liversage, *Land Tenure in the Colonies*, Cambridge University Press, 1945; and the writer's *Agricultural Reconstruction in the Far East*.

† Among those who compare religious and ethical criteria in occidental and oriental countries mention may be made of Max Webber, F. S. C. Northrop and Guy Wint in works referred to earlier.

eye of the needle has become greatly enlarged so that the affluent pillar of the suburban church need no longer fear, if he ever did, that his entry into the Kingdom of Heaven will be impeded. There is no necessary conflict between wealth and piety, and it is very helpful to economic development that he can feel both affluent and good.

As a reflection of the differences in mores, in part at least resulting from religious attitudes, the differences in the attitudes towards labour are important. Thus Boeke,* Chih-i-Chang and Tsaio-Tung Fei,† and other writers comment on acceptance of labour as a necessary evil rather than as a virtue which brings its own reward. The low elasticity of demand for commodities in terms of work is in part a reflection of this attitude.‡ Other writers comment on the high value placed on leisure, contentment and participation in the gossip, recreation and ceremonies of the village, and some preference for discontinuity in labour to give freedom to enjoy these things; and on their effects on attitudes toward labour and the desire to increase consumption.§ It is perhaps a pity that material advancement requires some sacrifice of these pleasures.

Religious ritual, folklore, tradition, magic,‖ and social ceremonials also have their part to play. Thus in India, the sacredness of the cow, and vegetarianism, are rituals which not only impose a heavy cost in terms of soil exhaustion and deprivation of land for human foods, but also lower nutritional levels by preventing the use of a valuable supply of animal protein. The ritual obser-

* *Oriental Economics*, p. 7.

† *Earthbound China*, p. 82.

‡ *Earthbound China*, p. 107; Boeke, *op. cit.*, p. 29. But this must not be pushed too far. It is no doubt affected also by the absence of incentive goods appropriate to the culture and within the means. In one factory in India an increase in wages led to absenteeism. In another it reduced absenteeism. The reason appears to have been that in the latter case the increase was larger so that it now became possible to purchase a bicycle by instalments.

§ Raymond Firth, *op. cit.*, p. 11; and Boeke; Chih-i-Chang and Tsaio-Tung Fei; and Northrop's works cited.

‖ See, for example, Ram Lal Bhalla, *Report on an Economic Survey in Bairampur*, Punjab Board of Enquiry, Publication No. 1, Lahore, 1922, pp. 134 *et seq.*

vances and relations associated with caste are also a serious impediment to improvements in consumption levels for the mass of the people, if only because they impose barriers to the division of labour according to ability.

The high levels of cultivation and craftsmanship often achieved with the means available in under-developed countries, indicate that folklore and tradition are, at least, not to be sneered at, for they embody the results of centuries of experience. But this experience is frequently local in range,* and the very completeness of the adjustments to environment which the techniques often express is an impediment to the acquisition of new knowledge, and the adoption of a scientific attitude in the sense of empirically trying out new methods. The influence of ceremonials has already been touched on in respect of ostentatious expenditure, saving and debt, and little more need be said, except that they are important elements in prestige and status. They add colour to life, but costs are often high in relation to income and they are not conducive to the accumulation of capital.†

The above sketch lists a forbidding array of obstacles to innovations, and when considered with the shortage of capital might be conducive to extreme pessimism. But the obstacles are not insuperable, and recognition of their existence, especially by foreign technical experts, might be conducive to greater success in technical assistance programmes designed to help governments and people help themselves, and to better judgments on where to

---

* Cf. Tawney, *op. cit.*, p. 52, in respect of China.

† Ram Lal Bhalla (*op. cit.*, p. 96) states that in the district covered by the survey (*c.* 1920) the total cost of betrothal and marriage to both parties (much of it in the ceremonial exchange of gifts) was 1,200 rupees, the net annual income of a typical Jat family being about 670 rupees. The importance of ceremonial expenditure as an impediment to economic improvement is such that some co-operative authorities give 'Better Living' co-operatives as agencies for co-operative agreement on its curtailment a high priority in co-operative systems, largely on the grounds that successful credit and other types of co-operative are unlikely as long as members are competing in extravagance. Cf. W. K. H. Campbell, *Practical Co-operation in Asia and Africa*, Heffer, Cambridge, 1951, pp. 96, 182, and the Foreword by C. F. Strickland, p. xxi.

begin, what to aim at, how to proceed and how fast to go. In any case, not all obstacles are equally important or obstinate, or equally to be found in all countries. Many of them are being weakened or dissipated by events, and success has been achieved in more than one place in overcoming some of them.* The problem, while taking them into account, is to develop viable plans in which a central place is given to the organization of leadership whose primary object is to promote participation of the people in programmes for their own betterment.

* E.g., in community development projects in India and Ceylon.

CHAPTER X

INNOVATIONS AND GROWTH: SOME REQUIREMENTS

J. A. Schumpeter,* in his classic formulation of one theory of economic development gives innovations the central rôle. This also is the position taken in this essay, but our approach is different in important respects. This is largely because our purpose is different. In what follows we are not concerned with criticizing Schumpeter's theory, but with making use of it by way of contrast in relation to the applied problem of using innovations to raise consumption levels in under-developed countries. Schumpeter abstracts away 'non-economic' elements, and is concerned with developed economies having a high degree of specialization of functions, and a rationale of behaviour typical of individualistic societies. He excludes 'growth' through small continuous modifications in the flow of production, and limits the concept of economic development to 'spontaneous and discontinuous change in the channels of the flow, disturbance of equilibrium, which for ever alters and displaces the equilibrium state previously existing.'† These innovations lead to new combinations of the factors of production. Schumpeter further excludes the use of unused resources, which however may be a 'contributing circumstance, a favourable condition, or even an incentive to the emergence of new combinations.'‡ Even past savings are excluded except in so far as they result from previous development. The

---

* *The Theory of Economic Development, op. cit.* In what follows I have elaborated on certain points discussed in 'Economic Development in Asia,' *Economia Internazionale*, November, 1952, and at times used the same phraseology where appropriate.
† *Ibid.*, p. 64.
‡ *Ibid.*, p. 67.

means for economic development are extracted from the flow of production in the main through credit creation by the banks.

Schumpeter classifies innovations into five types: (1) the introduction of a new good or quality of a good; (2) the introduction of a new method of production; (3) the opening of a new market; (4) the conquest of a new source of supply; (5) the carrying out of a new organization of an industry.* He excludes changes in consumers' tastes, which are regarded as changes in the data to which businessmen must respond. Leadership in economic development is exercised by entrepreneurs, *not in the successful management of the production flow, but in seizing possibilities to conceive and create new combinations.* The possibilities already exist, and the entrepreneur does not create them, but he surmounts legal, political and other forms of opposition, obtains the necessary co-operation of others and the resources required, and wins over consumers.

The less developed societies which concern us are societies in which the specialization of functions has not proceeded so far, and in which behaviour is less individualistic. Partly, but not entirely for these reasons, we must formulate the approach (in Schumpeter's terminology), in terms of growth and not simply of development; or, rather, our definition of economic development is synonymous with growth in levels of consumption. Discontinous innovations occur and are of importance in breaking down barriers to change, or in putting people in the mood to accept or want change, or in providing resources to make changes with. The war, the assumption of independence in India and other countries, communism in China, western democratic ideology, technical assistance programmes, and capital aid programmes (which are usually 'packages' embodying improvements in physical techniques, and in organization) are all of this character. But their main (though not exclusive function) is the preparatory one of weakening barriers to change and of helping people to help themselves in beginning the process of growth. They start, or lay the foundations for, the successive accumulation of small improvements.

* *Ibid.*, p. 68.

As Kroeber* points out, even the significant inventions which strike the public imagination, such as the telephone or television, have long and complex lines of antecedents. Hence even in Schumpeter's model it will usually only be the final applications which are discontinuous. The small accretions at last become congealed in something big or even dramatic. What we are concerned with in under-developed societies is the problem of transferring some ideas (or their concrete embodiment) which are the culmination of a long process in developed societies, in such a manner that they may not only be absorbed but also set in motion, or contribute to, this cumulative growth process.

The previous discussion of investment also strengthens the emphasis we are placing on continuous accretions to productive power, as the capacity of a community to innovate is progressively accelerated. The low income and, in general, the immaturity of banking systems will restrict the absolute and relative amounts which can be extracted from the flow of production through credit creation to bring about massive reconstructions as in Schumpeter's model. The shortage of entrepreneurs and technicians for large-scale enterprise, the necessity for balanced investment in a wide variety of fields, and the desirability of giving special consideration to enterprises with low capital intensity, all indicate the need for laying main stress on the accretion of technological improvements in concerns of modest size: in other words, for bringing about such improvements as in ploughs, in the use of fertilizers, or in the organization and technology of small industries, rather than in being unduly seized of the necessity for doing things in a big way so as to promote a technological leaping forward of the Schumpeterian type.

If our earlier description of obstacles to innovations is reasonably valid it lends further support to this approach. The *major* preliminary task is to remove these obstacles, strengthen the propensity to innovate among a large number of individuals, and put them in the way of innovating. The new process must be within the means and not be too repugnant to the culture. As far as

* *Op. cit.*, p. 357.

specific innovations are concerned, it is largely a matter of modest beginnings which by their success make possible an acceleration of the tempo of change. Moreover, obstacles often reside in elements in culture which are not economic in any usually accepted sense of the term. So we can hardly follow Schumpeter in abstracting away non-economic elements, even though this means a less rigorous and tidy formulation.

There are differences also in the rôle and location of leadership. Continuous growth, as distinct from discontinuous innovations, requires better management to promote gradual improvements in efficiency, adjust to growth as it occurs and seize the new opportunities which growth may offer. So we do not exclude better management of the production flow from our concept of leadership, but attach importance to responsiveness to economic change in plans and organization, whether in private concerns or government, and to alertness in absorbing and applying innovations made in other places. It used to be customary to belittle the Japanese as being imitative of western technology; but in the early stages of 'modernization' this is to be expected. By and large technical assistance programmes are an invitation to be imitative. Selective imitation plus adaptation is a form of flattery which may pay handsomely. So, one form of leadership is to discover and apply what can be usefully absorbed from elsewhere. An important requirement for technological advance is to increase absorptive capacity for suitable ideas and processes from other countries. Another major responsibility of leadership is to promote and administer types of organization designed to persuade and assist others to make economic improvements. This is the essence of agricultural extension which is concerned with all phases of human betterment.

Of recent centuries in economically developed communities, economic leadership has been located mainly in entrepreneurs, though governments are playing an increasingly important rôle. But in under-developed countries, as we have stressed, entrepreneurs of the western type able to manage large enterprises are fewer in number and in absolute and relative power, and they are seldom able to command large resources and manœuvre them into new positions. Even in India, which is better served by entrepreneurs than most under-developed countries, there is still a shortage of those competent to manage large-scale bureaucratic enterprises. This is shown in the attempt to meet needs by the establishment of managing agency firms which have generally been partnerships or private companies, though many are now public companies. These combine the functions of company promotion, issuing and under-writing fixed capital, provision of working capital, and the management of companies. A recent report states that 'although investment habits, and a capital market, have developed considerably, the dearth of business leadership still appears to leave a need for the services of managing agents.'* In virtually all under-developed countries the financial, marketing, advertising and other economic institutions and agencies which entrepreneurs must use are less developed. They operate in a milieu less conducive to the western type of entrepreneural imagination and more resistant to it, while at the same time their means of persuasion are less pervasive and potent.

As R. Richard Wohl points out in an article already quoted,† the disparity between what may be socially desirable and individually prudent for a given businessman is determined substantially by his environment. 'Like his confrères in the economically advanced countries he has a keen regard for self-interest, and measures his self-interest against his estimates of the economic conditions under which he operates. Knowing that his capacity to estimate, control, and shift uncertainty is limited, he may, more often than not, be especially sensitive to the risks to which a venturesome investment decision exposes him,' rather than 'be

---

* *Financial Institutions in India with Special Reference to the Mobilization of Domestic Resources for Development.* S. L. Simha, International Monetary Fund, 1950, pp. 70–71. This report draws attention to defects and deficiencies in the system, especially through the entry into the field of inexperienced people since the war, but considers that the system should be reformed, not eliminated. See also, S. K. Basu, *Industrial Finances in India*, Third Edition, University of Calcutta, 1953, Chapter VI.

† 'The Formation of Entrepreneural Groups in Under-developed Countries,' *op. cit.*, p. 99.

coaxed by the prospect of ultimately high profits if his long shot comes in. He does not see enterprise impeded by cool temperaments or by an inappropriate set of attitudes, but by structural, institutional limitations which narrow what he conceives to be feasible, economic alternatives.'

Certainly larger entrepreneurs in under-developed countries are neither equipped for the work of generating the mood to make technological changes among the host of small producers, nor able to provide them with the means. It is not usually their task.

So, by comparison with the West, governments must exercise a more positive rôle and entrepreneurs a less important rôle. Governments must not simply prepare over-all plans, but also, as part of them undertake massive projects, prepare a general economic and social climate conducive to private innovations, and give positive help to small-scale producers, especially peasants, in making technical and other changes conducive to economic improvement. Given the generation of a suitable economic and social climate, and positive leadership and direction by government, entrepreneurs may then have a leadership rôle to play. As in Japan, this might take the form of the integration of small enterprises with large, and the provision of technical and other forms of help to the smaller concerns. But farmers and many small industrial enterprises would be outside their orbit.*

Whether or not we describe management as a function of leadership may be a matter of terminology; but adequate recognition of differences of the sorts referred to between developed

---

* Wohl, *op. cit.*, p. 102, expresses a similar conclusion:
'The formation of a functioning and fruitful entrepreneurial group would, therefore, seem to be dependent on certain favouring historical conditions which foster its growth (and which do not now seem generally prevalent in under-developed countries), or else on the initiative of the State undertaking to foster economic development deliberately. . . . Of all present alternatives, however, the initiative of State . . . seems the most likely to produce a situation favourable to the emergence of entrepreneurial talent bent on rapid growth.' We are applying this generalization, not merely to the rôle of the State in preparing a suitable economic climate for entrepreneurs in larger enterprises, but also in itself promoting change and exercising economic initiative and leadership among farmers and small-scale producers.

and under-developed countries, might greatly affect the direction and content of development plans and programmes and the emphasis in technical assistance projects.

Two other important differences may be noted. First we should not exclude the use of idle resources, but, on the contrary, as our earlier discussion has shown, give them a special place. Second, we do not regard changes in consumers' tastes merely as changes in the data. Earlier references to the demonstration effects of western consumption levels, hint at the importance of raising *consumption standards* so that people may be more disposed to accept the changes needed if consumption levels are to be raised. Why should people want economic development sufficiently to do something about it, if the standards are unchanged? This is not merely a rhetorical question; for emphasis tends sometimes to be placed too exclusively on restraining the rise in consumption levels so that more can be saved. This is important, but sooner or later comes into conflict with the need both to raise wants and open up the prospect of satisfying them, so that people will work harder, and adopt new ways. Changes in consumer tastes, therefore, are among the means to be used, and not simply alterations in the data.

We conclude by considering some of the requirements in encouraging and promoting innovations directed to improving the efficiency of labour and capital. In large measure we are rearranging ideas already expressed.

As in the case of material investment, a balanced or integrated approach is required. A recent report concerned especially with rural betterment emphasizes that the approach should be 'multi-purposed', 'multi-processed' and 'multi-focused'.* The jargon is ugly, but useful. The effectiveness of promoting improved agricultural techniques is limited if the people are too ill to apply them, or if they so suffer from intestinal parasites that they benefit little from more food. While, with limited resources it is not possible to improve everything at once, so that a scheme of priorities is

* *Community Organization and Development in South and South-East Asia*, pp. 19–22.

required,* it is still necessary to bear in mind that successful action on one front will usually require complementary action on others. This applies not only to elements in welfare such as more food, health, education and so on, but also to balanced growth in different economic sectors. So the objectives are multiple.

In the same way a variety of processes is needed, each reinforcing the other. Persuading people to want things and showing them the techniques to use may be useless or positively harmful if necessary supplies are not available, or if the state of the law makes it possible for others to seize the fruits of the improved technology. To awaken aspirations before they can be satisfied may promote unrest and revolution rather than growth. Similarly, success in a programme of technological change is likely to be greater if efforts are made to obtain the support of different groups and assist them to participate. In rural communities, for example, this requires working with women and young people as well as with men; but the need goes further in bringing in different occupational groups and classes. Thus the I.L.O. Productivity Mission in India worked with and through trade unionists as well as employers, and those who were being professionally trained as production technicians.

Within this framework we again reiterate the obvious. Since it is people, and not machines, who innovate and apply the results of innovations, a first requirement is to improve the capacity of people as individuals, particularly by improved health and education, and training in specific skills. Without a general system of education, not indeed merely scholastic, but related to the life and needs of the society, and providing a ladder from the elementary school to the University or Technological Institute, continued progress is unlikely.† In higher education it is not simply a matter

---

* Cf. *ibid.*, pp. 22 *et seq.*, for an attempt to list criteria for the establishment of priorities.

† This opens up so large a subject that one is all too conscious of the platitudinous nature of so meagre a statement; but the necessity for such a general system which eschews mere learning by rote and is linked in purpose and methods with community life is becoming increasingly recognized and made the subject of experimentation. Recognition of the inadequacy of

of increasing facilities for training in the necessary arts and applied sciences, but also of changing attitudes so that those trained in the professions are less set apart and accept the responsibility for participation in 'action programmes': when for the agriculturist, for example, dirty boots as well as a desk piled with documents are the hallmarks of service.*

But while formal education, with literacy as one major aim, is a requirement for cumulative technological progress, literacy is not a necessary requirement for education and training in the early stages. Indeed, as has been suggested, quicker results may be achieved by intensive specialized training schemes and by education of the 'extension' type. In this, group methods, demonstra-

present or recent systems is expressed, for example, in the 'basic education' of Gandhian inspiration (described in *Basic National Education*, Hindustani Talimi Sangh, Sevagram, Wardha, 1938(?)) which is one of the reforms embodied in the Indian approach to Economic Development; in the Community Centred Schools in the Philippines (*The Community School of the Philippines*, Department of Education Memorandum No. 77S, 1952), and in the vocational approach under UNESCO Fundamental Education Projects in Thailand. A highly interesting approach to develop something more than 'mere literacy' schools in countries where there are few trained teachers was attempted through the so-called Nuclear Schools in Guatemala and other Latin-American countries. Trained teachers in the 'nuclei', usually in market towns, supervised and guided untrained teachers in rural schools in the surrounding area. The project method was used as a teaching technique and the aim was to use the teacher as a leader in social work, and the school as a centre of extension education by linking it with Parents' and Neighbours' organizations (cf. article by Ernest E. Maes in *Educational Approaches to Rural Welfare*, FAO, Washington, 1949). H. B. Allen uses his wide experience and knowledge of the problems to make a valuable contribution to their solution in *Rural Education and Welfare in the Middle East*, H.M. Stationery Office, London, 1946.

* In respect of development projects in rural areas, *The Report on Community Organization in South and South-East Asia* (pp. 66 *et seq.*) suggests for consideration the example of the North China Council on Rural Reconstruction which organized a project, the administrative responsibility for which was undertaken by the faculties of five University colleges. The project area became a field for research and training, and staff and students became familiar with the economic, sociological, agricultural, public works and other problems by doing something about them.

tion, learning by doing, the use of visual aids and a wide range of educational devices and techniques may be used.*

Extension education has been developed mainly in rural areas, but its principles may be applied more widely. Properly conceived and applied it embodies many of the general requirements for technological progress. We use it to illustrate these, with the reminder that they are of general significance not restricted to farming, and not simply part of a particular complex of education techniques first evolved in the United States and oriented to the culture and requirements of that country.† To apply them outside of rural areas may be more difficult and will require modification in emphasis.

A fully developed extension system integrates three main elements: research and testing, professional training, and advisory services or extension activities in the field. In the United States, the first two are undertaken by the Land Grant Colleges, the third by the County Agent.

Research both pure and applied is a necessary foundation for continued economic progress. The research of scientists in the Universities, and the sporadic or *ad hoc* research associated with action programmes will help. But for it to make its full contribution to planned innovations, research itself must be planned and consciously oriented to development requirements. In the circumstances of under-developed countries this requires co-ordination of effort, and the avoidance of the waste likely to be associated

---

* Extension education is perhaps the outstanding American contribution to agricultural improvement and rural betterment, cf. E. de S. Brunner and H. P. Yang, *Rural America and the Extension Service*, Columbia University, 1949; USDA, *Contribution of Extension Techniques to Rehabilitation of War Torn Countries*, Washington, 1945; and various FAO reports, including *Organization and Activities of 4H Clubs, Teaching Better Nutrition, Home Economics Education in the Caribbean, Educational Approaches to Rural Welfare, Social Welfare in Rural Communities, National Agriculture Improvement* and *Reports of Agricultural Extension Conferences in Europe and Central America*.

† The Community Project Approach, discussed further in Appendix I, is an elaboration of the extension approach in rural areas oriented to the culture and requirements of less developed countries.

with the establishment of numerous research projects or institutes for separate purposes. In the absence of large industries which can afford to spend considerable sums in research, or endow research institutions, government must again assume major responsibility for providing the funds and facilities, and establishing the appropriate agency. Such an agency may not only directly engage in research, testing or advisory services, but also stimulate and co-ordinate work undertaken by others, and keep a watchful eye on research findings in other countries and make them available.*

In under-developed countries a somewhat smaller relative emphasis on pure research, and a greater relative emphasis than in developed countries on applied research related to their particular requirements, would seem appropriate. Research facilities and personnel are usually very limited, and the results of pure research are normally readily available from wherever they originate. Moreover, the best prospect for improvement may often be in the discovery, testing and extension of the best known methods, either local or foreign, rather than in discovering something new. There are great and obvious benefits in continuous liaison with research organizations and activities in other countries to economize in local research facilities, and take advantage of research results from elsewhere.

There are also special requirements as to training in under-developed countries. Very often there is a highly qualified corps of technicians, professional men and administrators at the top, but a great gap between them and the people who are to be served and stimulated to innovate. To fill this gap there is a great need for less specialized and less intensively trained intermedaries or 'foremen' of various grades. Recognition of this need in the rural programmes in India is expressed in special training schemes for

* Such, for example, are the functions performed by the Department of Scientific and Industrial Research in a small country such as New Zealand. Note also the general discussion of the problem of organizing and conducting research, the description of the approach to it in Mexico, and the proposal to establish an Institute of Applied Research in Ceylon in the IBRD report on *The Economic Development of Ceylon*, pp. 797 *et seq.*

'village level' workers who are the active agents in close touch with the people.

In considering the appropriate field processes and procedures (which are essentially directed to persuasion and education) it is difficult to make a satisfactory compromise between a collection of cliches in tabloid form and a detailed formulation which is more appropriately a task for the sociologist. To commence with felt needs makes sense as a means of promoting willing collaboration; but changes will not proceed far until there is an awakening of other needs, the importance of which may be apparent to the outside observer or expert, but not yet apperceived by the people. This applies especially to intermediary goals such as better sanitation and nutrition. But whether in the satisfaction of felt needs or of those newly generated, technical consciousness must be awakened, there must be specific incentives (such as a bigger yield of rice to which a technique is applied), rather than appeals to vague aspirations for betterment, and the specific techniques required must be transmitted. This demands a sensitive perception of differences in requirements and potentialities. There will also be occasions as has been shown in relation to capital formation, when, in addition to advisory services, direct technical help will be required before the peasant or artisan can himself apply a new technology. As emphasized, the risk of loss and resistances to change are so much greater than in the West that benefits must be more convincingly demonstrated.

In the United States and other developed countries, the county agent or his equivalent may stimulate the adoption of a new technique knowing that the machines or supplies are available from commercial sources. Even better strains of livestock or seeds can be bought from commercial breeders—as, for example, hybrid corn in the United States. This is often not the case in under-developed countries. Governments, or Universities, or other public institutions may have to improve breeds of livestock or seeds, or select types more suited to local conditions, or design new machines. They may either have to multiply these themselves, or make the necessary arrangements for multiplication, and establish channels of supply. Having done so, the cost of innovations must be within the means of those who are to apply them. Hence it may often be necessary to make credit available on terms which are not too onerous. The sequence of innovations must be related to progressive improvements in absorptive capacity.

Individual activities take place within a society, the climate of which must be conducive to innovations. This goes very far indeed. There must be a body of enforced law which enables the individual to enjoy the fruits of his labour, and as a corollary, prevents him from appropriating the fruits of the labour of others, a system of taxation which does not unduly deter enterprise, and a system of administration which is not conducive to arbitrary and unpredictable decisions by officials, petty or otherwise. The removal of institutional impediments such as in systems of land tenure, or merchandizing, or usury, or in caste, may require legal exactments, but these are seldom sufficient. They may have to be accompanied by educational programmes and propaganda to generate a public opinion favourable to the law. In the first three cases, effective enforcement of the law is unlikely unless alternative, effectively competing agencies are established, offering the services previously provided by the landlord, merchant or money-lender. So positive action is required in encouraging or establishing new institutions or agencies. This is necessary not simply to *provide* services, but also as a means by which self-help and mutual aid may be promoted. In rural areas these agencies may take the form of panchayats or other local authorities, rural development councils, women's or young people's clubs or (especially in commercial aspects) co-operative societies. They must be given the statutory powers necessary for the performance of their functions. Thus in the Philippines, the barrio, which is a natural communal unit for improving local amenities, has no legal self-governing status, and is therefore unable to levy taxes for these purposes.* In other fields they will include types of business

* Cf. Roland R. Renne, 'Agrarian Problems and Foreign Aid in the Philippines,' *Far Eastern Survey*, Vol. XXII, No. 13, December, 1953. In India the revived panchayats are given wide statutory powers, including financial powers, but the poverty of the people is such that taxable capacity

organizations, operating within a suitable company law, societies of professional workers and trade unions, as well as special agencies to promote particular objectives or types of activity,* and so on.

One need not accept the mystical concept of the social will to be impressed with the necessity for public support to government plans and policies. There must be a certain élan in a developing society. So much importance is attached to this in the Indian Five Year Plan, that in addition to promoting voluntary organizations for specific purposes, such as panchayats or co-operatives, there is an ambitious aim to establish a nation-wide voluntary movement by the co-ordination of existing voluntary organizations and the establishment of new organizations. While one may regard the prospect of success with some reserve, the very attempt to marshal public support and action is significant in terms of our discussion.

While, in every country there will be innovators ranging all the way from exceptional peasants who try out a new crop, or schoolteachers who stimulate and organize the villagers to improve amenities, to large-scale entrepreneurs, sufficient leadership sufficiently dispersed is not likely to emerge spontaneously. For this reason we have emphasized the rôle of government not only in helping to establish a socio-economic environment conducive to enterprise, but also, more positively, in planning and implementing development policies and programmes. It is not simply a question of an efficient cadre of technicians and administrators at the centre, or even of a sufficient number of these at medium or lower ranks, but also of an efficient *system* of administration

is very small indeed so that the main source of improvement must still be voluntary self-help activities requiring little finance. Panchayats also suffer the disadvantage that the elected members are likely to be the more conservative elders. So, at least as a transitional measure, there is the need for other forms of local organization.

* For example, municipalities, investment corporations or research foundations. On the importance of voluntary organizations of various sorts in respect of *rural* betterment, cf. *Community Organization and Development in South and South-East Asia*, Chapter II.

carrying services to the people. Equally, it is a problem of stimulating and assisting leadership among the people themselves, providing the minimum necessary training for local leaders, and promoting the types of organization referred to earlier.* Local organizations under local leadership can provide the foundations of the administrative pyramid, and there is the need for training at all levels. Existing shortages of finance and trained personnel limit the degree to which administrations can be enlarged. But by the extent to which local organizations and leadership can be stimulated they become, in effect, a part of government administration and contribute to economy by enabling springs of gratuitous service to be tapped. Put in another way, one of the major requirements in rural areas is to integrate the official administration with local government and voluntary groups. The former provides external leadership and the services needed to promote innovations, the latter provide the agencies through which the administration works, and the means by which the self-determination of goals may be encouraged and people co-operate to help themselves.

If economic development is not to be held back by mass-inertia (especially in rural areas), widely dispersed and decentralized centres of local organization and leadership are needed. But, as previously illustrated, if the resources directed to promoting technological change are spread too thin they become uneconomical. A compromise has to be made between the optimum degree of concentration, and the urgency of the need to create widespread centres of leadership and change. In the community project under the Indian Five Year Plan this compromise is attempted by establishing some fifty-five community projects covering some 11 million people with a relatively intensive concentration of personnel and services, and a much larger number of

* Some countries, such as India, have highly efficient central administrations in the Federal Government and the States. These are ably surveyed in a recent report full of penetrating observations and recommendations (Paul H. Appleby, *Report of a Survey on Public Administration in India*, 1953). But in all under-developed countries, including India, there is the problem of extending and developing public administration in the ways indicated.

people by less intensive extension methods. It is anticipated that the projects will become centres radiating propensity to change over surrounding areas. As resources permit, the more intensive projects will be increased until they cover the whole of rural India. By beginning in this way it is possible to gain experience on techniques and methods of organization, and experiment with different degrees of concentration, so that improvements may be made as the programme is extended.

The community projects also have another practice, which is a desideratum of all development plans, in making provision for evaluation. A separate evaluation agency has been set up which will continuously survey and review programmes and compare different approaches and methods. Indeed, the community projects as designed, so conveniently illustrate many of the principles and requirements touched upon that they are summarily described in Appendix II.

It becomes quite apparent that economic development is a 'packet deal' and that changes in labour, capital and technology are complementary. Increasing the supply of labour by improved health measures or putting idle people to work requires both capital and improved technology. Some technical improvements are congealed in the material things created when capital formation occurs. Technical improvements require more capital, or its diversion from other purposes. So we have not been able to discuss labour, capital and technical improvements as if they were independent variables, but where the occasion has demanded, have indicated the mutual dependence.

But capital formation and improved technology are also competitive. In addition to extracting resources from the flow of production to create more concrete capital, we must extract resources to undertake research, make people healthier, educate and train them, organize them, persuade them to make changes, and provide them with technical knowledge. Supplies of goods must be diverted to these purposes instead of using them directly for production, and people must be employed to provide the services. The use of symbolic models in the formulation of requirements for growth, and in particular the tendency of western economists to discuss capital formation as if it possessed of itself the power to generate income, often obscure the importance of services of these and other kinds, and so give a distorted view of the whole process. Western preconceptions, be it noted, originate in societies in which there is already a substantial allocation of national income for services, and their adequacy can be largely taken for granted. In such circumstances there need be no great harm, and there may be something to be gained in converting capital into a sacred cow. But in under-developed societies the adequacy of services should not be taken for granted. Even 'social services' should be looked at, not simply as concessions to the impatient desire of human beings for betterment now, instead of later when they can be more comfortably afforded, but as something necessary to improve the capacity of the people who are the real source of generating power. Of course, there is, again, a question of balance, and the immediate effect of increasing services is to reduce the scant savings out of which the finance comes for capital formation. But the early increase in services is imperative if capital is to be more fruitful over the longer period, and if the development process is not to peter out.

PART III

CONCLUSIONS

CHAPTER XI

SOME CONCLUSIONS AND INFERENCES

A. Summary Recapitulation

In the final chapters we summarily recapitulate the main conclusions, draw certain inferences and make some observations on international assistance to promote economic development. We have described the position as follows:

Except in Japan, there is a strong tendency in Asian countries for population increase to absorb increases in national income so that consumption is close to the subsistence level. Some differences exist in levels of real income, but the very general existence of levels of nutrition below those required for health and efficiency is one symptom of the pressure of population. This conclusion is based on estimates which take account of such factors as environmental temperature, body weights, and age and sex composition of populations. Food production per head is still below the inadequate pre-war levels. Inadequate nutrition increases susceptibility to other diseases as well as nutrition-deficiency diseases. Consumption levels for other necessaries of life are also low. Deficiencies in housing, sanitation, water supply, and health and other services also increase the prevalence of disease. Fluctuations in the rate of natural increase are common, but they are due mainly to fluctuations in mortality. There is as yet little evidence of the widespread adoption of preventive checks, positive checks being the main demographic controls, at consumption levels not far from subsistence.

It is highly probable that the rate of population growth will accelerate in many countries, as a result of the extension of comparatively inexpensive mass preventive measures such as malaria control, mass vaccinations or inoculations and improvements in sanitation and water supply, especially in the villages, as well as measures to prevent famine. These may be expected to occur *before* development plans substantially increase *per capita* productive power, and before any significant change occurs in favour of family limitation. The familial attitude among peasant communities generates resistances to family limitation, and cheap and effective means of controlling conception acceptable within the culture do not seem to have been discovered as yet. Changes in attitudes from now on may occur more rapidly than they did in Europe, but they are not likely to slow the rate of population growth very much within the short space of two or three decades.

The ratio of effective supply of labour to population is lower than in developed countries. This arises first from morbidity reasons, second from the existence of a large volume of unemployed and under-employed labour. This latter is due not so much to a shortage of effective demand as to conditions of economic organization and institutional conditions. There is no need to recapitulate the causes in detail.

If constant returns to scale in an economy exist, capital must increase more rapidly than the labour force to increase production per head, in the absence of innovations. There is then diminishing factor returns to labour. Unless capital increases more rapidly than labour under constant returns, an increase in production per head can only come from innovations. If there are economies of scale but capital increases less rapidly than labour, these economies must be sufficiently large to off-set diminishing factor returns to labour. But again, innovations may change the situation, and lead to increased production per head. In particular enterprises or sectors, or for the economy as a whole in pioneer societies, increasing factor returns to labour are possible, or economies of scale even when labour increases proportionately less than capital. For reasons discussed at some length, especially the great predominance of peasant agriculture, such a situation is highly improbable for economies as a whole in Asia, and diminishing factor returns to labour, at a substantial rate, are virtually certain. This means also that economies of scale to population growth *per se* are virtually certain not to occur. Economies of scale may perhaps result if there is an increase in capital equivalent to the increase in labour; but the likelihood of substantial diminishing factor returns to labour carries the implication that economies of scale are unlikely if growth of output results from an increase in labour combined with a less than proportionate increase in capital.

If growth occurs in such a fashion that income per head increases, whether because capital increases more than in proportion to labour, or because of innovations, this is likely to change the structure of the economy so that manufacture and tertiary services (including the use of social overhead) are relatively more important and agriculture is relatively less important. The fuller use of labour is an important advantage accruing from the process. The increase in capital may enable additional output to be produced at a higher technological level. Such changes increase the possibility, even the probability that subsequent increase of output will be associated with greater economies of scale than before. In the absence of significant innovations, such changes in the structure of the economy as occur when capital increases less than population, are not likely to be conducive to any degree to economies of scale with subsequent expansion, more especially because of an increase in the relative importance of agriculture.

Such considerations serve to increase the emphasis to be placed on capital increase or innovations, not only because of their immediate effects, but also because of their contribution to the cumulative process of growth through their effects on the structure of demand and of the economy.

Such information as is available suggests that, on any reasonable assumption as to capital coefficients, rates of financial savings and of capital formation in under-developed countries are so low in relation even to current population increase that the prospects that growth in output will be greater than in population are not great; at best they are precarious. Even though improved health measures will reduce wastage and lost time and improve the quality of labour, the increase in population and in dependency consequent on the same measures will raise a difficulty in providing sufficient capital to increase consumption levels other than those embodied in health improvements. Moreover, improvements in the labour situation take some time to work out, in so far as they depend on health measures. This throws an additional responsibility on innovations to promote a break through, in the form not only of improvements in techniques as narrowly interpreted, and in organizations and institutions, but also of changes in attitudes.

B. Approaches

The above analysis suggests the following lines of approach to increasing levels of consumption:

(a) An increase in the rate of capital formation.

(b) The most effective use possible of available capital in terms of its ability to generate income.

(c) An improvement in the utilization of the potential labour force.

(d) The promotion of innovations.

(e) A deceleration of the rate of population growth.

The difficulty in bringing about a deceleration in the rate of population growth in the early, critical stage, increases the relative importance of the remaining approaches. When once the process of socio-economic change leading to increases in consumption levels gets under way, the prospects of a decline in the rate of growth of population through family limitation are greatly increased.

An initial requirement of some difficulty is to increase the rate of capital formation above that ruling; thereafter to extract for capital formation an increasing proportion of income increases as these occur. The main approaches are more effective promotion, mobilization, and disbursement of voluntary savings, and forced savings through taxation and/or inflation. Generally, there must be an increase in the marginal propensity to save and the use of forced savings by the extent to which this proves inadequate. Since much of the concrete capital must normally be imported, a corollary is the necessity to provide foreign exchange for this purpose. One of the investment criteria which, however, we have not discussed, is the effect on the balance of payments both as investment is occurring and after it begins to earn income. Some control over foreign exchange transactions may well be needed.

Low income, the importance of non-investment motives in saving, the tendency for financial investment to take forms which do not increase the ability of the economy to produce further income, or to only a small degree, and the lack of suitable agencies or credit instruments to aggregate and channel savings are among the obstacles to an increase in voluntary savings. They require not only the establishment of suitable agencies and instruments, but also the promotion of an economic climate conducive to the emergence of private investment opportunities. Among the conditions contributing to these ends would be a satisfactory company law and provision for its enforcement. Another would be the establishment of specialized institutions to promote different types of investment (e.g., co-operative short-term credit institutions with primary societies integrated into the financial system through apex banks, long-term agricultural credit banks, insurance corporations and development corporations), an efficient central bank, and improvements in commercial banks to ensure adequate liquidity for working capital, and monetary stability. Small-scale decentralized industries might be expected to strengthen the investment motive in rural areas. Properly regulated, the managing agency, as developed in India, is worth consideration for larger types of enterprise.

A part of the problem is to regulate and control existing financial agencies such as money-lenders and indigenous types of bank so that their charges are not unduly usurious. Frequently, high charges result from the risks and high costs of management of troublesome types of transactions, but they result also from a monopoly element. There tend also to be geographical differences in costs. The larger urban concern, for example, may often obtain working capital from western type commercial banks at rates comparable with those in the West, but the smaller concern, and those in rural areas, may have to pay high rates to money-lenders and indigenous bankers.

Larger concerns will also find it easier to obtain fixed capital by share flotation or debentures, especially if a share market exists.

But the smaller concern cannot resort to these sources. One effect of such conditions may be to distort investment because of the greater difficulty which small or medium concerns have in obtaining capital, and the higher cost. This is all the more important in countries in which such types of enterprise are of greater relative importance. Moreover, if smaller enterprises have to rely on institutions mainly concerned with short-term finance for their intermediate or long-term needs, this tends to have a destabilizing influence because a given proportionate contraction of credit means a greater proportionate contraction of working capital than if fixed capital is obtained outside the short-term system.* While an improvement and extension of commercial banking is desirable to improve sources of working capital for small, as well as large enterprises, it is also important to develop institutions to meet the long term and intermediate requirements of small and medium concerns.

Regulation alone is not likely to succeed in curbing usury by money-lenders and indigenous bankers, but the establishment of competing institutions would help. The former will continue to have a part to play, and more may be achieved by establishing competitive institutions and by extending and strengthening the commercial banking system and making its facilities available to them, than by concentrating on regulating them into good behaviour. These measures would also facilitate the geographical flow of funds.

When all is said and done, attitudes towards savings for investment are of crucial importance. The sort of approaches listed should help a great deal in changing these. In large measure changes in attitudes towards savings are involved in the whole process of promoting innovations. Integrated approaches to betterment, such as through the 'multi-purpose' community projects, may be expected to contribute substantially both by providing new investment opportunities, and by increasing

---

* This is of some importance in developed societies also. I have touched on the problem in respect of New Zealand in 'Stability and Growth,' *Economic Stability in New Zealand* (edited R. S. Parker), N.Z. Institute of Public Administration, Whitcombe and Tombs, Wellington, 1953.

general propensity to change. In addition education and propaganda specifically directed to savings and investment, and to encouraging the resort to such new institutions as are created rather than to the money-lender, are needed. Discouraging conspicuous consumption on ceremonials, and promoting co-operatives to provide both the means to save and the opportunity to invest are important in rural areas.

Existing tax structures reflect economic, political, and other social conditions. Low incomes, the high relative importance of subsistence production, lack of accounting, political pressures, and the inadequacy of fiscal administrations are conducive to a high relative importance of indirect and a low relative importance of direct taxes, and to a great deal of evasion. Frequently local authorities do not have adequate taxing powers. The high relative importance of public investment needs, and the necessity for an extension of services, make it desirable to reform tax systems in many countries. A substantial contribution might sometimes be made by reducing evasion through a tightening up of fiscal administration. But greater resiliency and progression is required through the revision of tax structures. Much reliance will have to be placed on sales taxes, export and import duties, and other forms of commodity tax, which would grow with growing income, but increased attention to income and other direct taxes which can be graduated is also needed. Since many works and services are better provided locally, local governments require adequate fiscal powers. The encouragement of private savings and investment by business concerns may conflict to some extent with an increase in forced savings through taxation; but a tax system adjusted to encourage private savings may possibly increase total net savings because of the smaller disincentive effect of taxes, encourage the habit of ploughing back profits, and increase subsequent taxable capacity.

There is a conflict of opinion on the efficacy of inflation as a means of increasing *net* capital formation through forced savings. A mild inflation through deficit financing for public investment might increase net capital formation; but any degree of inflation may reduce net capital formation by discouraging voluntary savings. Distributional effects and resulting industrial unrest may be more serious, and curbing inflation will be more difficult, once it gets under way, than in developed countries. The deliberate use of inflation as a means of increasing net capital formation is, therefore, hazardous.

Difficulties in increasing net capital formation out of voluntary or forced savings direct attention to the use of unemployed and under-employed labour for capital formation. In seasonally employed labour, in rural areas, there is a large potential source of labour power which could be directed to this purpose, either individually or collectively. Community projects in Ceylon and India, demonstrate the possibilities in this approach. While some finance capital may be required by way of loans or grants-in-aid, the problem is primarily one of organization as part of the composite process of promoting innovations. The small space given to this matter is no criterion of the great significance which should be attached to it.

We have stressed the importance in determining investment criteria, of the shortage of capital and the redundance of labour. In general, such conditions support the case for giving preference to types of investment with a high ratio of output to capital invested. These will usually be small or medium scale enterprises, of low capital intensity. For this reason, and because of the incentive effects of an increased supply of consumers' goods, a normal desirable sequence would be light consumer goods→medium→ heavy industries. Such a sequence is also supported because one stage helps provide markets for the next. Moreover, the criterion is consistent with the general arguments which have been advanced in favour of decentralized industries in rural areas. Such arguments are concerned, not only with the advantage of avoiding the social and economic costs of urban concentration, but also with strengthening the investment motive for saving, promoting dispersed centres of leadership and change, and providing employment opportunities, *in situ*, for unemployed or under-employed labour. Even if such industries are seasonal, low capital intensity would mean comparatively small diseconomies through idleness of the capital.

Shortage of capital also strengthens the case for using labour intensive methods of capital formation, for example, in public works, where practicable.

But the criterion of low capital intensity can be applied only as a general rule, or 'rule of thumb' to which there are important exceptions. One of these is the fact that in some industries the technological superiority of the more capital intensive types is so great as to override arguments in favour of types of structure with low capital intensity. To get the best of both worlds it is desirable to give special attention to promoting technological improvements in small- or medium-scale types of enterprise of low capital intensity, and similar improvements in capital investment in agriculture.

Another exception to the rule arises from the necessity for investment in social overhead, in which the capital coefficient is low, and investments in which are very often capital intensive. These make their contribution in improving the marginal net product and the capital coefficient in other industries or sectors. Balance of payments requirements may sometimes shift the emphasis in favour of capital intensive types of investment.

More generally, the need for balanced investment may sometimes make it undesirable or impossible to avoid capital intensive types. On the other hand, attention must always be given to the extent to which capital-hungry types of investment starve others and promote unbalance. They must be judged in terms of the net effects, which include the deterrent to expansion and the reduction in output per head in other industries or sectors. In the early stages, especially, it may be more economic to import the products of industries where capital intensive structures have great technological superiority. But in any case, the possible divergencies between individual and social marginal net products seem likely on the whole to be greater than in developed countries. This applies especially because we are concerned with the requirements for growth, and not simply with the static criterion of comparative financial costs. Many criteria in terms of growth are intangible or difficult to assess in financial terms. They include, for example, the employment of otherwise idle labour, encouragement of entrepreneurship, and promotion of receptivity to change. They are affected by the desirability of placing emphasis on the short-run results not only to increase the incentives, but also to promote an early increase in income as a source of capital formation for further growth. Such conditions, as well as differences in the whole economic climate which affect absorption capacity for technological change, make it extremely hazardous merely to transfer the investment criteria appropriate to developed societies.

Frequently, preconceptions based on western experience cause industrialization to be over-stressed. In part this arises because developed societies are more highly industrialized. But it is one thing to argue that when societies become more developed they also become more industrialized, and another to deduce that in consequence heavy emphasis should be placed on industrialization at any particular stage in the process. This is a delusion to which western economists with little direct acquaintance with under-developed countries are particularly prone, but it is shared by some governments in such countries. In part over-emphasis on industrialization by governments (especially in large-scale types of enterprise) is a question of prestige; but it arises also from failure to stress sufficiently that industrialization is a consequence, as well as a cause, of increased real income per head. It results in the negative danger of under-emphasis on agricultural improvement. Indeed balanced growth will often, perhaps usually, require a larger increase in relative emphasis in the early stages on agriculture than on industry. This is recognized in the Indian Five Year Plan.

Of primary importance, in the present connection, are improvements in the quality of the labour force by improved nutrition, the necessity to provide a surplus of food over rural requirements for workers diverted to capital formation or non-farming industries, and the need to increase the market for industrial products by raising rural income. The consumption function for industrial goods imposes a limit on balanced expansion of non-farming sectors. Relief of rural pressures by industrialization requires that prior, or at least parallel, attention be given to increasing production within the existing agricultural structure. Policies over-emphasizing the pull of industrialization as a *means* of increasing agricultural production are very likely to be self-defeating and lead to waste in investment.

We have argued that the two main means of improving the effectiveness of labour are measures to improve health and to employ unemployed and under-employed labour. The rhythm of the seasons is the main cause of unemployment. The utilization of under-employed labour will follow mainly from the development process as a whole. The increase in productive power per head, through its effects on demand per head, leads to substitution by types of enterprise in which there is greater labour continuity. The same process, as it reduces the relative importance of farming, will also reduce the proportion of occupied workers subject to the seasonal rhythm. There are considerable potentialities in utilizing unemployed labour; first by extending the farming season by new crop practices; second in local capital formation; third in small-scale decentralized industries of low capital intensity. While these approaches will require some finance capital they will enable the small volume of financial savings to go further.

Our general line of argument suggests that in many under-developed countries in Asia it is unlikely that the rate of capital formation will increase sufficiently to keep ahead of prospective population increase. Apart from external aid, an improvement in levels of consumption then requires that such increase in capital as takes place be greatly supported by innovations.

Massive, discontinuous innovations of the Schumpeterian type will occur from time to time, and on occasion may be of considerable importance—such, for example, as multiple-purpose river projects of the TVA type covering large areas. But the socio-economic conditions described in previous chapters, including the relative shortage of capital in which many technological innovations must be expressed, cause us to place major emphasis on the cumulative effect of continuous innovations of modest dimensions.

Innovations cover not only improvements in capital and processes, but also the growth of new forms of organization and improvements in the quality of labour. We have stressed the importance of health programmes (covering also nutrition) as innovations of great importance from this point of view, as well as of education and training. But economic attitudes must also be changed, so that stress must be laid on developing the means of persuasion. Research is needed to discover and test new methods. Adoption of technological innovations requires the organization of supplies of the things needed in the new techniques. So we have emphasized the necessity for a 'multi-purpose' approach, and cited the community projects as embodying this principle, especially in respect of rural areas.

The relative shortage of entrepreneurs and the resources at their command, together with the need to promote greater economic efficiency among a larger number of small-scale producers make it necessary for governments to play the main part in promoting innovations. So the strengthening of government administration is normally a requirement if economic development is to succeed. An important task of governments is to prepare a general climate conducive to innovations in the private sector.

An important general conclusion has emerged that in the extraction of resources from the flow of production, capital formation and the provision of services are both complementary and competitive. The development process may not be initiated (in the sense of an increase in levels of consumption), or if it is, will be exhausted unless there is adequate investment in 'human capital'. This means an adequate allocation of resources to services, not merely as ends, but as means. Because capital is expressed in concrete things or conventionally can be measured in accountancy units, its importance is not likely to be overlooked. This is less true of services which affect more intangible and less measurable elements in the development equation.

CHAPTER XII

SOME OBSERVATIONS
ON INTERNATIONAL AID

A. Capital Aid

Recognition of the importance of international aid is manifested in the establishment of the International Bank for Reconstruction and Development, and proposals for the establishment of new international financial agencies, in the Expanded Technical Assistance Programme of the United Nations and Specialized Agencies, in the Colombo plan, and in the bi-lateral programmes of the United States and other governments. The arguments advanced in this essay reinforce the urgency of the need for additional international assistance to promote a break through. This is all the more so if the rate of population growth is accelerated. While health measures may eventually increase labour power in relation to population especially by improving its quality, the first effects are likely to be an increase in dependency and in the rate of growth of capital required.

In arguing the need for additional capital aid and technical assistance, it is necessary first to issue a caveat against exaggerated estimates of the amount of capital or technical assistance required, or which could be absorbed; second, to suggest that it is as much a matter of kinds and sequences as of amounts; third to stress that the complementariness of capital and technological innovations requires a close co-ordination of capital aid and technical assistance.

The primary purpose of international loans, or grants, is to provide foreign exchange to procure concrete capital or technical services. They do not increase local resources available for capital formation, with the qualification that loan or grant-financed imports may divert additional resources to public purposes by the creation of counterpart funds through their sale to private citizens. Loans under commercial conditions such as those given by the International Bank must pay interest, and it is desirable that they be repaid so that the Bank's resources become, in effect, a revolving fund for development. This at once imposes a limit on absorptive capacity; for economic development does not necessarily and automatically lead to a proportionate improvement in the balance of payments. A second limiting factor is the necessity to 'marry' the imported capital with local capital formation. This will differ according to the kinds of capital imported, and to the way in which domestic capital formation occurs. For example, by the extent to which idle labour can be used, absorptive capacity on this particular score would be increased. But over-importation of capital goods may generate inflationary pressures by forcing the pace of domestic capital formation. On the other hand, it may distort investment by causing an undue proportion of domestic capital to be drawn away from investments not requiring imported capital, to whose which do.

Other factors limiting the absorptive capacity for capital imports include the ability of governments to plan and operate development programmes,* and the availability of managerial and technical skills. For reasons such as these, as well as because the (implicit) capital : output ratio is too high, I have argued elsewhere† that the estimates by the United Nations experts of the capital imports needed by under-developed countries were excessive.‡ Nevertheless, on any reasonable assumption as to capital coefficients the capital imports required are much in excess of the current volume of international capital aid.§ In many

* Cf. *Fourth and Fifth Annual Reports of the International Bank for Reconstruction and Development*, Washington, 1948–9 and 1949–50.

† *Economic Development in Asia, A Preliminary Approach*, op. cit., pp. 18–19.

‡ *Measures for the Economic Development of Under-developed Countries*, p. 76.

§ *Supra*, Chapter VII, p. 113, where we estimate that with a capital coefficient of 0·25 loans of $5,600 million would have been required for Asia (on the basis of estimated 1949 incomes) to promote an increase in real income of 2 per cent per head for a population growing at the rate of 1½ per cent.

countries also, it is highly likely that carefully selected capital imports substantially in excess of those being received could be absorbed.

The kinds of imported capital required will depend on the circumstances of each particular country. It is futile, or at least wasteful, to provide capital assistance for types of enterprise for which technical skills and managerial qualities are insufficiently developed, or having regard to existing consumption functions, to develop industries too much in advance of expanded demand for their products. Both of these obvious considerations reinforce the general, though, of course, not the universal case, for capital imports for small-scale types of enterprises. They are more likely to be consistent with existing technology and they can be expanded in a less discontinuous fashion.

Frequently absorptive capacity will be improved if a special agency is established which distributes imported capital supplies, and arranges local finance for their purchase. Sometimes it may be necessary to make arrangements for servicing. These desiderata might apply, for example, to imported farm machinery. Such an approach also facilitates the collection of counterpart funds.

The effective operation of an institution dispensing commercial loans such as the International Bank, requires in the main that they be for specific projects. They may not directly generate export income, but there must be exchange available for servicing. There is a self-liquidating element in the transactions. Our discussion has stressed the importance of investment in social overhead. This is often a type of investment in which returns are long deferred, and which has a low ratio of output to capital. The effects in improving the balance of payments may be so indirect and conjectural that they should not be taken into account. As well as to social overhead this might apply, for example, to irrigation or land development which improves nutritional levels, but may neither increase exports nor reduce imports. Such investments might not be suitable objects for commercial loans, but a necessary part of the development process, requiring both capital imports and domestic capital formation. In some cases the imports might appropriately be foodstuffs which sustained labour during capital formation. For these various types of investment there is a strong case for grants, or loans at low rates of interest.* Even though not suitable for commercial loans, they might complement them, provide foundations otherwise lacking, and increase absorptive capacity for commercial loans.

In developed societies this side of the Iron Curtain, the strong tradition of private enterprise causes much emphasis to be placed on the desirability of private international investment. Its significance arises, not so much out of the volume of funds, which have probably only occasionally been large in proportion to the national incomes of recipient countries other than those settled by Europeans, but out of the complementariness which we have stressed as being necessary. With the capital have gone administrative and technical competence, business and technological connections with more developed countries, and, in the case of export industries, economies of scale consequent on integration with world markets, finance and transport. Ideally also, they offer scope for the training of executives and technicians in recipient countries, but, by and large, their rôle in this respect can hardly be described as having been impressive.

Private international investment in the past has not succeeded to any marked degree in promoting economic development in the sense of rising levels of consumption, and it did not set in motion any markedly successful process of innovations.† The countries we are considering remain under-developed, and subject to population pressures. Conditions might have been worse without it, but even past experience when the volume of private investment in real terms was much greater than now, suggests that even under favourable conditions private foreign investment could not

* Cf. United Nations *Report on a Special United Nations Fund for Economic Development*, New York, 1953.

† For useful observations on the impact of foreign investment and reasons why it was not more effective in promoting economic development, cf. A. E. Kahn, 'Investment Criteria in Development Programmes,' *Quarterly Journal of Economics*, Vol. LXV, February, 1951; and H. W. Singer, 'The Distribution of Gains between Investing and Borrowing Countries,' *American Economic Review*, Vol. XL, No. 2, May, 1951.

be expected to play more than a minor part in raising consumption levels. In fact the current obstacles to private investment are well known, so that equally with the slogan 'trade not aid' the patent impossibility of promoting any significant expansion of private investment hints at a disingenuous element in much current advocacy.*

Nevertheless, every effort should be made to promote the flow of private funds. In lending countries this points to the desirability of tax exemptions and forms of guarantee, and of exploring further the possibility of an international agency to facilitate private investment.† In recipient countries it points to the relaxation of many of the conditions which deter direct and portfolio investments, especially the former. Some requirements, such as that a certain proportion of nationals should be employed in responsible positions, are reasonable from the point of view of long run development needs. But many countries are deprived of useful help because restrictions and rigidities go further than is necessary.

The specific problems and requirements are well known and

---

* I refer to the slogan of 'trade not aid' first because over the short period it is unlikely to improve the balance of payments sufficiently to remove the need for international loans of some size; second, because of the great difficulty in diverting additional exchange earnings in under-developed countries to capital imports without import controls or other trade barriers the removal of which might be expected as a *quid pro quo* for trade liberalization in developed countries; third, because, rightly or wrongly, the world at large has doubts of the continuity of American trade policy in the direction of liberalization; fourth, because the destabilizing effect on world trade of American agricultural price support policies through the disposal of agricultural surpluses is itself prejudicial to the steady expansion of world trade in primary commodities and conducive to measures in other countries to protect their primary producers. I would add, however, that the liberalization of trade and greater stability in markets for primary products are among the desiderata for the economic development of under-developed countries. Price instability is a major threat, for example, to the establishment and successful operation of rural credit and marketing institutions.

† See, for example, *Report on the Proposal for an International Finance Corporation*, International Bank for Reconstruction and Development, Washington, April, 1952.

well traversed, so that we need not elaborate further. But there remain certain obstacles such as instability in governments, the possibility of nationalization, inconvertibility of currencies, and the high returns possible in developed countries, which are not likely to be removed by international agreement. So both the nature of the development process in under-developed countries, and the unlikelihood of any great expansion of private international investment mean that the preponderance of international finance must be inter-governmental. This includes the possibility, however, that an increasing volume of private investment in lending countries may be channelled through inter-governmental agencies such as the International Bank, and that as development proceeds conditions will be more favourable for private investment.

The other side of the picture is the use of inter-governmental loans for domestic private investment in under-developed countries. International agencies or governments do not normally lend to private enterprise; but public development corporations in recipient countries may be used as agencies through which private enterprises may borrow to obtain foreign exchange for capital imports.*

B. Technical Assistance

Technical assistance, of course, takes a variety of forms; training programmes, fellowships, surveys, technical meetings or seminars, as well as advisory missions, and demonstration or pilot projects. International organization of these on a large scale is something new, and it is understandable that many difficulties have arisen. Administrative organizations and procedures had to be established with little experience as a guide. There have been problems of overlapping and co-ordination among different agencies. Solution of these particular problems requires not so much formal delimitation of areas of operation as positive procedures for co-ordination in the field, as well as at headquarters.

* Such, for example, as the loan of the International Bank to the Industrial Development Bank of Turkey for the Development of Private Industry, *Seventh Annual Report*, 1951–52, p. 25.

At the operational level this must be extended by similar procedures with and between the departments or agencies of recipient governments.*

Even with a certain amount of financial flexibility, reliance on annual budgets has made it difficult for the responsible agencies to develop long-range plans with the necessary continuity. This has added to the problem of recruitment and been a factor in short-term contracts causing disturbing changes in personnel, even in programmes which, to succeed, would have to operate over a period of years. Delays in the completion of agreements with governments have also added to recruitment difficulties. In any case the supply of experts in a wide variety of fields who are technically competent, and able to get along with people of another culture and modify their techniques to suit different environments, is limited in relation to needs. There is not yet a cadre of experts who can be transferred from one assignment to another and thereby be given continuity in employment, or who would wish to make a career of this sort.

On the other hand, there is a limit to the number of programmes or foreign technical experts which recipient governments can take care of. Local costs may become burdensome. Staff must be diverted from their normal tasks to receive and apply the technical assistance. Technical assistance programmes carry the implication that they will be continued under local leadership, and out of local resources, and ability to do this must be assessed. Despite such difficulties there have been gratifying successes in many fields and countries. If it were possible to remove the handicap of annual budgets to enable longer range planning, one would expect the difficulties to become progressively less, as both agencies and recipient governments gained in experience. In what follows there is perhaps a certain element of implicit criticism at times, but it is made with due appreciation of the sort of difficulties referred to.

* This problem is briefly touched on in United Nations *Report on Community Organization and Development in South and South-East Asia*, Chapter VI.

Imported capital goods such as machines will themselves usually embody what are technological improvements for the recipient country. They are thus an indirect form of technical assistance. But, as we have stressed, it is also not unknown for western types of capital to be unsuited to under-developed countries. A corollary is that much may often be gained by a combination of western technical 'know how' with local knowledge, including the folklore of the peasant, so that either imported or locally produced capital may be better designed to suit local conditions. For example, an improved plough must be capable of being pulled by the draught animals of the peasant, under existing soil conditions, and this may necessitate differences in design even in different parts of the same country.

A further corollary is the desirability of combining capital assistance and technical aid in one operation. Failing such a combination capital may go to waste. As its annual reports show, this is well recognized by the International Bank. The problem may go very far. Applicant governments may need help in discovering relevant facts, establishing priorities, generally in planning programmes of which particular projects requiring imported capital are a part, and often even in formulating requests, as well as in the techniques of establishing and operating particular projects. Usually also more will be required than the mere designing of capital goods or processes to suit local needs. Demonstrations of their superiority over those existing may be necessary. If our plough is to be made locally, it may be desirable to organize mass production and a supply system, integrate the village blacksmith into the production line, and provide credit so that the farmer may be able to buy it. Even such a simple illustration indicates that effective technical assistance may be a complex socioeconomic process.

The obverse is that technical assistance must be appropriate to the over-all investment potentialities, and not simply to the capital required for a particular project. Technical assistance suited to advanced types of enterprise is of doubtful value if they can only be established by withdrawing capital from other purposes where the contribution of investment may be much greater. This is a variant of the problem of determining appropriate investment criteria.

The complementariness of capital and technology goes further, in requiring that technical aid continues long enough for the necessary skills to be learned by the local people who must carry on the programme, and for the necessary organization and administration to be firmly established. This applies even where no external capital aid is involved. One significant general approach to ensure sufficient duration and continuity is in the 'co-operative programmes' or 'servicios', especially between the United States and Latin-American Governments. Agencies of the United States Government collaborate with agencies of recipient governments in health, agricultural or other programmes. Teams of American and local technicians or administrators, in effect jointly operate the programmes, with the intention that the Americans progressively withdraw as the local 'counterparts' are trained and the administration operates smoothly as a going concern.*

Recognition that technical assistance is a co-operative venture between foreign advisers and local administrators or technicians, and that there must be continuity over a period of time, is necessary if technical assistance is to achieve the overriding objective of promoting self-help in under-developed countries, so that they may develop their own supply of experts and institute their own process of innovations. In Schumpeter's terminology, technical assistance is a discontinuous innovation, the major purpose of which is to start a *stream* of innovations. Increasing absorptive capacity for capital imports is one element in this objective, but a major requirement is to give special attention to developing *general preparedness for* innovations. While specific *ad hoc* projects have their place, main emphasis is needed on starting and encouraging an indigenous cumulative innovatory process.

Technical assistance agencies operate through governments,

* Among references note: Kenneth R. Iverson, *The Servicio in Theory and Practice*, Institute of Inter-American Affairs, Washington, 1951; *Foreign Agriculture* (US), Washington, April, 1952; *Foreign Commerce Weekly* (US), February 4, 1952; and *Team Work in World Agriculture*, USDA, Information Bulletin, 21, Washington, 1950.

and except by way of demonstration or training the foreign experts do not do the work themselves. Hence, the specific requirements include an *élite* who will absorb the techniques, and exercise leadership in applying them and in promoting further innovations. There must be an effective public administration through which they will function, and this implies a sufficient measure of continuity in office of responsible ministers and senior officials. Instability in government is not simply a question of changes in government, but of frequent changes in ministers and senior officials.

'Technical assistance programmes can do little about stability in government, except indirectly, but they may help a great deal in establishing a cadre of leaders in administration and technology, and improving administrative systems where the will exists that these be done. Promotion of general preparedness for technological and other necessary kinds of change requires that certain things be antecedent to any general technical assistance campaign, or at least should be embodied as major elements in the early phases. These things will include the strengthening of administrative systems and improvements in administrative procedures, training schemes,* and in the agricultural sector, the development

* I am tempted to enlarge on the problem of training, but content myself with one or two observations. By and large, the main approach should be in the establishment of training facilities in recipient countries. Fellowships abroad have their place; but often the level of techniques abroad is inapplicable in the fellow's home country, or the approach required is different. Mature people with experience may be able to apply the knowledge gained and make the necessary adjustments; but others may be bewildered rather than helped, and may become less adjusted to their own culture. So arrangements must be made by those who know both the circumstances of underdeveloped countries, and what the developed countries have to offer—a by no means common combination. In the social fields especially, more attention might be paid to the possibility of in-service training in under-developed countries which are doing a good job and where socio-economic conditions are similar. For example, more will usually be gained by studying co-operatives in Ceylon or Cyprus than co-operatives in Denmark or the United States. Where developments have gone far enough, technical meetings of responsible officials in the countries in a region may provide an invaluable means of mutual education.

of agricultural extension systems, or community projects, to provide agencies through which specific techniques may be extended. Many such approaches have in fact been made, but the writer's observations in a number of countries suggest that their basic importance in improving receptivity to specific forms of technical assistance has not always been fully appreciated. Because they have not come early enough in the chronology of technical assistance programmes, or proceeded far enough, there can scarcely be a country in which technical experts have not experienced frustration over the shortage of 'counterparts', and administrative inadequacies.

An essential requirement if technical assistance is to be fully effective is that the experience gained in a circumscribed locality, or by a group of people, shall be capable of wider extension. This usually necessitates that the existing administrative machinery shall be capable of doing the work of extension or duplication, that there shall be people trained to undertake the task, and that extension is within the economic capacity of the country. Technical assistance demonstrations sometimes do not conform to the test of duplicability, nor sufficiently recognize the integrated nature of the development process. They may possess some value in demonstrating specific techniques, such as improved cultural practices for rice, or malaria control. In some cases, foreign advisory services very properly have a restricted function; but adequately conceived the demonstration or pilot project may be one of the most effective ways of giving technical assistance, especially in rural areas. So we conclude by suggesting certain desiderata for a project of this sort.*

The purpose of a pilot or demonstration project of the type we have in mind is not simply to demonstrate specific techniques but also, and more important, to formulate an approach which can be made administratively viable for a much larger area, and which it is economically possible to extend. For reasons discussed earlier,

---

* I have drawn here on *Community Organization and Development, op. cit.,* Chapter VI, and on experience gained as a member of the Mission which prepared this report, and in other connections in various countries.

it should represent an integrated approach to rural betterment (covering agricultural improvement, health, education, village improvement and so on). If it covers only one aspect, it is apt to be unbalanced and lose much of its value as a demonstration. In essence it is a community project, exploring the possibilities for the co-ordination and economical functioning of the various national services in the demonstration area. It may reveal what changes are required if these services are to be effectively provided within the means available. The goal is that it continue as a model and as a training centre for other areas after the technical assistance personnel are withdrawn.

If these objectives are to be achieved, the demonstration should cover an area comparable with at least the smallest administrative area of a size sufficient for economy in operation, and should be used as a training centre as well as for demonstration. The area selected should, as far as possible, be representative, presenting neither special advantages nor peculiar difficulties. Establishment should be preceded by a clear formulation of objectives, and a survey to ascertain the major characteristics and problems, and provide measures for subsequent evaluation of progress. There should be an assessment of the normal staffing of such an area as it would exist as part of the general administrative system. Provision should be made in advance for local counterpart officers, facilities and supplies.

The staffing by technical assistance personnel should not be greater than is possible as a continuing administrative unit, when the project is fully transferred to the local administration, except to the extent that higher concentration is needed for training purposes. Otherwise it merely demonstrates what can be done by more resources than the country can afford. Since a function of the technical assistance team is to demonstrate to governments and to train future workers, personnel should be selected, not merely in terms of technical competence in specific fields, but also of ability to train, and interpret their objectives and requirements to governments. Local counterparts should be of a status equivalent to that required of officers having administrative responsibility in a representative administrative unit. Indeed, the combined team should be fully responsible for the services covered by the project in the area, and not an adjunct, or subordinate to the existing officers. Otherwise the demonstration team tend to be regarded as intruders, and there is no basis for continuance as a demonstration and training centre. Those selected should be of the best available quality. Initial plans should provide for the continuance of the demonstration for a sufficient period of years to soundly establish the project and adequately train the local personnel. As far as possible, too frequent changes in technical assistance personnel should be avoided. These might be withdrawn progressively. A system of evaluation should be set up, not only to assess the project, but also because of its value in national programmes as the experiences gained in the demonstration are used to establish projects elsewhere.

A demonstration of the type outlined requires the collaboration of a number of technical assistance agencies and agencies of government. This necessitates first that administrative responsibility be clearly defined, second that effective arrangements be made for consultation and co-ordination by a national committee, including representatives of the agencies of government and technical assistance agencies.

APPENDIX I

NOTE TO CHAPTER VI ON THE UTILIZATION OF IDLE LABOUR

James E. Duesenberry, 'Some Aspects of the Theory of Economic Development,' *Explorations in Entrepreneural History*, Vol. III, No. 2, gives some support to the argument used in respect of the use of idle labour for capital formation, and to the adoption of less capital-intensive methods, in the following passages which are worth quoting *in extenso:*

'Thus the dilemma of the backward countries is not their inability to withdraw resources in general from consumers' goods production. Rather it is the lack of balance in the unemployed resources available to them.

'There are some ways out of the impasse, however, which make it possible for capital to be formed without cuts in current consumption. The simplest in principle, though not perhaps the simplest in application, might be called the "unit multiplier" solution. Certain types of capital can be formed with a maximum of labour and a minimum of capital resources. Some types of construction such as the building of irrigation dams and canals and the construction of roads require (technologically) only very small amounts of equipment. (Cement production does not require much capital.) The methods of construction which do not use much capital are inefficient in western countries because of the high transfer price of labour. But in situations in which much labour and very little capital is available, they are the only feasible methods. They may even appear uneconomical in the East from a financial standpoint. The real transfer price of labour may be zero, but some wage must be paid to induce labourers to give up their share of family income. This minimum is probably more than the disutility of labour. In some cases, therefore, in India capital has been raised abroad for purchase of equipment which could have been dispensed with or spread more thinly over a greater range of projects, because of the financial illusion which makes financial labour cost exceed the real transfer price of labour.

'If, however, a country wishes to form capital quickly it will engage in construction projects using as little capital as possible. But if wages are paid to those working on the construction projects they will wish to spend them on consumption. They can be used to buy food from farmers with whom the labourers formerly lived since the latter will have excess food supplies (by their old standards). However, if food is sold in that way the farmers will have increased money income which they will want to spend on industrial products which will not be available. If an inflationary process is to be avoided the farmers must be taxed to prevent their incomes from increasing. If taxes, just sufficient to pay for the construction, are levied there will be no change in anyone's consumption but income will have increased by the amount of the investment made. When the projects are completed there will be an increase in agricultural output. This was more or less the procedure used by the British in India but there most of the gains have been eaten up by the population increases. It will be noted that the scheme suggested here is the same as that suggested by Haavelmo* for raising employment with a balanced budget in capitalist countries.

'The unit multiplier method is the only one available to a country with no saving or a very low rate of saving if inflation is to be entirely avoided. But that method has the disadvantage that it puts the whole burden of development on the government. If a certain amount of inflation can be tolerated other methods can be used. Bank loans can be raised or idle balances tapped by private firms engaging in capital formation. The funds thus raised can be used to hire idle labour as before and to import capital equipment from abroad. That part of the capital expenditure which is used to hire local labour will produce an increase in demand for consumption goods. In addition increased expenditure on capital imports will tend to depress the exchange rate and produce a rise in import prices (in terms of the local currency). Thus the initial capital formation will tend to have an inflationary effect. No actual cuts in total consumption need result since there is no need of a fall in production. But prices must rise sufficiently to prevent any immediate increase in consumption as a result of the increased incomes being dispensed by the investors. This can be avoided if the idle balances tapped take the form of gold, as might be the case in India.'

But Duesenberry does not quite appear to visualize the institutional set-up in most under-developed countries, at least in Asia, and some modifications seem necessary:

(1) The problem facing under-developed countries is both 'inability to draw resources in general from consumers' goods production' and 'lack of balance in the unemployed resources available.' Some resources, either in goods or services or both, are needed to put idle labour to capital formation.

(2) Much of the capital formation possible is *collective* and the community projects in India and Ceylon show that a great deal of it can be stimulated

* Haavelmo, T., 'Multiplier Effects of a Balanced Budget,' *Econometrics*, Vol. XIII, October, 1945.

without wages, though grants in aid of other forms may be needed, reinforcing the point made under (1) above.

(3) The argument is expressed mainly in terms of a withdrawal of labour from other uses—e.g., labourers formerly living with farmers. The main source would be the families of farmers during their seasonally idle time. The inflationary effect still occurs, however, if they are paid wages or the finance capital needed to stimulate the works is credit-created.

(4) Levying taxes 'just sufficient to pay for the construction' would in most cases prove difficult under existing tax systems. Reform of tax systems (local as well as central), and encouragement of voluntary savings in rural areas, must be attempted; but these will take time. Meanwhile, the use of idle labour should be proceeded with (if possible by organizing collective action which avoids wage payments) even though some mild inflation results.

(5) Whether placing on governments the burden of development of the sorts under discussion is a 'disadvantage' is largely a matter of political philosophy. It is a necessary condition to put idle rural labour to work. Except for landless labourers, or except in the long run as a cumulative process of development pulls rural labour to the cities, the 'idle' labour is needed on the farm at seasonal peaks. Private enterprise is generally unsuited to the task of employing the great bulk of the idle labour, which is seasonal, in capital formation, except near cities. Duesenberry's argument would, however, have more point in relation to small-scale decentralized industries, and to this extent reinforces the case we have presented. But such industries require prior research, inventions and organization which are functions more appropriately undertaken by government.

(6) It is difficult to see how the release of gold would differ from credit creation except in the financing of imports.

Duesenberry then advances arguments (pp. 5–6) more favourable to the use of inflation than those raised in the following chapter. He is also more optimistic as to the prospects of additional capital formation out of the added *profits of capitalists* (p. 6).

APPENDIX II

THE COMMUNITY PROJECT APPROACH*

Since completing this essay, I have attempted a fuller schematic examination of the approach summarily described below in *The Communities Project Approach to Economic Development*. South Pacific Commission, Technical Paper No. 84, Noumea, New Caledonia, July 1955.

The community project approach is especially suited to rural areas. It is less appropriate to urban areas because the 'community' in the sense of a group of people who, by virtue of living in a locality are conscious of having interests in common, is less characteristic, or less vital. In rural areas in under-developed countries the village is normally a community in this sense, though care must be taken not to idealize the village, and neglect factions, or other groupings which may cut across the village and affect its solidarity, or that the sense of belonging may extend beyond the village.

Voluntary organizations in different parts of the world have applied the community project approach over several decades. They have been pioneers in the development of techniques and of integrated programmes for rural betterment. But it is only of recent years, for example, in Ceylon, Egypt and India, that the community project has been adopted as a major agency for rural betterment in national programmes.

The growing interest in the community project approach and recognition of its potential importance is reflected in a Resolution of the Economic and Social Council.† This, *inter alia*, requested the Secretary-General of the United Nations to compile documentation on the objectives and methods, and the successes achieved by 'community welfare centres' and on the difficulties met, and invited the Technical Assistance Board to give sympathetic consideration to the applications from governments for technical assistance in this approach. Missions were appointed to survey community organization and development in various areas, and a series of country monographs is in preparation.

Voluntary agencies (other than village organizations) have a useful rôle to play in supporting national programmes in a variety of ways; but they do

---

* This appendix draws substantially on *Community Organization and Development in South and South-East Asia*.
† Resolution 390D, (XIII), 9th August, 1951.

not themselves have the resources necessary to develop and operate national programmes on a sufficient scale and covering a wide enough area to meet the requirements for economic development. Such programmes must be the responsibility of government and the rôle of voluntary agencies is subsidiary though it may be important. Accordingly, we examine the community project in the setting of national programmes.

It seems best to attempt a summary schematic account, which describes one type of organization, rather than describe various possible approaches or go into detail. We select the Indian Community Project approach as being most developed and most amenable to schematic description. Even in India there are variations, so that our picture is a simplified and generalized outline of the main elements.*

The national administrative requirements will be lightly touched upon. They include a central agency which will formulate policies and plans, promote the co-ordination of the various national services, ensure supplies and personnel and provide adequate facilities for training and evaluation. In India, the problem of administration is complicated by the Federal Structure. But the States are responsible for the projects in their territories, and the relations between central and State Governments are not especially germane to the community project approach as such. Some functions, such as evaluation, are undertaken at the Federal level, but there is no need in a generalized account to consider the division of responsibilities.

The State Organization is usually headed by a Development Committee consisting of the ministers concerned with development, the Chief Minister as Chairman, and a Development Commission as Executive Officer. The *Secretaries* of the departments concerned act as an Advisory Committee. The *Directors* of the various departments are an advisory committee to the Commissioner. The Deputy Development Commissioner is responsible for Community Projects. At the District, the next administrative level, is a District Development Committee, consisting of senior departmental officers, with the Collector as Chairman and a District Development Officer as the executive official. Each project is under the administrative responsibility of a Project Officer responsible to the District Development Officer, with two Assistants. There is a project advisory committee consisting of officials, voluntary workers, members of the Legislature, and others.

The community project programme began with fifty-five projects, covering between 11 million and 12 million people, late in 1952. A typical project covers about 300 villages, with a population of about 200,000. The area and population covered approximate to a *tahsil* or sub-division of an administrative district. It is, therefore, likely that the community project organization

---

* More detailed discussions of various aspects can be found in the selected references given at the end. Note, for example, *Community Organization and Development in South and South-East Asia*, Appendix D.

will become a reorganization of the national services for the whole of India within the existing administrative State framework of districts and sub-districts. It is important to note that, on the basis of present experience, a population of about 200,000 is normally deemed to be necessary to ensure economy of administration, and that any substantially larger number would normally be too great.

The organization of the project is a pyramid with the project officer at the apex and village level workers at the base, the total staff being about 125. At the administrative centre are the senior supervisory and technical staff in agriculture, health, education, village industries, engineering, social services, etc., and also the major facilities, such as a hospital, high school, veterinary centre, and supply depots. Each project area is divided into three blocks covering about 67,000 people at the headquarters of which are located the second level of supervisory and technical staff, secondary health centres, middle schools, and other facilities. A typical project will have some sixty village level workers, one for each five or six villages, or about 3,000 people.

The supervisory and technical staff have a greater or less measure of specialized training. The village level worker is not a highly trained specialist, but a 'multi-purpose' worker who has received some training in the elements of agriculture, sanitation and other skills, and especially, in working with villagers. Some village level workers are graduates, but more generally they will be of the level of matriculants. It is they who are in closest contact with the villagers. Their task is to give such technical assistance as is within their powers, and beyond this to draw on the services of the more qualified specialists in the various fields. The organization is designed to transmit the needs of the villagers through to those who can best help in satisfying them, and provide a channel of technical service and supplies from the project or block headquarters through the village level worker to the peasants. But the village level workers have a wider responsibility in promoting receptivity to new ideas and methods by demonstration and other extension techniques, stimulating and assisting local leadership, and persuading and assisting the villagers to organize for self-help and mutual help. They must see to it that supplies are available to meet wants which their efforts have stimulated.

The primary importance attached to self-help activities, both in capital formation and in activities directed to current production and welfare, causes special emphasis to be placed on various types of village organization such as the *panchayat*, or council of elders, the village development council, the co-operative society, the women's institute, or youth club. In some projects development councils have been organized on 'cabinet' lines with different villagers responsible for promoting and organizing separate activities, such as improving village sanitation, adult education, or the extension of particular farm practices. In some, also, representatives are elected to 'circle' councils covering several villages, from these to block councils and from these to project councils. In this way it is hoped to stimulate road building, drainage, or other works of benefit to several villages, enable the project authorities at various levels to receive the advice of villagers as to their needs, and familiarize the villagers with official policies and plans and obtain their co-operation.

The success of community projects requires a supply of people who are both trained in particular techniques and able to work with villagers, and stimulate them to innovate and to help themselves. To ensure an adequate supply of such personnel is one of the most difficult problems to overcome. Adequate training facilities are required at four levels: for 'professional' workers, such as the doctor, engineer, agriculturist, educationist or co-operative officer; the 'vocational' workers with a lower level of professional skill, such as the nurse, or sanitary inspector; the 'multi-purpose' village level worker; and the 'auxiliary' villager helper who will usually be a voluntary worker. Except for the very important need to pay special attention to field training in the villages, training for the two former groups may be given in familiar types of institution such as the university, hospital, training college or specialized training school. The two latter will usually require developments along less familiar lines, and instructors who have a special understanding of the problems of work in the villagers. The need for special training for village level workers is being met in India by the establishment of some thirty training centres under a scheme in which the Ford Foundation is collaborating with the Government of India. In both India and Ceylon, training for the fourth group is being provided in experimental schemes under which selected villagers are brought together at intervals for periods of a few days to two weeks, special emphasis being placed on the mastery of a few simple techniques such as construction of latrines, or the performance of an improved farm operation. The aim is to equip them to become leaders in promoting the adoption of particular new techniques.

Continuing evaluation of technique and approaches, indeed of all aspects of community project activities, is of great importance, the more so as the resources available are so small that under-developed countries cannot afford to waste them. This has been recognized by the Indian Planning Commission by establishing a separate evaluation agency.

We may summarize the objectives as follows:

(i) To provide for the *economical* extension of the national development and welfare services in a co-ordinated way such that each supports the other. The estimated total cost of a rural community project in India for a period of three years (in 1952) was 6,500,000 rupees, or 2,170,000 rupees a year. This amounts to about 33 rupees a head over the three years. But of the total amount 5,201,000 rupees is non-recurring, and 1,299,000 recurring. Presumably, therefore, the average annual non-capital expenditure is about 433,000 rupees for all the services covered, say a little over 2 rupees per head. This would be very much less than a single visit to a doctor in most western countries.

(ii) To promote innovations in the villages, not only in respect of agricultural and industrial production, but also in improving other elements in welfare. In essence the community project is a particular form of organization, not only to provide services which the villager cannot provide for himself, but also to apply the principles of extension education to production and general betterment. There is the specific recognition that improved health, education, and production are mutually dependent, that a variety of techniques and methods are needed, and that all sections of the village community must be stimulated and helped.

(iii) To stimulate and assist rural people in helping themselves by promoting technical consciousness, providing technical assistance, and organizing supplies, or grants in aid where these are necessary, and especially by organizing villagers the better to utilize idle labour and other potentialities for self-help.

(iv) Generally to promote agricultural expansion and expansion of other production in conformity with over-all development plans.

Some References

There is a growing but sporadic literature on community projects in under-developed countries, but as yet I am aware of no systematic over-all analysis. *Approaches to Community Development* (edited by Phillips Ruopp: W. van Hoeve Ltd., The Hague, Bandung), is a symposium dealing with sociological, economic, and educational aspects of community development, and providing interesting case studies, but has little to say on the requirements for national programmes. The United Nations is systematically compiling information. Reports of Survey Missions are available on Community Organization and Development in the *Caribbean Area and Mexico, Selected Arab Countries of the Middle East,* and *South and South-East Asia. Community Development Programmes in Greece* gives special consideration to labour utilization. A number of country monographs have been prepared and others are in preparation. The United Nations has also prepared a 'Study Kit' entitled *Social Progress through Local Action* which is a collection of useful reprints, and also a report entitled *Principles of Community Development. Social Progress through Local Action.* This is the fullest discussion of the various problems and approaches in community projects. For India there is a great deal of pamphlet material. The projects at Etawah and the Firkas in Madras, which we have referred to as prototypes of the Community projects, are reported on in *Interim Reports on Pilot Development Projects, Etawah and Gorakhpur,* Government of the United Provinces; and *Annual Administration Reports of the Rural Welfare Department,* Government of Madras, respectively. The Community projects Administration of the Planning

Commission and India has published *Community Projects: A Draft Handbook* (1952), outlining objectives and plans of organization. The Programme Evaluation Organization of the Indian Planning Commission has recently published *Evaluation Report on First Year's Working of Community Projects*, Delhi, May, 1954, which gives much valuable information. The periodic news-letters of the Ford Foundation in India, frequently deal with aspects of community project activities and give an impressive picture of a well-designed technical assistance programme. In Ceylon, the *Annual Administration Reports of the Director of Rural Development* describe community project activities. UNESCO has published a report (*mimeographed*) by Dr. J. D. N. Versluys on *Village Development Schemes in Ceylon and India* (1952).

A much fuller list of reference is to be found in a United Nations bibliography: *Selected List of Books, Pamphlets and Periodicals in English on Community Organization and Development* (March, 1953).

INDEX

For Product Safety Concerns and Information please contact our EU
representative GPSR@taylorandfrancis.com
Taylor & Francis Verlag GmbH, Kaufingerstraße 24, 80331 München, Germany

www.ingramcontent.com/pod-product-compliance
Lightning Source LLC
Chambersburg PA
CBHW050419280326
41932CB00013BA/1919

* 9 7 8 1 0 3 2 5 4 8 3 6 4 *